CLASSROOM-BASED INTERVENTIONS ACROSS SUBJECT AREAS

Classroom-based Interventions Across Subject Areas explores cutting-edge educational research that has real potential to support the improvement of classroom practice. Written by expert researchers and practitioners, it provides empirically tested and theory-based approaches that practitioners can use to improve learning in classroom settings.

This edited volume provides examples of classroom-based interventions in English, mathematics, science, languages, history, and geography. Taking as its basis research which has been conducted in actual classrooms with close collaboration between researchers and practitioners, this text will help researchers and practitioners understand how and why interventions can be successful or not. The text further considers the broad theoretical and practical issues that derive from intervention studies, including the nature of collaboration between researchers and teachers and ways of adapting effective classroom-based interventions for use in different contexts.

Offering insight into the methodology behind successful classroom-based interventions, this text will be essential reading for students of education, trainee teachers, and all those concerned with how educational research can impact on teaching and learning.

Gabriel J. Stylianides is a Professor of Mathematics Education at the Department of Education and a Fellow of Worcester College at the University of Oxford, UK. He is the convenor of the Subject Pedagogy Research Group and has conducted a number of intervention studies with a focus on mathematics. He was an Editor of *Research in Mathematics Education* and is currently an Editorial Board member of the *Elementary School Journal* and the *International Journal of Educational Research*.

Ann Childs is an Associate Professor of Science Education at the University of Oxford, UK. She is joint course leader of the science strand of the Post Graduate Certificate in Education and Director of Masters in Teacher Education (mathematics and science).

CLASSROOM-BASED INTERVENTIONS ACROSS SUBJECT AREAS

Research to Understand What Works in Education

Edited by Gabriel J. Stylianides and Ann Childs

Routledge
Taylor & Francis Group

LONDON AND NEW YORK

First edition published 2019
by Routledge
2 Park Square, Milton Park, Abingdon, Oxon, OX14 4RN

and by Routledge
52 Vanderbilt Avenue, New York, NY 10017

Routledge is an imprint of the Taylor & Francis Group, an informa business

British Library Cataloguing-in-Publication Data
A catalogue record for this book is available from the British Library

Library of Congress Cataloging-in-Publication Data
A catalog record for this book has been requested

ISBN: 978-1-138-04862-1 (hbk)
ISBN: 978-1-138-04863-8 (pbk)
ISBN: 978-1-315-17007-7 (ebk)

Typeset in Bembo
by Out of House Publishing

CONTENTS

FIGURES

TABLES

CONTRIBUTORS

Nick Andrews
University of Oxford, UK

Daniel Brocklehurst
English tutor, Sydney, Australia

Katharine Burn
University of Oxford, UK

Jaya Carrier
Bishop Challoner Catholic Federation of Schools, Tower Hamlets, UK

Ann Childs
University of Oxford, UK

Anna Fielding
St Edward's School, Oxford, UK

Roger Firth
University of Oxford, UK

Merrilyn Goos
University of Limerick, Ireland

Alexandra Haydon
The Castle School, Thornbury, UK

Judith Hillier
University of Oxford, UK

Jenni Ingram
University of Oxford, UK

Laura Molway
University of Oxford, UK

Trevor Mutton
University of Oxford, UK

Andrea Pitt
University of Oxford, UK

Katherine Porter

Jo Rudd
University of Oxford, UK

Elizabeth Samuel
Queen Katherine School, Kendal, UK

Shirley Simon
University College London, UK

Alexandra Strutt
Bristol Grammar School, Bristol, UK

Gabriel J. Stylianides
University of Oxford, UK

Richard Taylor
Gillingham School, Dorset, UK

Ian Thompson
University of Oxford, UK

Christina Watson
Queen Katherine School, Kendal, UK

Robert Woore
University of Oxford, UK

1

AN INTRODUCTION TO CLASSROOM-BASED INTERVENTIONS ACROSS SUBJECT AREAS

Gabriel J. Stylianides and Ann Childs

Several researchers have expressed concern that educational research has not played a greater role in supporting improvement of classroom practice, especially improvement of students' learning of key concepts in different subject areas (e.g., Cai et al., 2017; Ruthven & Goodchild, 2008). Some complementary reasons that have been offered for this state of affairs include the inadequate theorisation of classroom phenomena (e.g., Sierpinska & Kilpatrick, 1998), the insufficient understanding of the theory–practice relationship (e.g., Malara & Zan, 2008), the ineffective sharing of meaning across researchers and practitioners (e.g., Wiliam & Lester, 2008), and the inadequacy of certain common approaches to professional development (e.g., Cai et al., 2017; Gurski, 2002). Regarding the latter, some examples of shortcomings of professional development programmes include a top-down approach where the focus is working on problems identified by researchers versus problems identified by teachers (Cai et al., 2017) or professional development programmes that fail to take account of what motivates teachers to engage in the programme as well as the process by which teacher change can occur (Gurski, 2002).

What can be, then, some important features of educational research with good potential to support improvement of classroom practice? Stylianides and Stylianides (2013) identified the following three features which, although they were discussed by the authors in the domain of mathematics, can apply equally well to other subject areas of the school curriculum:

1. The research is conducted in the 'world' of practitioners (i.e., in actual classrooms) and with close collaboration between researchers and teachers, thus increasing the likelihood that the results of the research will be directly applicable (instead of merely potentially relevant) to practice;
2. The research directly addresses problems of student learning and how this learning can be better supported by teaching (including teaching resources

such as curriculum materials), thus tackling key issues of current ... classroom practice; and

3. The research seeks to develop empirically-tested *and* theory-based solutions to alleviate problems of student learning in order not only to show that things 'worked' (or 'can work') but also to explain how/why things 'worked', thus shedding light on the mechanisms of success.

Stylianides and Stylianides, 2013, p. 334

These three features generally characterise research studies on effective *classroom-based interventions* which helped promote important learning goals that typical classroom practice had difficulty supporting. Despite the importance of classroom-based intervention studies, especially in terms of their potential to help develop research-grounded solutions to problems of practice, it is widely accepted (Cai et al., 2017; Kane, 2016; Snow, 2016; Stylianides & Stylianides, 2013, 2017) that there is a need for more studies in this area.

The previous statement does not suggest that educational research is lacking good examples of classroom-based interventions in different subject areas. For instance, some notable exceptions to the point we mentioned earlier about the inadequacy of certain common approaches to professional development are certain classroom intervention research studies conducted in collaboration with primary and secondary teachers to develop effective strategies in formative assessment (see, e.g., Torrance & Pryor, 2001; Black et al., 2004); these studies have theoretical underpinnings and have proved to be strong models for professional development rooted in teachers' concerns. Rather, our concern as well as a major motivator for this book is that the number of research-informed classroom-based interventions is small and acutely disproportionate to the number of studies that documented important problems of practice for which solutions are needed.

This book takes a step towards addressing the aforementioned concern by providing examples of classroom-based interventions in different subject areas: English, Modern Foreign Languages, science, mathematics, history, and geography. The book consists of eight main chapters written jointly by university researchers (all of whom are also teacher educators) and teachers (Chapters 2–9), and two commentaries (Chapters 10–11) from internationally acclaimed researchers, Merrilyn Goos and Shirley Simon. We will not say much about the content of particular chapters as the commentaries provide a discussion of them in addition to identifying themes and other issues that emerge from the entire collection. Rather, we will focus on making some overall comments about the book.

We begin by clarifying our use of some key terms in the book. While the term 'intervention' has been used in different ways, our use of it in this book is similar to its standard use in medicine where an intervention denotes 'action taken to improve a situation' (Stevenson & Lindberg, 2012); in our case the situation in need for improvement relates, of course, to classroom practice. Different chapter authors unpack or problematise the notion of intervention in their chapters. For coherence across the book, however, the basic meaning and starting point of the different conceptualisations was the same: 'action taken to improve a situation.' The terms 'action' and 'situation' were open for the chapter authors to discuss and explain how they are being interpreted in their chapter. We also clarify that we use in this book the term 'classroom' broadly to denote a formal learning setting at any level of education, including teacher education.

The book is aimed at engaging in an academic debate as well as helping teachers improve classroom practice. This dual aim is well served by the fact that the core book chapters (Chapters 2–9) are written jointly by university researchers and classroom teachers. In more detail, we aim for the book to be pedagogically useful to teachers through exemplars taking place either in school or teacher education settings. We also aim for the book to be thought provoking on fundamental research issues of teaching, learning, and curriculum design. The book, therefore, is expected to have both academic and professional appeal and is aimed at researchers, teacher educators, teachers, trainee teachers on both undergraduate and postgraduate courses, and curriculum developers (such as textbook authors). Although the exemplars are based on data drawn from the UK context, special care was taken to make clear the applicability of the issues to other cultural contexts. The two commentaries (Chapters 10–11) help make the broader applicability of the ideas as clear as possible.

The book, as a collection of chapters, is interdisciplinary and so it can appeal to a broad audience. Also, each core chapter, in addition to addressing important issues in a particular subject area, also addresses at least one issue that applies across subject areas; the latter characteristic makes each chapter separately and the book as a whole of interest to international readers independently of the particular subject area of primary interest to them. Chapter 2 by Brocklehurst and Thompson in English represents an example of a theoretically driven reading intervention in a particularly challenging context. However, the chapter also shows how the study has design implications for research on classroom activity that considers the relationships between mediated activity, students' development, and the classroom environment. Chapter 3 by Molway, Mutton, Woore, and Porter, in addition to providing a research-informed approach to address practical classroom problems in Modern Foreign Languages, shows how small-scale research studies can be a valuable first step in a wider process of systematically developing and evaluating pedagogical innovations. Chapter 4 by Haydon and Childs, focused on science classrooms and student questioning, also provides insights for all teachers into how to get students in classrooms to ask more higher level questions. Chapter 5 by Hillier and Taylor, again focused on science, provides an example of how to gain complementary insights for both school students and prospective teachers' learning by applying separate frameworks of analysis and for different purposes. Chapter 6 by Ingram, Andrews, Rudd, and Pitt, in addition to considering how talk can be developed in mathematics classrooms, also addresses broader issues of language use in all classrooms. Chapter 7 by Burn, Carrier, and Fielding, in addition to its focus on developing history teaching and learning, also explores the potential of small-scale studies to generate empirically tested and theory-based solutions to alleviate challenges to student learning. Chapter 9 by Samuel, Watson, and Childs raises broader methodological issues about the use of randomised control trials in educational research and speaks to debates taking place nationally and internationally (see, e.g., Goldacre, 2013; Lingard & Gale, 2010). Finally, Chapter 8 by Firth and Strutt, as well as its focus on prospective teachers' planning in geography, also reflects more generally on the nature of teacher preparation courses, professional learning, and the role of collaborative reflection and research in developing beginning teachers' practice.

Overall, the book as a whole engages with a number of broad theoretical or practical questions, such as the following:

- What is the nature of collaboration between researchers and teachers on classroom-based interventions? What are the difficulties and possibilities of this collaboration? The chapters provide insights into the diverse ways collaboration can be productive in classroom-based intervention research. For example, Chapter 5 (Haydon and Childs) and Chapter 6 (Ingram, Andrews, Rudd, and Pitt) both show how collaboration between researchers and school teachers brought different but complementary knowledge to the design and implementation of the classroom-based research. Chapter 9 (Samuel, Watson, and Childs) show how collaboration in a nationwide randomised control trial extended the teachers' repertoire of research skills to the work of the school's Teacher Learning Communities. Finally, Hiller and Taylor (Chapter 7) show how the collaborative process of writing their chapter allowed them to see the value to two constituencies of learners, school students and prospective teachers, of writing science explanations in developing their conceptual understanding of science.

- What might be involved in trying to adapt a classroom-based intervention – which was shown to be effective in a particular context – for use in different contexts? What are possible ways of facilitating this adaptation process? Chapter 3 (Molway, Mutton, Woore, and Porter) and Chapter 7 (Burn, Carrier, and Fielding) particularly look at how the findings from their small-scale interventions could speak to practitioners and researchers in different contexts. However, we would also argue that, in reading all of the chapters, the richness of detail provided of the contexts in which the interventions took place have the potential to provide readers with enough detail to judge the relevance/resonance of the interventions and their findings to their own context. For example, the strategies described in Chapter 5 (Haydon and Childs) about an intervention to develop student questioning in science secondary classrooms are presented in adequate detail to facilitate adaptations to different classroom contexts.

- What are the key factors that led to classroom-based interventions being undertaken in the different contexts? In all chapters the interventions were carried out as 'action[s] taken to improve a situation' (Stevenson & Lindberg, 2012). However, there were also other key motivations that drove the intervention work discussed in the chapters beyond the need to address important problems in the local contexts. For example, for Samuel, Watson, and Childs (Chapter 9) their involvement in a nationwide initiative using randomised control trials provided an opportunity to extend the range of methodologies they were employing to research the work in their Teacher Learning Communities. For Firth and Strutt's work (Chapter 8) an additional motivation was an opportunity to challenge the status quo in geography education on the nature of subject knowledge. For Molway, Muttion, and Woore (Chapter 3) a key motivation for their intervention came from a national change in assessment policy. Finally, for Burn, Carrier, and Fielding (Chapter 7) the dearth of research in history education was an additional key motivating factor for their work.

- How do these studies mitigate against the shortcomings of current professional development programmes and take account of what motivates teachers to engage in the interventions? Many of the chapters show significant professional growth through engaging in the interventions, particularly as often the interventions relate to a particular policy/professional need that motivated the teachers and researchers to engage together in the design and implementation of the intervention. For example, Chapter 4 documents Haydon's dissatisfaction with the level of questioning and engagement by her students as a key motivation which drove the intervention. There is significant evidence in this chapter that documents her professional growth and of the other teachers in her department. Chapter 3 (Molway, Mutton, Woore, and Porter) also shows how involvement in the two interventions described in this chapter led to significant professional growth of both the teacher and the teacher educators involved.

We hope that readers will find the contributions in this book inspirational for further research on classroom-based interventions in different subject areas. Prior research has extensively documented numerous problems of students' learning and we believe that the time has come for research to place more emphasis on seeking solutions to these problems, thereby promising a better future for students' learning at all levels. To make real progress in this area, however, the close collaboration between researchers and teachers is necessary. As Cai et al. (2017) pointed out, '[f]or research to have an impact on practice, teachers must be consciously and deliberately positioned as part of the greater community of those who generate as well as consume knowledge' (p. 4). The joint authorship of the core chapters of this book between researchers and teachers is not only a unique feature of this book, but is also telling of the close collaboration that took place in conducting the reported research.

To conclude, we wish to thank all the contributors to this book as well as the numerous teachers and students who allowed aspects of their classroom practice to be analysed and discussed in the book. Without the generosity of those teachers and students this book would not have been possible.

References

Black, P., Harrison, C., Lee, C. Marshall, B., & Wiliam, W. (2004). Working inside the Black Box. *Phi Delta Kappan*, 86(1), 8–21.

Cai, J., Morris, A., Hwang, S., Hohensee, C., Robison, V., & Hiebert, J. (2017). Improving the impact of educational research. *Journal for Research in Mathematics Education*, 48(1), 2–6.

Goldacre, B. (2013). *Building evidence into education*, London: DfE. Downloaded from: www.gov.uk/government/news/building-evidence-into-education

Guskey, T. R. (2002). Professional development and teacher change. *Teachers and Teaching: Theory and Practice*, 8(3), 381–391.

Kane, T. J. (2016). Connecting to practice: How we can put education research to work. *Education Next*, 16(2), 81–87.

Lingard, B., & Gale, T. (2010). Defining educational research: A perspective of/on Presidential addresses and the Australian Association for Research in Education. *The Australian Educational Researcher*, 37(1), 21–49.

Malara, N. A., & Zan, R. (2008). The complex interplay between theory in mathematics education and teachers' practice: Reflections and examples. In L. D. English (Ed.), *Handbook of international research in mathematics education* (2nd edn) (pp. 535–560). New York, NY: Routledge.

Ruthven, K., & Goodchild, S. (2008). Linking researching and teaching: Towards synergy of scholarly and craft knowledge. In L. D. English (Ed.), *Handbook of international research in mathematics education* (2nd edn) (pp. 561–588). New York, NY: Routledge.

Sierpinska, A., & Kilpatrick, J. (Eds.). (1998). *Mathematics education as a research domain: A research for identity (An ICMI Study)*. London, England: Kluwer Academic Publishers.

Snow, C. E. (2016). The role of relevance in education research, as viewed by former presidents. *Educational Researcher*, 45(2), 64–68.

Stevenson, A., & Lindberg, C. A. (Eds.). (2012). *New Oxford American Dictionary* (3rd edn). Oxford University Press. Retrieved 12 February 2013, from www.oxfordreference.com/view/10.1093/acref/9780195392883.001.0001/acref-9780195392883.

Stylianides, A. J., & Stylianides, G. J. (2013). Seeking research-grounded solutions to problems of practice: Classroom-based interventions in mathematics education. *ZDM – The International Journal on Mathematics Education*, 45(3), 333–341.

Stylianides, G. J., & Stylianides, A. J. (2017). Research-based interventions in the area of proof: The past, the present, and the future. *Educational Studies in Mathematics*, 96(2), 119–127.

Torrance, H., & Pryor, J. (2001). Developing Formative Assessment in the Classroom: using action research to explore and modify theory. *British Educational Research Journal*, 27(5), 615–631.

Wiliam, D., & Lester, F. K. (2008). On the purpose of mathematics education research: Making productive contributions to policy and practice. In L. D. English (Ed.), *Handbook of international research in mathematics education* (2nd edn) (pp. 32–48). New York, NY: Routledge.

2

DOUBLE STIMULATION FOR RELUCTANT READERS

A literature circle intervention in a secondary school English classroom

Daniel Brocklehurst and Ian Thompson

Introduction

The question of how to encourage reluctant secondary school students to read is a complex one. Strong reading skills are vital for academic success in most secondary school subjects. There is also widespread agreement amongst English teachers that reading widely is beneficial for both the cognitive and emotional development of young people. Yet English teachers confronted by students who say that they 'hate' reading or who claim to have never read a book face a challenge. How do they get their students to do more, and more effectively, of the very thing they dislike doing?

This chapter reports on a research intervention carried out by the first author of this chapter, then a practising English teacher, that aimed to address questions of how to stimulate reluctant readers in a Year 7 (aged 11–12) English classroom. This focus arose from discussions on a master's in learning and teaching course between the teacher and the second author, his university academic supervisor. The university lecturer had also been the teacher's tutor on a teacher education programme three years earlier and both authors shared a conception of learning as being both a social and situated activity. Although the chapter is primarily aimed at both teachers and researchers of secondary school reading, the broad interest of this research lies in providing a worked example of practitioner interventionist research conducted from a Vygotskian theoretical perspective. In particular, it is argued that Vygotsky's (1987) principle of double stimulation is an effective method for focusing research on the dynamic and historical processes of learner transformation and development.

The site of the research was a school operating under the particular constraints of a recent negative government inspection report. The English department in particular was under great scrutiny and carrying out an intervention under these circumstances was very challenging. The school had identified the need to create a more prominent culture of reading amongst their students. In order to develop students' reading for pleasure, as well as to help reluctant readers to acquire new ways of thinking about and interrogating texts, the teacher became interested in the idea of implementing literature circles, a collaborative reading activity he had been made aware of during his teacher education programme.

A central concern for this research was the need to design a classroom-based intervention that focused on the interactions between the development of individual learning competences and social learning within the setting of the classroom. This form of research involves a combined focus on the dialectic between social interactions and individual development. Accordingly, we drew theoretically on the ideas of Vygotsky (1987) and post-Vygotskian researchers because of their focus on the social contexts of learning and its relationship with the formation of mind and activity. Thus the research reported here represents an example of a theoretically and research-informed intervention aimed at an identified issue of whole school improvement.

Before describing the research, we therefore begin by outlining some key concepts from Vygotskian theory in relation to researching learning. We then explore the potential of a literature circle intervention as a site for stimulating reading development.

A Vygotskian approach to researching learning

Vygotsky (1987) conceived learning as both a social and situated cultural activity. Learning involves mediated activity through psychological tool usage and in particular the culturally acquired conceptual tool of language. In English classes, activities of writing, reading, and speaking and listening are both distributed in the sense of many participants contributing to these specific acts of literacy and situated within the specific context of the classroom and school environment (Thompson and Wittek 2016).

The *Zone of Proximal Development* (ZPD) (Vygotsky 1987) is probably both the best-known and least understood concept in Vygotsky's thought. Unlike the predominant model of children's learning that sees the function of learning as acquisition of knowledge, Vygotsky's theory of the ZPD stresses the importance of the educative process in the psychological development of higher order thinking. Vygotsky's emphasis in the concept of the ZPD was on the development of the individual child in their social situation of development. For Vygotsky, the ZPD is the difference between existing and potential levels of development revealed through an analysis of how far a student is able to master a task by themselves or with help from a more knowledgeable other, such as a teacher or more capable peer. Vygotsky's concept of the ZPD defines the potential *development* of a child rather than an abstract metaphor for learning. For Vygotsky, real learning is that which is in advance of current levels of development and is mediated through interactions with other people and through the social and cultural acquisition of sign systems.

Vygotsky's (1987) *principle of double stimulation* grew out of his search for new methodological tools to research interaction and development within social situations of development. The aim of this tool was to focus the researcher on the dynamic and historical processes of development as learners use culturally and socially acquired knowledge to make sense of the world. The principle of double stimulation describes a situation in which an individual is confronted with a researcher-set problem or dilemma that they do not yet have the knowledge or the psychological tools to solve without the secondary stimulus provided. The problem constitutes the object of the activity and the secondary stimulus, in the form of tools or artefacts, which provides the potential means of solving the dilemma. Vygotsky argued that by studying the ways in which people appropriate these tools to try to solve the problem, it is possible to reveal the ways in which they interpret the environment and contexts they act in.

As Sannino (2015) explains, the process of double stimulation begins with a conflict of motives which is resolved through volitional action or will. The concept of object motive is a key element in Vygotskian research not least because of the possibility of conflicting or contradictory object motives within an activity. The object motive for teachers and the reason they design classroom activities are their students' learning trajectories. The object motive for the students involved in these activities may well be very different. This theoretical framework views individual psychological development as being rooted in culture and society (the social situation of development). It is both through interaction with others, and our response to the contexts within which we develop, that we attempt to make sense of the world around us.

Engeström (1999, 2007) has extended Vygotsky's concept of action constituting a subject, an object and mediational tools in order to account for the social relations that affect the mediational process. In particular, he highlights the importance of rules and division of labour within activity. Engeström's *theory of expansive learning* views joint activity, as opposed to individual actions, as the central unit of activity. Internal contradictions of this activity are 'the motive force of change and development' (Engeström 1999: 9). Mediated activity changes not only the subject but also the social context of the activity system. This analysis of collective activity is linked to an 'emphasis on action or intervention in order to develop practice and the sites of practice' (Edwards and Daniels 2004: 108). Vygotskian research in this tradition is interventionist and aims to study contradictions within processes of learning through the process of double stimulation or by changing the division of labour within an activity system. This involves both transforming the activity and expanding the agency of the participants.

The literature circle as a site for double stimulation

In the English classroom, the literature circle represents a potential site for transforming the activity of classroom reading (Thompson 2015a). Literature circles are small classroom discussion groups based around a literary text that they have chosen. The students meet regularly to discuss what they have read and organise the amount of reading they will do for the next session. Although the model is flexible, there are three essential elements found within any literature circle: independent reading, reader response, and collaborative learning (Daniels 2002). In most models of literature circles, students are assigned roles – for example, illustrator, summariser, questioner – designed to mirror the analytical and cognitive decoding tools used by experienced and successful readers (Peterson and Belizaire 2006). Students read chapters from the point of view of their particular role and then join a group discussion on the chapters in question. Roles are rotated as the literature circle progresses. Talk is generally perceived to be student-centred in that discussions are led by the students through their reading roles. These roles are designed to be temporary supports and aim to recreate the cognitive reading processes of mature readers. Students' choices of books can be used to create the literature circle groups themselves.

Literature circles promote independent reading, fully encourage reading as a transactional process, and allow processes central to social learning, such as exploratory talk (Eeds and Wells 1989; Mercer 1995). Importantly, they encourage personal response and enjoyment of reading as well as receptive vocabulary (Allan, Ellis and Pearson 2005). Literature circles have been repeatedly praised for enabling students to decide on texts that engage them (Gambrell 1996; McMahon and Raphael 1997; Short and Pierce 1990) and increase motivation (McElvain 2010). Research has shown that it is important that groups meet regularly and that the students are treated as much of a learner and teacher as their class teacher; this setting encourages independence (Scott 1994; Owens 1995) as well as social and leadership skills (Certo 2011). The groups achieve these outcomes and arguably work best when they are mixed ability. In their study, Elbaum, Schumm and Vaughn (1997) found that students – both strong and struggling readers – preferred to work in groups and pairs that were of a mixed ability, rather than whole class instruction or independent work, noting that they helped and encouraged each other more.

Literature circles heavily emphasise the need to respond in a personal way to a text (King and Briggs 2012). Literature circles, transactional by nature, allow students to understand that personal responses are a starting point to sophisticated analysis. This is an important first step in ensuring the success of perhaps the strongest aspect of literature circles, which is its reliance on discursive processes, in particular, the use of exploratory talk (Clarke and Holwaldel 2007). Researchers examining talk during literature circle discussions have often found it to be purposeful and critical (Latendresse 2004; Sandmann and Gruhler 2007).

Robinson and King (1995) argue that literature circles represent a Vygotskian approach to learning how to analyse and interpret texts. The collaborative nature of the activity enables more effective development in these skills and can also significantly improve students' attitudes to reading. The ZPD can be seen in the very structure of a literature circle: students – of a mixed ability – push each other to consider one another's opinions and so others are constantly driving their learning. In their study of the effects of literature circles, King and Briggs (2012) write that 'the children were able to explore both the texts and the reading process in ways they would not have been able to manage independently' (8). Vygotskian theory is drawn on to explain why: 'in the literature circle, the interpersonal dialogic nature of the talk was then internalised to become part of the independent thinking applied to texts read alone or with younger siblings' (8). This kind of talk encourages students to move beyond a narrow perspective on meaning and consider other points of view and to 'embrace language as a motivational tool for developing novel approaches to thinking' (Sanacore 2013: 120). It also helps to improve students' attitudes to reading in general. When students see others talk with interest about a book, they also want to 'be members of the "in" group' (King and Briggs 2012: 4).

Another form of talking – talking about talk – has also been shown to be useful in literature circles, allowing students to be 'reflexive' and study 'themselves to outgrow themselves' (Mills and Jennings 2011: 591). This is, in essence, metacognition: talking about one's own talk is another way of being aware of one's own cognitive processes, enabling oneself to regulate, evaluate, and monitor thinking, 'thereby affording more efficient and active learning' (Bonds, Bonds and Peach 1992: 56).

There are also arguments for, and some research showing, the positive contribution that literature circles can have on students' ability and performance in tests. King and Briggs (2012) argue that literature circles may not only increase a student's sight vocabulary but also improve their ability to use the three cuing systems: semantic, syntactic, and graphophonic. Almasi (1995) found that cognition growth occurred at a higher level in student-led discussions about literature as opposed to teacher-led ones. Sweigart (1991) noted that, by participating in literature circles, students' comprehension improved. Moreover, Blum, Lipsett and Yocom (2002) concluded that literature circles could help improve students' skills in problem solving and making decisions.

However, Daniels (2002) points out that literature circles actually go against the idea of testing and assessment; while there is growing research about its strong positive effect on students' reading ability, it is difficult to see this improvement instantly. Due to their indirect effects, literature circles can therefore be easy to criticise and difficult to see the worth of. Indeed, there are problems not only with how literature circles are perceived, but also within the model itself. Daniels (2006), one of the key proponents of assigned roles in groups, came to realise that in many classroom scenarios the reading roles were often dominating the work of literature circles and often limiting the type of talk about text that the circles were designed to foster. Excessive concentration on roles leads to a series of reports rather than a genuine discussion. To combat this, Daniels advocates a form of continuous teacher assessment of small group student-led discussions. This then becomes an important purpose for the teacher in setting the task of collaborative reading. From a Vygotskian perspective, this involves direct mediation with students as they talk about reading with their peers. Another problem with literature circles is that its name has been erroneously used to refer to any reading group, including those that do not contain the three essential elements outlined. While flexibility is a good thing, literature circles can be done badly. For example, Ellis (2007) described a situation in which a group of trainee teachers implemented what they thought were literature circles but, in the end, only 'spent an awful lot of time devising teacherly questions specific to each novel' (196).

More worryingly, some studies have found problems within literature circle discussions. In their own study, Clarke and Holwadel (2007) experienced behavioural problems, with group cohesion dissolving as soon as teachers left the group, students even resorting to bullying and arguing. Sanacore (2013) also found that some peer-led discussions were mediocre because group members often wasted time, argued their point of view in a bullying manner, focused on irrelevant points, and did not consider each other's perspectives about the text. It has also been observed that students can create their own social positions in terms of ability level (Allen, Möller and Stroup 2003) and gender (Clarke 2006; Evans 1996), going against the aimed characteristics of equality and egalitarianism.

When considering the benefits of literature circles alongside the potential problems within them, it is perhaps most useful to look at arguably the most valuable aspect of literature circles: collaboration with more capable peers within a ZPD. Although Eeds and Peterson (1991) show how important it is for the class teacher to monitor student reading groups, suggest reading and encourage certain lines of enquiry, Daniels (2002) and Whittaker (2012) argue that once students know how literature circles operate, the teacher should allow the students to take charge. Barnes (1976) also rightly points out that, in the classroom, there is a great deal of difference between the effect of questions asked by pupils of one another, and the effect of a teacher's questions, partly because the pupils expect that the teacher usually '"knows the answer" already' (43). Indeed, as Barnes writes, 'the very presence of a teacher alters the way in which pupils use language, so that they are more likely to be aiming at "answers" which will gain approval than using language to reshape knowledge' (Barnes 1976: 78).

However, Vaughn, Gersten and Chard (2000) and Thein, Guise and Sloane (2011) argue that when students move beyond a personal response towards a critical examination of a text then more teacher guidance is needed. In fact, Daniels explains the benefits of the class teacher joining a group and playing the role of a fellow reader 'honestly reading, responding, predicting, and sharing meaning-making processes right along with the students' (Daniels 2002: 24). This allows the students to see how a mature reader responds to a book for the first time, reacts, interrogates and shares ideas.

King and Briggs (2012) argue the importance of the teacher listening to the students with a belief that what they say is important. Questions should not be used to check understanding but be used for the teacher to be informed by the children. Thompson (2015a) notes how prospective teachers in the teacher training course at the University of Oxford are 'encouraged to sit with the groups and intervene as part of their assessment of both actual and potential levels of students' understanding' (102). This role represents mediational guidance within the child's ZPD; the teacher is the aid that can help realise the full potential of the child's development through modelling and probing the activity of both voicing inner speech so that thought can be reworked, and promoting exploratory talk among peers so that ideas can be challenged. In a similar vein, Miller (2003) has argued that teacher mediation in open discussions about literature can create a ZPD, or 'assistive social space' (290) that can lead to development. The ZPD indicates both the presence of maturing psychological functions and the potential for meaningful interventions that can stimulate reluctant readers' conceptual development (Thompson 2015a).

Older student as more capable peer

The question for the practitioner researcher was whether they could introduce an older student such as an older student (aged 16 to 18) to work within a literature circle and become a fellow reader in a class that held many reluctant readers. It was hypothesised that there might be significant benefits in integrating into a literature circle someone who was passionate about literature, willing to read and discuss alongside younger peers, eager to model to the students what a thoughtful, inquisitive reader might look and sound like. Cross-age peer support has recently become popular within schools in the form of mentoring, which can help with problems of bullying and create a more positive ethos within the school (Cowie and Smith 2010; Willis et al. 2012). It has been defined as an 'interpersonal relationship between two youth of different ages that reflects a greater degree of hierarchical power imbalance that is typical of a friendship and in which the goal is for the older youth to promote one or more aspects of the younger youth's development' with an aim to go beyond academic difficulties (Karcher 2005: 266). The older student in a literature circle would be aiming to encourage reluctant readers to read. This is arguably both focusing within and going beyond academic interest as it would involve factors such as attitudes, motivation, and ways of thinking about reading. The older student, as a more capable peer, could model and elicit developed talking and thinking about a text, but also act as a mentor in the more traditional sense by helping students talk through reasons why they are reluctant to read and address these deep attitudinal and motivational problems. The older students could lead learning and development in attitudes within literature circles without harming the exploratory talk, as a teacher might risk doing. They would also constitute a secondary stimulus for the reluctant readers within the primary stimulus of the activity system of the literature circle.

It has become apparent in this literature review that a number of problems can occur when literature circles are implemented, especially into a class of reluctant readers. The possibility of adding older students as facilitators to literature circles allowed this unique research study to focus on three research questions:

1. Can older students act as 'more capable peers' in literature circles in order to allow reluctant readers to develop and learn at a greater rate than they would on their own, and, if so, how might they successfully do this?
2. Can older students encourage and motivate reluctant readers to read and how might they do this?
3. Ultimately, how might older students help change reluctant readers' attitudes towards reading from negative to positive?

The study proposition (or hypothesis), with Vygotskian theory as a basis, was that older students have the potential to both accelerate younger students' development in reading skills, and positively affect students' attitudes and motivation, *if* they truly play out the role of a 'more capable peer' as described by Vygotsky.

Methods

The research was carried out with a Year 7 class (aged 11–12) in a medium-sized comprehensive school in a small town in south-east England. In a survey of the reading views of the chosen research class conducted before the intervention, just over half expressed a dislike of reading with only around a third claiming to actively enjoy reading. The research involved a literature circle intervention with two older students attached to two groups of reluctant readers.

A case study method was chosen as the most appropriate form of research design because of the need to observe change and development during the literature circle intervention. The strengths of the case study method allowed a focus on the 'how' aspects of the research questions: *how* might the older students interact with the students; *how* might they be effective or ineffective. It would not have been useful to gauge the effectiveness of the model without knowing exactly how it was effective. By looking closely at this reading strategy in action through case studies of the two groups of five younger students that each worked with their own older student, the researchers could observe the details that would best illuminate *why* this approach may or may not be effective. This case study approach involved examining a 'contemporary phenomenon in depth and within its real-life context' (Yin 2014: 18). The case study approach was also suitable for the reason that the research began with a particular theoretical proposition: if an older student played the role of 'a more capable peer', in the true Vygotskian sense, and promoted exploratory talk, then the younger students would begin to understand the worth of reading and become intrinsically motivated to read.

As a piece of practitioner research conducted for an academic purpose, the project aimed to give implications for the school in which it was set, as well as the wider educational context. However, it was also looking at something for the first time – something very context-dependent with many variables. A thorough examination of older students working with younger students in literature circles could not be done alongside the introduction of other variables. There was so much to consider by examining the literature circles with older students on their own, that valuable insights – useful to both the school and the field of educational research – were best gained in a more thorough manner, with more focus on what actually happened within the focus groups.

An important part of the intervention was the introduction of the older students to the reading circles as a form of secondary stimulus. Double stimulation describes a situation in which an individual or groups are confronted with a researcher-set problem or dilemma that they do not yet have the knowledge or the psychological tools to solve without the secondary stimulus provided. In the research reported here, the teacher and academic researchers identified two groups of seven reluctant readers aged 11–12 who were each assigned an older student. The primary stimulus for reading was the division of labour within the activity system of the literature circle. The intention was for the older students to act as a secondary stimulus within the activity system of a collaborative reading group to support processes such as inference and criticality employed by successful readers. Data for the analysis of the two case studies include observations, transcripts of discussions, questionnaires, younger student group interviews and semi-structured interviews with the older students.

As mentioned earlier, an initial questionnaire was implemented to ascertain the younger students' attitudes towards reading. Reluctant readers were identified as students who had responded by circling 'I don't like reading at all' or 'I don't really like reading', and had also claimed not be reading anything in their own time. Over two lessons, the practitioner/researcher explained in detail to the class what literature circles were, read out the openings to eight novels, and allowed students to vote for their favourites. From students' choice, literature circle groups were set up of four to six students, giving students their first preference whenever possible. Five groups were formed, two of which had a significant number of reluctant readers. Two older students, Emily and Jack (all student names used in the chapter are pseudonyms), who were enthusiastic about the project, volunteered to take part and were assigned to these two groups. Jack was assigned to group A and Emily group B. Both older students were known to the teacher to be hardworking and trustworthy students with a passion for literature. They were given full details about the project and its aims, the nature of literature circles, and were instructed in their role as 'capable peers'. They were also given an advice sheet to help them during discussions. They worked closely with the teacher throughout the running of literature circles, regularly talking and sharing thoughts after each lesson. Their feedback helped in the implementation of needed changes to make the literature circles work better.

It was anticipated that the audio recordings of the literature circle discussions during the first five weeks would provide the richest data, capturing the complexity and subtle nuances within the relationship between older and younger students. If the questionnaire and interview data indicated that the reading strategy was successful, or otherwise, the recordings of the discussions, transcribed for analysis, would allow one to explore reasons as to *how* this might be the case. These recordings were arguably the only reliable data tools from which one could measure the effect that the older students might have had, in Vygotskian terms, as more capable peers. It was only through these discussions that one would be able to detect any exploratory talk or movement along the ZPD. The full findings of the research are reported elsewhere (Brocklehurst 2015) but here we concentrate on an indicative sample of the data from these discussions augmented by the other data sources.

Findings

There was a marked difference in the effectiveness of the two literature circle groups. Group A, led by Jack, in many ways mirrored a managerial relationship of teacher to class whilst group B, involving Emily, provided an effective stimulus for reading through transforming the activity and expanding the agency of the participants.

Jack's Group A was made up of Andy, Cassie, Clark, Jasmine and Jimmy – all students who initially claimed to dislike and avoid reading. Jack struggled to develop a strong relationship with the students who saw him in a managerial or administrative role in the group. Despite Jack trying to get the students to decide roles, no substantial talk about their chosen book – *Holes* by Louis Sachar – ever really started, despite Andy's evident enthusiasm. In one instance, Jimmy said that he was in trouble. Jack asked why, prompting Jimmy to talk about a detention that he received, passionately going into great detail about the nature of the punishment. Even though Jack initially showed interest, he suddenly got back on track, seemingly ignoring Jimmy's anecdote: 'so now we've got to decide how much to read.' Jimmy's own interest could have been tactfully linked to the book that they were reading, which was about a boy wrongfully accused of something he did not do. Jimmy's own thoughts and knowledge (his action knowledge) could have served as a platform to begin thinking about the novel. However, Jack, playing the role of manager in the group, did not think to pursue this direction and swept the conversation aside.

Similar instances occurred throughout the discussions, for example when Jack asked whether everyone did the reading:

> **Jack:** so what do you think of it
> **Andy:** it's all right (0.5) not bad
> **Jack:** and did everyone do the work?

It was only Andy who responded apathetically to Jack's question. No one else was given a chance. Jack, enacting his role of manager, moved on to checking whether the students did the role work. The talk was not centred on the text itself.

In the discussions without Jack, however, there was a complete loss of order. There were virtually no real in-depth discussions about the novel beyond the administrative checking of roles. Although it was hardly productive with Jack present, it became even more ineffective when Jack left. It was evident that the students were very resilient and disillusioned with reading.

Jack was certainly useful in encouraging, or perhaps pushing, students to read more, as Jasmine noted in the group interview: 'chapter three (0.5) so (.) this is for the entire week (0.5) so (.) if you want to push yourself (1.0).' Often this role of checker could be useful:

> **Jack:** what have you done as summariser?
> **Jimmy:** well (.) he got into trouble for stealing the shoes
> **Andy:** then he has to go to a camp for bad boys
> **Clark:** he's sort of like getting [done
> **Andy:** [this kid
> **Jasmine:** Stanley Yelnats

Here it was evident that the students wanted each other and Jack to know that they had done the reading: they all offered their own knowledge about what happened. Jack was arguably creating a culture of expectation; students expected each other to have done the reading and they wanted to prove that they had done it. This was something that Jack made clear in his interview: 'they've at least always read the book' although his additional comment – 'or at least they've told me that they have' – gives an indication of how little depth there was in any of the discussions about the book.

Overall, Jack was not effective in encouraging students to discuss texts; as a consequence, it would seem, their motivation to read did not improve. In effect he acted the role of manager of the task, not of an older, more capable peer working alongside the students. In this sense, Jack's potential role as a form of secondary stimulus for the students was limited.

The students in Group B – who also shared a dislike towards reading – were Chris, James, Kara, Omar and Sarah. The older student, Emily, was skilled in creating different levels of rapport, which led to the younger students effectively engaging with her. Without this level of rapport, important characteristics such as trust, honesty, safety and community could not occur. She was not fulfilling a teacher role, monotonously warning students to get back onto the topic; she was arguably one of them and allowed talk about, for example, computer games to serve as a way into talking about their book.

Emily worked tirelessly to encourage students in Group B to give reading a chance, especially in the first session. Chris and James repeatedly expressed their indignation at the prospect of reading their chosen text – *Madame Doubtfire* by Anne Fine – repeating that they were 'not reading'. Chris appeared to be very reluctant at the beginning: 'I'm not reading thirty-two pages' and 'I hate reading'. Emily responded in a patient, positive, and persistent manner without becoming argumentative or confrontational. She used collective language, 'let's read to', and, significantly, consulted them about this. Chris and James's refusal to read thirty-two pages were made to seem exaggerative by Emily: 'it's only thirty-two pages.' The meaning in 'only' seems to be understood by Kara, who adopted Emily's role for a small moment, echoing her words before being interrupted by James. Emily, during the first meeting, was already becoming Kara's role model. Emily's phrase 'if you start tonight you can get it over and done with' (which she repeated later) did not seem that inspiring but was perhaps used to offer a practical way for the boys to deal with this sudden challenge of having to read. It was a temporary, pragmatic solution. Her declarative retort to Chris's 'I hate reading' at the end – 'reading's fun' – is indicative of the persistent influence she would have over him over the course of the weeks, eventually helping to radically transform his views. Emily allowed students to be honest and feel safe expressing their genuine opinions, and she established herself as one of the group by using inclusive language to begin to create a small community of readers built on trust.

The level of trust that Emily described in her interview can be seen in the discussions. Moreover, it appears that Emily was directly responsible for establishing and maintaining this safe environment. During the first session, Emily immediately addressed the theme of trust while becoming an encourager, enthusiastically and ambitiously working to change the students' outlook on reading for the better. In fact, Emily explicitly communicated to the group the importance of trust and honesty. After she asked if they wanted to read aloud, James replied: 'I wouldn't want to read (0.5) if I can be completely honest (.) I actually really don't want to do it', adding that 'last lesson you told us we have to be honest about it'. James's honest attitude to reading aloud can be heard and, in this situation, served as groundwork for trust. Without Emily to accept these negative attitudes constructively, it would be difficult to see the students using negativity as a basis for trust rather than as a basis for doing anything but engage with the reading. Another important point about Emily's behaviour here is to be seen when she said that it would be 'awesome' if they could choose to read together, communally, in a supportive way. She encouraged communal activity.

However, Omar and James's reluctance to reading aloud was strong. Emily seemed to understand this reticence as being connected to their confidence: 'you don't have to worry about pronunciation (0.5) you don't have to read that much (1.0) it could just be about that much at a time.' She was communicating to the group that this will be a friendly, safe environment – a place to try, to build confidence slowly and at one's own pace. Later, she reminded them that 'you don't have to read out aloud if you don't want to'. Chris already began to react positively to the safe, communal environment established by Emily: 'I want to read the whole paragraph.' Chris also noted that Emily corrected him at times during reading aloud for which he was grateful, not hurt. This also later allowed Chris to accept corrections from others, for example Kara, as noted by Emily during her interview: 'Kara explained that she was just trying to help him (.) he actually felt like quite happy about it.' Emily actively and successfully created trust among the students themselves to accept and value each other's corrections and criticism. Chris quickly became enthusiastic about reading aloud ('I want to start') as any potential embarrassment was diminished, not insignificant given that he was assessed as having a reading age of only seven years and three months at the age of eleven. He rapidly switched from 'I'm not reading' and 'I hate reading' to 'I want to start'. This would arguably have been most unlikely without Emily's involvement. Omar, like Chris, also seemed to become more willing, interrupting Emily: 'why don't I be the man who reads stuff out.'

Later in the discussion Emily modelled how to talk respectfully; when Chris rudely said 'shut up' to the inaudible conversation between Omar and James, Emily gently reprimanded him: 'there's a nice way (0.5) you can say please can you listen to me.' Emily also made it apparent that students should not just be kind to one another and take criticism well but work together on problems: 'can anyone help James find a simile.' She offered Omar to share her own book when he forgot his own. Time and time again, the expected communal spirit was reiterated and modelled.

Discussion

The contrasting examples of the ways the two literature circle groups operated are presented here to illustrate the ways that in certain circumstances older students can mediate younger students learning through acting as a form of secondary stimulus. From a Vygotskian theoretical perspective, learning leads development and is mediated through interactions with other people and through the social and cultural acquisition of sign systems. For Vygotsky (1987), the ZPD indicates both the presence of maturing psychological functions and the possibility of meaningful interventions through mediated activity that can stimulate conceptual development. The two literature circle examples suggest that this process of learner development is not an automatic one. Derry (2008) has pointed out the importance of the design of the learning environment constructed with a clear conceptual framework. This conceptual clarity includes the role of the mediator in the learning process.

Overall, literature circles were not effective for group A and there were no real in-depth discussions about the book. Jack only enacted the role of administrator and manager, and only at times encouraged, which was ineffective in terms of the quality of discussion. Rather than push them along their ZPDs by aiming learning in advance of development, it seems that Jack actually did the opposite. As a result, the students were unable to use his role as a mediator of reading as a secondary stimulus in any meaningful way. This is not to blame Jack in any way: the level of collaboration provided in preparation and instruction was clearly not good enough. He was with a difficult group of non-readers, who sought opportunities to misbehave. Jack did his best to keep the students reading and finish a number of books – this is certainly an accomplishment. However, the students' motivation to read did not improve, as was evident through all of the data sets, because there was virtually no exploratory talk of any kind; Jack did not act as 'a more capable peer'. The students did not engage, did not see the worth of the task and so their attitude to reading did not improve: they were not encouraged to read.

However, group B's final meeting shows how productive, thoughtful, and engaging discussions *can* be in literature circles. A comparison of the students' lack of engagement during the first meeting to their enthusiasm at the end shows the progress that they made. Emily was largely responsible for this outcome. She did this through her active encouragement, establishing and maintaining trust and honesty, community and safety, and perseverance. Most importantly, from our theoretical perspective, she became the more capable peer and secondary stimulus that was needed for growth in each student's ZPD. By the end, thanks to her modelling, questioning, and encouragement to use exploratory talk, the students had learned to discuss, interrogate and imagine in ways that they could not do at the start. Crucially, this had a dramatic effect on Chris and Kara's attitude, which greatly improved. As Emily pointed out in the interview, although Omar and James maintained that they still disliked reading, their attitudes may actually have shifted, as evidenced by their greater involvement in discussions by the end. In this way, group B transformed the activity of the literature circle and expanded the agency of the participants.

In summary, the key findings of this research in relation to the research questions were that within the activity system of a literature circle:

- older students can act as more capable peers in literature circles and allow reluctant readers to develop and learn at a greater rate than they would on their own;
- older students can encourage and motivate reluctant readers to read; and
- older students can help change reluctant readers' attitudes towards reading from negative to positive.

However, these developments are only made possible if:

- the older student focuses less on playing a managerial role and focuses more on being the secondary stimulus of 'a more capable peer', modelling and encouraging exploratory talk and questioning, to enable younger students to develop along their ZPDs in terms of how they think about, analyse, interrogate, and experience the texts that they read; and
- the older student is sociable, willing, and enthusiastic, reading alongside the younger students and showing genuine interest in reading.

Concluding remarks

King and Briggs (2012) argue that reading is a social process: 'in this respect, the literature circle is an extension of most children's earliest reading experiences, which are essentially social in nature [...]' (3). Thompson (2015a; 2015b) has previously argued that the teacher's role is to design tasks and learning environments that challenge students and enable them to acquire and internalise the learning tools necessary for them to develop conceptual understanding. The key to this development is collaborative or joint activity that engages students in mediated activity. This process of conceptual development involves co-operation and collaboration between the teacher and the learner, or between learners at different levels of development.

The research reported in this chapter represents an innovative attempt by a practitioner to introduce a secondary stimulus for reluctant readers' development. The research also suggests potential fruitful future avenues for English classroom teachers and researchers of double stimulation interventions aimed at studying development by changing the division of labour within an activity system. This study has research design implications for researchers of classroom activity concerning the relationship between mediated activity, students' development, and the classroom environment. The collaboration between the two researchers, and the mixed results from the two groups, raises the importance of the need to design both the nature of the intervention and the role and function of the more capable older student as a mediator of learning.

This study also has another important implication, namely the mutual benefits derivable from a practising English teacher conducting research under the supervision of a university academic. The process itself was beneficial to the teacher in question in developing his understanding of, and skills in, conducting research to benefit not only his own practice but also the English department at the school. In turn, the university researcher was able to be involved in an intervention that required the contextual knowledge and professional understanding of the teacher. Although there are limitations in regards to the sustainability of the particular type of literature circle using double stimulation as investigated here, the study serves as an example to other teachers of how research can be undertaken in other settings to create potentially developing connections between students in different year groups in schools.

References

Allan, J., Ellis, S. and Pearson, C. (2005) *Literature circles, gender, and reading for enjoyment*. Edinburgh, Scotland: Scottish Executive Education Department Research Report.

Allen, J., Möller, K. J. and Stroup, D. (2003) 'Is this some kind of soap opera?': A tale of two readers across literature discussion contexts. *Reading & Writing Quarterly*, 19 (3): 225–251.

Almasi, J. F. (1995) The nature of fourth graders' sociocognitive conflicts in peer-led and teacher-led discussions of literature. *Reading Research Quarterly*, 30 (3): 314–351.

Barnes, D. (1976) *From Communication to Curriculum*. Harmondsworth: Penguin.

Blum, H. T., Lipsett, L. R. and Yocom, D. J. (2002) Literature circles: A tool for self-determination in one middle school inclusive classroom. *Remedial and Special Education*, 23 (2): 99–108.

Bonds, C. W., Bonds, L. G. and Peach, W. (1992) Metacognition: Developing Independence in Learning. *The Clearing House*, 66 (1): 56–59.

Brocklehurst, D. (2015) *Encouraging reluctant readers to read: Sixth-form led literature circles for Key Stage 3 students*. Unpublished MSc dissertation. University of Oxford.

Certo, J. L. (2011) Social Skills and Leadership Abilities Among Children in Small-Group Literature Discussions. *Journal of Research in Childhood Education*, 25 (1): 62–81.

Clarke, L. W. (2006) Power through voicing others: Girls' positioning of boys in literature circle discussions. *Journal of Literacy Research*, 38 (1): 53–79.

Clarke, L. W. and Holwadel, J. (2007) Help! What is wrong with these literature circles and how can we fix them? *The Reading Teacher*, 61 (1): 20–29.

Cowie, H. and Smith, P. K. (2010) Peer support as a means of improving school safety and reducing bullying and violence, in B. Doll, W. Pfohl and J. Yoon (eds.) *Handbook of youth prevention science*. New York, NY: Routledge, pp. 179–195.

Daniels, H. (2002) *Literature circles: Voice and choice in book clubs & reading groups*, 2nd edn. York, ME: Stenhouse.

Daniels, H. (2006) What's the next big thing with literature circles? *Voices from the Middle*, 13 (4): 10–15.

Derry, J. (2008). Abstract rationality in education: From Vygotsky to Brandom. *Studies in the Philosophy of Education*, 27: 49–62.

Edwards, A. and Daniels, H. (2004) Using Sociocultural and Activity Theory in Educational Research. *Educational Review*, 56 (2): 107–111.

Eeds, M. and Peterson, R. (1991) Teacher as curator: Learning to talk about literature. *The Reading Teacher*, 45 (2): 118–126.

Eeds, M. and Wells, D. (1989) Grand conversations: An exploration of meaning construction in literature study groups. *Research in the Teaching of English*, 23 (1): 4–29.

Elbaum, B., Schumm, J. and Vaughn, S. (1997) Urban middle elementary students' perceptions of grouping formats for reading instruction. *The Elementary School Journal*, 97: 475–499.

Ellis, V. (2007) More than 'soldiering on': realizing the potential of teacher education to rethink English in schools, in V. Ellis, C. Fox and B. Street (eds.) *Rethinking English in Schools: Towards a New and Constructive Stage*. London: Continuum, pp. 185–198.

Engeström, Y. (1999) Activity theory and individual and social transformation. In Y. Engeström, R. Miettinen, and R. L. Punamäki (Eds.) *Perspectives on Activity Theory*. New York: Cambridge University Press, pp. 19–38.

Engeström, Y. (2007) Putting Vygotsky to work: The change laboratory as an application of double stimulation. In H. Daniels, M. Cole and J. Wertsch (Eds.), *The Cambridge Companion to Vygotsky*. New York: Cambridge University Press.

Evans, K. S. (1996) Creating spaces for equity? The role of positioning in peer-led literature discussions. *Language Arts*, 73 (3): 194–202.

Gambrell, L. (1996) Creating classroom cultures that foster reading motivation. *The Reading Teacher*, 50: 14–25.

Karcher, M. J. (2005) Cross-age peer mentoring, in D. L. DuBois and M. J. Karcher (eds.) *Handbook of Youth Mentoring*. Thousand Oaks, CA: Sage, pp. 266–285.

King, C. and Briggs, J. (2012) *Literature Circles: Better Talking, More Ideas*. Hertfordshire: UKLA.

Latendresse, C. (2004) Literature circles: Meeting reading standards, making personal connections, and appreciating other interpretations. *Middle School Journal*, 35 (3): 13–20.

McElvain, C. M. (2010) Transactional literature circles and the reading comprehension of English learners in the mainstream classroom. *Journal of Research in Reading*, 33 (2): 178–205.

McMahon, S. I. and Raphael, T. E. (eds.) (1997) *The Book Club Connection: Literacy learning and classroom talk*. New York: Teachers College Press.

Mercer, N. (1995) *The Guided Construction of Knowledge: Talk Amongst Teachers and Learners*. Clevedon, England: Multilingual Matters.

Miller, S. M. (2003) How Literature Discussion Shapes Thinking: ZPDs for Teaching/ Learning Habits of the Heart and Mind, in A. Kozulin, B. Gindis, V. S. Ageyev and S. M. Miller (eds.) *Vygotsky's Educational Theory in Cultural Context*. Cambridge: Cambridge University Press, pp. 289–316.

Mills, H. and Jennings, L. (2011) Talking about talk: Reclaiming the value and power or literature circles. *The Reading Teacher*, 64 (8): 590–598.

Owens, S. (1995) Treasures in the attic: Building the foundation for literature circles, in B. C. Hill, N. J. Johnson and K. L. S. Noe (eds.) *Literature Circles and Response*. Norwood, MA: Christopher-Gordon, pp. 1–12.

Peterson, S. and Belizaire, M. (2006) Another look at roles in literature circles. *Middle School Journal*, 37 (4): 37–43.

Robinson, M. and King, C. (1995) Creating a community of readers. *English in Education*, 29 (2): 46–54.

Sanacore, J. (2013) 'Slow Down, You Move Too Fast': Literature circles as reflective practice. *The Clearing House: A Journal of Educational Strategies, Issues and Ideas*, 86 (3): 116–120.

Sandmann, A. and Gruhler, D. (2007) Reading is thinking: Connecting readers to text through literature circles. *International Journal of Learning*, 13 (10): 105–114.

Sannino, A. (2015). The principle of double stimulation: A path to volitional action. *Learning, Culture, and Social Interaction*, 6: 1–15.

Scott, J. E. (1994) Literature circles in the middle school classroom: Developing reading, responding and responsibility. *Middle School Journal*, 26 (2): 37–41.

Short, K. G. and Pierce, K. M. (eds.) (1990) *Talking About Books: Creating literate communities*. Portsmouth, NH: Heinemann.

Sweigart, W. (1991) Classroom talk, knowledge development, and writing. *Research in the Teaching of English*, 25 (4): 469–496.

Thein, A. H., Guise, M. and Sloan, D. L. (2011) Problematizing Literature Circles as Forums for Discussion of Multicultural and Political Texts. *Journal of Adolescent & Adult Literacy*, 55 (1): 15–24.

Thompson, I. (2015a) Communication, culture and conceptual learning: Task design in the English classroom, in I. Thompson (ed.) *Designing Tasks in Secondary Education: Enhancing Subject Understandings and Student Engagement*. London: Routledge, pp. 86–106.

Thompson, I. (2015b) Researching contradictions: Cultural historical activity theory research (CHAT) in the English classroom. *English in Australia*. 50 (3): 21–26.

Thompson, I. and Wittek, L. (2016) Writing as a mediational tool for learning in the collaborative composition of texts. *Learning, Culture and Social Interaction*, 11: 85–96.

Vaughn, S., Gersten, R. and Chard, D. J. (2000) The underlying message in LD intervention research: Findings from research syntheses. *Exceptional Children*, 67: 99–114.

Vygotsky, L. S. (1987) Thinking and Speech. In L.S. Vygotsky, *Collected Works* (Vol. 1, pp. 39–285). New York: Plenum Press.

Whittaker, C. R. (2012) Integrating literature circles into a cotaught inclusive classroom. *Intervention in School and Clinic*, 47 (4): 214–223.

Willis, P., Bland, R., Manka, L. and Craft, C. (2012) The ABC of peer mentoring – what secondary students have to say about cross-age peer mentoring in a regional Australian school. *Educational Research and Evaluation*, 18 (2): 173–185.

Yin, K. R. (2014) *Case Study Research: Design and Methods*, 5th edn. California: SAGE Publications.

3

WHAT ARE THE POSSIBILITIES AND LIMITATIONS OF SMALL-SCALE, MEDIATED CLASSROOM INTERVENTIONS?

Two cases from Modern Foreign Languages

Laura Molway, Trevor Mutton, Robert Woore and Katherine Porter

Introduction

This chapter sets out to explore the possibilities and limitations of small-scale, mediated intervention studies taking place in Modern Foreign Language (MFL) classrooms in the UK. We begin by defining and elaborating on the key terms in this statement of aim.

First, we use the term 'intervention' to denote a conscious change in classroom practice aimed at improving learning and teaching. For example, a languages teacher might alter their usual practice to address a perceived problem such as low attainment in a particular skill area, such as reading. In a research context, the term assumes that there is some systematic assessment of outcomes before and after the change in practice, in order to provide an answer to the question 'has the intervention made a difference?'

Second, in relation to our focus on UK MFL classrooms, we would note that teachers in this context are, in theory, able to draw on a strong tradition of classroom-based interventions in the field of Second Language Acquisition (SLA) to inform their practice: see, for example reviews of intervention studies covering a range of different areas by Saito (2012), Lyster, Saito & Sato (2013), Schmitt, (2008) and Boers & Lindstromberg (2012). In many published SLA studies, however, the participants are high proficiency and/or adult learners of English. These participants differ from MFL learners in terms of their age, linguistic proficiency level and motivational profile – partly because the languages learned in classrooms in the United Kingdom (UK) may not have the instrumental or cultural value that English often carries for foreign language learners in other contexts. There have been some published intervention studies conducted in MFL contexts, but so far these have tended to focus on language learning strategy instruction (reflecting the particular interests of the small number of researchers who are active in this context – see for example Macaro & Erler, 2008; Graham & Macaro, 2008). There is much ground left to cover.

Third, our chapter focuses on classroom interventions which are small in scale. Using the terminology of the Education Endowment Foundation (EEF),[1] a major funder of recent classroom-based research, existing interventions range from large-scale 'effectiveness trials' (involving 40 or more schools), through medium-scale 'efficacy trials' (10 or more schools) to small-scale 'pilot studies' aimed at providing proof of concept (typically three or more schools). Finally, there are also practitioner-led studies based in individual classrooms. Many of the latter are conducted each year within the framework of Initial Teacher Education (ITE) and Master's assignment projects. Despite robust criticism (see for example Oancea & Pring, 2008; Thomas, 2016) it is sometimes assumed that large-scale Randomised Control Trials (RCTs) – large-scale because of the need for adequate statistical power – are the 'gold standard' of evidence concerning what works in the classroom. In this chapter we argue that smaller-scale studies which produce rich yet more tentative findings can also be very valuable.

Associated with the issue of scale is the question of the status of the knowledge arising from different kinds of intervention studies, and how the findings are disseminated. Large-scale intervention studies conducted by professional academics will routinely be published. Increasingly, smaller-scale interventions (e.g. Master's or doctoral theses) may also be included in systematic reviews or meta-analyses (in the field of SLA research, for example, see Plonsky, 2011; Hassan et al., 2005). However, we would question who the readers of these publications might be, beyond the research community itself, and the extent to which such publications are accessible to teachers (even given recent increases in open access to research publications). By contrast, practitioner research often fails to be published or more widely disseminated, and in the UK at least, MFL teachers do not currently have a systematic outlet for this kind of research in the way that teachers of some other disciplines do: for example, the Historical Association journal *Teaching History* regularly publishes single practitioner case-study research.

Finally, we explain what we mean by a 'mediated' classroom intervention. We argue that the strongest classroom interventions at any scale should be both research-informed and practitioner-informed. To take two 'straw man' examples, we could envisage on the one hand a teacher trying out an intervention in their classroom but failing to draw on existing theories or research; and on the other a professional researcher coming up with an intervention based on theoretical concerns but which is not adequately grounded in practice. In the former case, the teacher may unwittingly be 're-inventing the wheel' or failing to capitalize on what has gone before; in the latter, the intervention may founder simply because it fails to take adequate account of the practical realities of the classroom. By contrast, we can envision a third kind of intervention, grounded in both theoretical and practical perspectives, such that practical concerns are mediated by research understandings, and vice versa. As we shall see, however, this balance is not easy to achieve in practice.

Underpinning this concept of mediation in intervention research is a wider vision of teacher professionalism. We adopt Winch, Oancea and Orchard's (2015) conceptualization of professionalism, which includes an emphasis on research literacy (see also BERA, 2014). That is to say, teachers should be 'equipped to engage with and be discerning consumers of research' and 'equipped to conduct their own research, individually and collectively, to investigate the impact of particular interventions or to explore the positive and negative effects of educational practice' (BERA, 2014, p. 11). We would not necessarily expect research findings – even those of large-scale, appropriately mediated intervention studies – to be directly applicable to other classrooms 'off the peg'. Rather, teachers would need to use a critical, informed understanding of a given study's findings and, further, to consider these findings in the light of their contextual knowledge of their own classroom.

The current chapter focuses on two small-scale mediated classroom intervention studies. The factor linking the studies is that each focuses on the development of classroom-based assessment practices in light of recent changes to the National Curriculum in England (DfE, 2013), resulting in the removal of the previous, well-established assessment framework (the National Curriculum 'levels') and the consequent requirement for schools to determine their own assessment frameworks. In discussing these two studies, we will consider questions around the nature of research expertise, professional autonomy, the status of the knowledge produced (and the potential for wider impact) and the potential benefits of teachers' engagement with and in research for their own professional learning.

Background: assessment as a focus for classroom-intervention

Assessment serves a fundamental role in any teaching and learning process as a means to diagnose a pupil's particular strengths and weaknesses, leading to the identification of areas for improvement. Research into the types of assessment that have the potential to promote learning has led to the foregrounding of formative assessment, widely referred to as Assessment for Learning (AfL). Assessment can be considered to be formative when classroom evidence is used to 'adapt the teaching work to meet learning needs' (Black et al., 2003, p. 2). Research into formative assessment suggests that it has the potential to produce significant learning gains (Black & Wiliam, 1998).

Muijs and Reynolds (2010) note that the aims of formative assessment may frequently be in tension with other conflicting uses and purposes of assessment in schools. These include: evaluating the quality of teaching and learning of individuals and whole school communities for various purposes; using this information to hold individuals to account for standards of teaching and learning; controlling the curriculum (via the 'washback effect' of high stakes examinations); and providing multiple stakeholders with assurances that an individual has reached a designated level of achievement.

Some of these conflicting purposes of assessment have been evident in MFL classrooms in England. In common with other school subjects, assessment of language learning has been shaped for many years by external assessment requirements: for example, the National Curriculum 'levels'[2] at Key Stage 3; GCSE and A Level specifications at Key Stage 4 and sixth form respectively.[3] In this chapter, we focus particularly on Key Stage 3, where both the interventions we report were targeted. In this phase of education, the National Curriculum 'levels' were deeply embedded in schools' practice, even though they were heavily criticized by SLA researchers for having a negative 'washback' effect on classroom practice. It was argued that they entrenched teaching methods that were not supported by research into how languages are learned (Macaro, Graham, & Woore, 2015).

The policy context surrounding language teaching and learning in England has undergone rapid change in recent years, and in relation to assessment at Key Stage 3 there have been several key shifts. First, the requirement to assess pupils' progress in Key Stage 3 via the National Curriculum levels was abolished in 2013 and no alternative statutory framework has been put in its place. Second, alongside the emphasis on communicative approaches which had characterized the National Curriculum for MFL since its inception (DES/Welsh Office, 1991), the 2013 National Curriculum placed a greater emphasis than had previously been evident on what might be considered more 'traditional' aspects of language learning. These include explicit reference to grammar, translation and the study of 'great literature' and a similar emphasis was to be seen in the revised subject content of GCSE and A Level examinations from 2015 onwards. Finally, these changes have been accompanied by a reduction in the availability of local and national support and advice structures previously accessible to MFL teachers, following the removal of most central funding for languages and the discontinuation of the National Languages Strategy (Johnstone, 2014).

All of these policy changes are recognized as having a significant impact on teachers' classroom practice (see Tinsley & Board, 2017). Our focus in this chapter is on two interventions that address specifically the removal of National Curriculum levels at Key Stage 3. As with all subjects, the lack of any prescribed assessment framework within the new National Curriculum has left behind a vacuum, resulting in some fragmentation of practice across contexts. This presents both opportunities and challenges for schools, with a clear need for the careful development and piloting of alternative assessment frameworks. In the case of MFL, this has posed particular problems for a number of reasons.

First, we would argue that the old NC levels were highly problematic in terms of the model of progression that they represented within each of the four language skills (Macaro, Graham, & Woore, 2015; Mitchell, 2003). Nonetheless, they cast a long shadow, continuing to exert a heavy influence on assessment practices in schools: for example, when we surveyed MFL departments in our own ITE partnership in 2016, 12 of 16 departments were either still using the old NC assessment levels, or were using modified versions of them.

Second, assessing language proficiency is highly complex. One problem is that pupils may be stronger in one skill (e.g. listening) than another (e.g. reading); therefore, trying to sum up pupils' performance in a single overall grade or level is inherently reductive. Even a pupil's level of proficiency within a single skill is itself a complex construct. Different learners may achieve the same level of communicative competence through different balances of linguistic knowledge and strategic behaviour: for example, two pupils – Pupil A and Pupil B – may get the same mark on a reading comprehension exercise, but for different reasons. Pupil A may have understood most of the words but been unsettled by the small proportion that they did not know, leading them to miss important elements of the text's meaning. By contrast, Pupil B may have known relatively few of the words in the text, but been able to compensate for this lack by using sophisticated comprehension strategies. The fact that both pupils might achieve the same 'level' in an assessment illustrates that this judgement is of little formative value in terms of helping them (and their teachers) know what they should do next in order to improve.

Third, SLA research has shown that progression in learners' linguistic output may follow a 'U-shaped' trajectory (McLaughlin, 1990), whereby they initially produce correct forms by reproducing memorized chunks of language (i.e. accuracy is high). As their knowledge develops, they may then begin to 'unpack' these chunks and generate language of their own, but thereby make more errors (i.e. accuracy decreases). Only later, when their knowledge of the language becomes more secure, do they return to producing correct forms (i.e. accuracy increases again to its previous levels). Some researchers have also identified a trade-off between complexity, accuracy and fluency, all of which are desirable features of language output and can be seen as different aspects of overall proficiency (see Housen & Kuiken, 2009). For example, learners may be able to produce language more accurately and fluently by restricting the complexity of what they are trying to say; but if they try to use more complex language, their fluency and accuracy may decrease. The fact that accuracy may actually decrease as learners progress is of course problematic for any assessment system which assumes that pupils will show a neat linear progression from one 'level' to the next.

Finally, it is difficult to assess progression in MFL when (in our experience) schools' schemes of work often adopt a topic-based approach, in which the assessment at the end of each unit is highly dependent on the particular vocabulary associated with that topic. There is often little recycling of this vocabulary in subsequent topics, and little emphasis on the high-frequency words and structures that provide a basis for communication across topics.

Therefore, we can see that creating a valid and workable assessment framework in MFL is a complex matter indeed. Yet, since the removal of the NC levels in 2013, teachers in MFL departments across England have been faced with the considerable challenge of creating (or choosing) and implementing new assessment frameworks for their own particular contexts. In a sense, they can thus be considered to be conducting their own 'classroom interventions': they are making conscious changes in classroom practice aimed at improving learning and teaching. Anecdotal evidence, however, suggests that many teachers found themselves having to implement assessment frameworks in a hurried and sometimes unprincipled way – either producing something new within a very limited time-scale, adapting the familiar old levels, or buying in a commercial assessment scheme. Further, there is often a requirement for these new assessment frameworks to comply with the constraints of generic frameworks which have been agreed at a whole-school level – even where teachers may consider these problematic for use in MFL classrooms specifically.

In response to these issues, the two studies that are the focus of this chapter take a more systematic and research-informed approach to investigating the effects of alternative models of assessment. The first was carried out by a practising MFL teacher who was also a student on a part-time Master's programme in Learning and Teaching. The study formed the basis for her final dissertation. The second study, led by university academics working in collaboration with student teachers and mentors in a range of schools, was an attempt to explore some of the possibilities of extending a multi-level school–university partnership (within the Oxford Education Deanery: see Fancourt, Edwards & Menter, 2015) beyond its traditional 'core' focus on Initial Teacher Education.

Intervention study 1 – Katherine's assessment study

Background to the study

The study in question was designed as an intervention to address a specific problem that had been identified in relation to both Katherine's own classroom teaching and the wider issues in MFL assessment raised by the reform of the National Curriculum in England, as outlined above. While the teacher had a general interest in developing her understanding of classroom-based assessment, she and her colleagues within the MFL department were also questioning more specifically the nature of the regular assessments that were being carried out in their school (every 6–7 weeks).

First, she was aware that, in the separate assessments for each of the four language skills (listening, speaking, reading and writing), pupils tended to perform at different levels for each, yet the score or 'level' awarded for each skill was aggregated to form one overall score for each pupil; she worried that this might not accurately reflect that pupil's actual skill-related performance. Second, she had concerns around the validity of the actual assessments being carried out, since assessment tasks for each skill were often presented in a way that made it difficult to determine an overall level of pupil competence. The mixing of different levels of questions within the same assessment required the teacher to make a 'best fit' judgement as to whether or not a pupil had achieved a particular level overall. Furthermore, Katherine was responding to concerns shared with colleagues within the MFL department that they needed to be able to give pupils a more accurate picture of their progress. However, this had to be done whilst at the same time satisfying the school's requirement for teachers to submit regular assessment data by which progress would be tracked at a whole-school level.

Finally, at a broader level, Katherine also wanted to develop her teaching in such a way as to incorporate more of the features of effective Assessment for Learning (AfL) within her classroom. Aware of the reported benefits of self-assessment and self-regulatory learning to both the learner and the learning process (Sadler, 1989; Assessment Reform Group, 2002; Swaffield, 2011; Black & Jones, 2006) she was keen to develop an assessment framework which included opportunities for her pupils to self-assess their own level of competence against specific criteria. An initial analysis of the pupils' workbooks indicated that there was little effective self-assessment taking place prior to the intervention and that the pupils were very dependent on the teacher for any feedback on their work, with little opportunity to engage with the feedback they were receiving.

Thus, there were a number of starting points for the intervention. However, all were closely related to the wider context of the removal of statutory assessment levels and the subsequent onus placed on schools, and individual subject departments within schools, to devise their own assessment frameworks to measure pupil progress. Furthermore, the teacher was interested in exploring her pupils' engagement with the process of learning a foreign language and felt that a more relevant assessment framework might lead to greater levels of engagement and motivation among some of her pupils. This view was influenced by Coleman's (2009) review of motivation studies, which identified a lack of confidence and an inability to perceive their own progress as some of the key reasons for low motivation amongst MFL learners.

The nature of the intervention

The two key research questions were:

1. Can an assessment framework be developed for the MFL KS3 classroom which enables pupils to feel at ease with the assessment, while at the same time ensuring that their progress is being accurately measured?
2. Can self-assessment be used effectively within such a framework?

It was decided that a two cycle 'action research' approach would allow the issues to be investigated in a systematic and practical way (Cohen, Manion & Morrison, 2007; Elliott, 1991; McNiff, 2002). Further, as Edwards and Talbot point out, this style of research gives 'scope for inventiveness and creativity' (1997: p 61). Their 'plan–act–monitor–review' approach was used as the basis for both cycles of intervention (Figure 3.1).

The first cycle saw the planning and implementing of an assessment approach that led to an increase in the amount of pupil self-assessment that was being carried out. This self-assessment was done against specific criteria devised by the teacher. The second phase developed these self-assessment criteria further, including the formulation and trialling of a more detailed and coherent framework for assessment. Here, pupils were able to assess their own performance against criteria that could

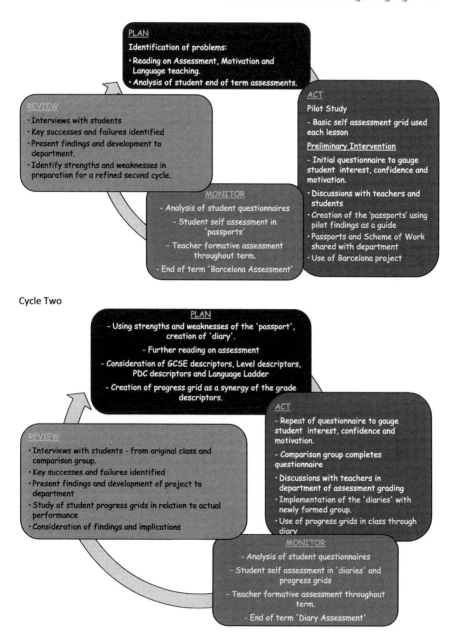

FIGURE 3.1 Overview of the action research approach

be equated to 'levels' or 'grades' (for the purposes of whole-school monitoring purposes), yet which also enabled them to judge whether they were currently working 'above', 'at' or 'below' expected levels of performance. For each of these three levels of performance and within each separate skill area (listening, speaking, reading and writing), the pupils were given a series of 'can do' phrases with which to assess their own performance, and these were aligned to designated levels, enabling the teacher to track progression in each of the four skills individually over time.

The assessment framework that was developed and subsequently applied was informed by a reading of the relevant literature and drew on four existing frameworks: the previous National Curriculum level descriptors (Qualifications and Curriculum Authority, 2007); the GCSE grade descriptors from one of the national examination boards (AQA, 2014); the Languages Ladder grade descriptors (DCSF, 2007); and the MFL Professional Development Consortium's assessment framework (PDC in MFL, 2013; see also below).

The participants

A class of 29 Year 8 (12–13-year-old) pupils learning Spanish was selected to be the focus of the study. This was a mixed-attainment class which Katherine had taught previously and one with which she felt she had a good relationship.

The first cycle of the intervention was conducted over one half-term, covering one unit from the MFL department's scheme of work; the second phase took place over the subsequent half-term, again covering one unit of work. A parallel class (taught by another teacher) acted as an informal 'comparison group'. This class was given the same assessment materials but they were not used regularly or explicitly in the lessons.

The first cycle focused on the topic of 'holidays' and an assessment record was produced that would be presented in the form of a customised passport, in which the pupils would record their levels of understanding and progress. For the second cycle (focussed on the topic of 'leisure time and activities'), customised diaries were created to fulfil a similar purpose. Data were collected from both the intervention group and the comparison group through questionnaires and interviews, as well as through analysis of the passports and diaries themselves. There was a limited amount of collaboration within the MFL department while the study was being carried out.

The outcomes of the intervention

The intervention indicated that the framework had provided an opportunity to develop the learners' capacity for self-assessment and that it was also sufficiently rigorous to enable teachers to report progress at both the individual and whole class level. The pupil judgements were moderated by the teacher and her colleagues, and as the pupils became more familiar with the processes involved, there was evidence that they were able to make reliable assessments of their own performance against the designated criteria.

What was particularly interesting was the gradual development of a greater focus on learning as being the key to higher levels of performance. In the first survey, a greater proportion of pupils identified appropriate classroom behaviour as a factor that could lead to improvement (74 per cent, with only 26 per cent identifying a learning focus) but by the beginning of the second cycle, the proportions were 59 per cent and 41 per cent respectively. (In the comparison group, the second survey revealed figures of 80 per cent and 20 per cent respectively.) The data also indicated that lower attaining pupils tended to identify more targets related to their behaviour, whereas higher attaining pupils tended to identify learning targets.

The initial cycle revealed that there needed to be greater clarity in relation to the assessment criteria by which the pupils were being asked to assess themselves, and also the opportunity for greater levels of independence when doing so. While some pupils began to use the language of the success criteria when discussing their progress, the study also revealed that such engagement might nevertheless mask underlying misconceptions in terms of what the assessment criteria actually meant. One pupil summarized her achievements at the end of the intervention as follows:

> … in writing I can include some tenses and different vocab and overall I can cope with unfamiliar vocabulary in a topic I know.

When asked, however, to give an example of this in practice, the pupil replied:

> What's vocabulary? I don't know what it is.

One other interesting outcome was in relation to the pupils' perception of the subject itself. Prior to the intervention many of the pupils were generally motivated to learn but nevertheless lacked confidence in their ability to perform in one or more language learning skills. There was some evidence that, in spite of continuing to find the subject challenging, pupils felt more confident is attempting to use the language productively, with some pupils commenting on the value of the self-assessment grids contained within the passports and the diaries, for example:

> It does give you a little bit of hints like saying what you need to do or what you have been doing so it just helps you in a sense and if you are in the middle and you look at the top and you realise you haven't done that then it's kind of helped you, not only to realise what you're meeting but also how to improve.

Dissemination of the results of the intervention

The teacher was able to disseminate her findings both within her school and beyond, since she moved to a teaching post at a different school the following academic year, where she discussed the study and its findings with her new colleagues. In addition, there was the opportunity to lead an ITE seminar at the university through which she was completing her Master's course, focusing on a number of assessment issues (including the validity and reliability of assessment data) with beginning teachers.

Case Study 2: trialling a 'Pedagogical Assessment Framework'

Background to the study

The second study was one in which student teachers on an Initial Teacher Education course trialled an alternative assessment framework in MFL, the 'Pedagogical Assessment Framework' or 'PAF' (Macaro, Graham & Woore, 2015). This framework was developed as part of the 'Professional Development Consortium in MFL' (pdcinmfl.com), a collaborative project involving secondary school teachers and university-based researchers. Over a period of six weeks, working with the support of their school-based mentors and university tutors (the current authors and other colleagues), the student teachers each used this framework to assess a specific language skill (either reading or speaking) with at least one class in Key Stage 3.

A brief description of the PAF is in order at this point. (A full copy of the framework can be found at pdcinmfl.com and in Macaro et al., 2015.) At its core is a twin approach to assessment for each language skill, comprising a 'main strand' (focusing on communicative competence) and a 'supporting strand' (focusing on the underpinning linguistic knowledge – e.g. knowledge of vocabulary and grammar – and strategic behaviour). The purpose of the main strand is to ensure that the principal focus is always on what pupils can actually do with the language. The purpose of the supporting strand is to provide diagnostic information to inform teaching and learning: it helps learners (and their teachers) decide on the priority areas to work on in order to develop their communicative competence further. To illustrate, Pupil A (in our example above) would benefit from developing their strategic competence, helping them to be more resilient when faced with unknown words. Pupil B, by contrast, is already an effective strategic reader, but this will only carry them so far: they must increase their vocabulary knowledge in order to progress to more complex texts.

Again, the launch of the new NC and its lack of any statutory assessment framework provided the immediate impetus for this study. The resulting fragmentation of assessment practices across partner schools presented a practical problem in relation to how the coverage of assessment on the ITE course would be addressed. Discussions of this issue in university seminars could no longer build upon a foundation of common practice in schools. Indeed, several student teachers raised this issue in end-of-course evaluations as an impediment to their progress on the course. Furthermore, informal observations and conversations with teachers in partner schools indicated that MFL departments were themselves grappling with the implications of the new NC and the urgent question of how to handle assessment in the 'post-levels' context.

These considerations led to the idea of an intervention study which could: develop the student teachers' understanding of assessment; develop assessment practices in schools across the partnership; and more broadly explore the viability and effectiveness of the PAF framework itself, including its washback effects on classroom teaching and learning. The project sought to address a number of questions but the ones focused on in this chapter are as follows:

1. What were the perceived strengths and weaknesses of the PAF?
2. What effects did it have on classroom teaching and learning?
3. What was the impact of the project on the student teachers' understanding of assessment?

Nature of the intervention

The project can be conceptualized as a 'dual' intervention operating on two levels. First, a change in practice in the ITE course was instigated, resulting in the student teachers being asked to try out the PAF with one of their classes, and being supported in doing this. Second, the student teachers' use of the PAF was itself an intervention in their own classrooms, since they were trying out a different assessment framework from the one otherwise in use in their school context.

For the first (ITE-based) intervention, it was considered important that the student teachers were not simply presented with the new assessment framework and a set of instructions to follow in order to implement it. Rather, university sessions were used help them to understand the PAF and its underlying rationale. It was hoped that they would then be empowered to use it in ways with which they felt comfortable and which fitted their own particular classroom contexts. In other words, they were able to take some degree of ownership over how the assessment framework was to be implemented.[4] For the second (school-based) intervention, student teachers were allocated randomly to one of two groups, the first of which focused on speaking and the other on reading. They then used the PAF to assess the relevant skill over one school half-term (March/April).

The school-based intervention had a number of limitations: for example, student teachers were being asked to experiment with a new system of assessment when they themselves were novice in matters of assessment generally. The intervention was also shorter than would have ideally been the case, being constrained by the ITE course calendar. Further, in light of the short timescale and the student teachers' status in school, it was not possible to embed the PAF as the 'official' assessment framework (the one used to communicate with parents and school managers about pupils' progress). These factors limited the effects of the intervention but nevertheless allowed a flavour of its impact to be obtained.

Methods of data collection

From the cohort of 28 student teachers, 23 participated in the project, spread across 15 schools. Twelve focused on reading and 11 on speaking. They were supported by 15 school-based mentors and five university tutors (including three of the present authors). Three schools opted out of the project, since they did not feel able to support their student teachers' use of the PAF when they were already in the process of implementing their own new assessment frameworks. This accounts for the five student teachers who did not participate.

Data were gathered from a range of sources. Both the student teachers and their mentors completed online questionnaires eliciting their views on the PAF (and on their participation in the project itself), and follow-up interviews were conducted with the student teachers. Samples of assessment materials which the student teachers created (e.g. reading comprehension tasks, speaking tasks and vocabulary tests) were also collected. This was to provide insight into how the framework was implemented in practice: i.e. how the student teachers translated the assessment framework into concrete assessment tasks. Finally, samples of pupils' work produced in response to these tasks were collected, together with any feedback provided by the student teachers. The findings presented in this chapter are based on the questionnaire and interview data.

The data collection (and indeed the project as a whole) presented some complex ethical issues relating to the power relations between the different groups of participants. Participation was optional for both the student teachers and their mentors, but given that the university tutors were not only the researchers, but also the course tutors, there was a risk that the student teachers might feel coerced into taking part. To guard against this, it was repeatedly stressed that their participation in the project was entirely unconnected with their own progress and assessment on the ITE course. Further, a research assistant was employed to manage and conduct the data collection, thus making it easier for the student teachers to opt out should they wish to do so. This mechanism was also designed to increase the likelihood of the student teachers giving their honest opinions on the PAF, rather than saying what they thought their tutors might want to hear.

A further tier of complexity was created by the mentors' involvement in the project. There was significant variability in the degree to which mentors were prepared to relinquish control of assessment procedures in their classrooms, in order to enable student teachers to experiment with the PAF.

Outcomes

Here, we provide a brief overview of some of the project's key findings; see Woore, Mutton, Molway, Macaro and Savory (in preparation) for a more complete account of the outcomes.

In relation to the first research question, the student teachers mentioned various weaknesses of the PAF, but these were disparate, with no particular patterns emerging. For example, they felt that: the PAF was time consuming to implement (n=2 respondents); it was unclear how to interpret some of the terms in the level descriptors, such as 'familiar language' (n=2); the levels were pitched too high for beginner learners (n=1) or were too broad to allow their pupils' progress to be documented effectively (n=1); and the label 'beginner' attached to the first level could be demotivating (n=1). Further, two participants mentioned difficulties with reliability, as illustrated by the following comment made in one of the interviews:

I know that there is a lot of criticism about the previous system [the old NC levels] (…) you tick this tense and you go up a level (…) However it does give you some clear criteria from the teacher's point of view and the students' perspective, when they are trying to complete tasks, when they are aiming for something.

This response is interesting, however, because it seems to acknowledge that the (perceived) greater reliability of the old system came at the expense of its validity as a model of progression in foreign language learning.

By contrast, there was clear agreement on a number of strengths of the PAF. The responses of 15 out of the 23 participants indicated that, in broad terms, they felt the PAF offered a valid model of progression in language learning, and was a useful diagnostic tool for understanding learners' progress and current learning needs; this understanding, in turn, could inform subsequent lesson planning. By contrast, the old NC levels (still in use in numerous partner schools at that time) were felt to embody an incomplete and inaccurate model of progression, placing artificial emphasis on particular aspects of language learning whilst neglecting other important aspects. The following quotations from two participants illustrate these views:

To me, what is best about the [PAF] framework is that it makes teachers think about what the exact building blocks for success in language learning are, as these are very different from what has been conveyed in the old NC levels.

I found the PAF really useful to work out what I needed to do to help improve the students. For example, I could address their overuse of cognates and give the students strategies. It gives me more information about the students' needs. The [old NC] levels in comparison are superficial. I would say the PAF provides a good diagnosis for future planning.

To address the second research question, the student teachers were asked whether (and if so, in what ways) their use of the PAF had influenced their wider classroom practice. Thirteen participants responded to this question. Two of these reported little influence on their classroom practice, because they had had insufficient time to engage with the PAF as thoroughly as they would have liked. One said that there had been a negative influence, because they felt that the PAF had compromised their ability to cover the school's prescribed scheme of work. However, ten respondents felt that the PAF had had a positive impact on their teaching. Specifically, they reported that they had put more emphasis on the following, when compared to the teaching they had been doing previously (before they started using the PAF): developing pupils' language learning strategies (n=4 participants); their knowledge of high frequency words (n=2); their proficiency in phonological decoding (n=1); and their ability to engage in spontaneous oral interaction (n=1). Another said that the PAF had led her to focus more instructional attention on the *processes* of language learning, rather than simply the product. It could be argued that all of these reported outcomes are highly positive ones, when seen from the perspective of research into language learning and teaching (for an overview see Macaro, Graham & Woore, 2015).

Five other student teachers, when asked about the influence of the PAF on their classroom teaching, reported that it had developed their understanding of the underlying components of language proficiency, of how pupils make progress in these areas and hence of how this might be reflected in their teaching. As one respondent noted:

> It made me think how best I could prepare students for an assessment based on those levels – just like when teaching for national curriculum level-based assessments, you teach students two tenses so they can get a level 5. It was much more positive than the latter situation, however, because I was more concerned with giving students the tools and practice they needed to successfully communicate, rather than focussing on being able to reproduce certain structures just because someone somewhere was dictating that they should.

Finally, in terms of impact of the project on the student teachers' own professional learning (research question 3), it is clear from analysis of their questionnaire and interview responses that they had developed a deeper and more critical understanding of the issues involved in assessing pupils' progress in MFL. This is evident, for example, in the four quotations above, in which the student teachers discuss the validity of the PAF in relation to the old NC levels, backing up their views with specific arguments relating to the nature of foreign language learning. Further, as had been hoped, the PAF provided tutors with a common point of reference when discussing assessment-related issues in university seminars.

Dissemination

The findings of the PAF project have been (or are being) disseminated by the university-based authors via various conference presentations and published outputs, as well as through local school–university partnerships.

It could, however, be argued that the intensive nature of the work undertaken with the student teachers as part of this project – for example, the detailed critical discussions of the PAF, its background and the issues arising in its implementation – may well have had a deep and potentially long-lasting influence on their classroom practice. Of course, this influence may extend, in the immediate term, only to the classrooms of those student teachers who participated in the project, or of those working directly with them in schools. However, this tension between 'breadth' and 'depth' of impact is something that, we would argue, merits further discussion.

Discussion

These two small-scale, mediated classroom interventions raise a number of interesting issues which potentially have a wider relevance beyond the MFL contexts in which the studies were carried out. These issues can be summarized in terms of three specific questions.

1. *What have we learnt about classroom-based interventions in assessment and the related challenges?*

Both interventions presented in the above case studies focus on the development of assessment practices in MFL classrooms following the removal of the statutory and well-established National Curriculum levels at key stage 3. In comparison to a more straightforward intervention that introduces, for example, a specific new teaching strategy over a period of time (the impact of which might be measured from data gathered through pre- and post-tests), both the interventions described above are complex. The process of devising and applying alternative assessment frameworks and then creating related assessment tasks is sufficiently complex, but then to try to evaluate the validity and reliability of these frameworks increases this level of complexity even further. In the PAF intervention, there was some attempt to 'triangulate' the student teachers' assessment judgements by asking the mentors working directly with them to moderate the assessments made. In Katherine's case, where the focus was also on developing the pupils' capacity to self-assess their language competence accurately, she used her own assessment to moderate the pupil judgements. In both cases, however, a certain degree of subjectivity was involved, raising questions as to the reliability of the approaches taken beyond the specific contexts in which the interventions were carried out.

A further factor in determining possible limitations of the two interventions relates to the validity of the assessment criteria that were developed in both studies. The validity of the assessment criteria within any given framework can only be evaluated through the fluent use of the framework and its criteria within the classroom, but such use presupposes pupil familiarity with the criteria and the ability of the teacher – and the pupils – to engage with them effectively. This, in turn, requires an initial process of introduction and familiarization. However, to do this, more time and resources would have been necessary than were available to either of the interventions described in this chapter.

The need for a shared understanding of assessment criteria is illustrated clearly in Katherine's study where one of the pupils *appeared* to be able to carry out the process of self-assessment effectively and to highlight areas which would serve as his future learning targets; in doing so he was able to articulate the language of the success criteria as expected, but demonstrated little understanding of the meaning of quite basic terminology used within those criteria (that is to say the meaning of the word 'vocabulary'). Questions are thus raised about the common level of understanding and interpretation of the criteria. Nevertheless, it could be argued that Katherine was only able to gain this greater insight into the pupil's lack of understanding because of the detailed data collection that accompanied the action research project. This misconception might otherwise have remained hidden.

Overall, whilst we recognize that assessment in any subject area is complex, we would argue that this is particularly so in MFL, where the principal aim of instruction is the development not of conceptual understanding, but of communicative competence. This complexity is further exacerbated by the pressure to satisfy institutional requirements to produce regular assessment data within a prescribed format for accountability purposes. Drawing on research into the way in which languages are learnt can, however, help us to devise assessment frameworks that are both valid and promote effective pedagogical approaches. In both the interventions described in this chapter, the focus is ultimately on learning and teaching, rather than on the wider issues around assessment policy and accountability issues, leading to a more positive 'washback' effect on classroom practice.

2.   *What have we learnt about the ways in which interventions of this nature contribute to teacher professional development and learning, and the related challenges?*

Professional autonomy

One key issue relates to the level of individual teacher autonomy within classroom intervention studies of this nature. In Katherine's case, although constrained by the requirement to submit regular assessments of her pupils' progress to senior leaders in the school, she was nevertheless able to take the initiative to devise a way in which such data could be generated through a more innovative approach. She was able both to create a new assessment framework (based on her reading of the literature and informed by her understanding of other such frameworks) and to create the tasks by which pupil progress would be measured, drawing on her own interests and capabilities (Benson, 2010).

In the case of the PAF, the student teachers did not have a hand in developing the assessment framework itself, and they also had to use the PAF within the constraints of the existing policies and practices of the schools in which they had been placed. Nonetheless, they were able themselves to devise assessment tasks which they considered appropriate for the specific contexts in which they were working, which again allowed them to make the most of their own strengths and to develop their own ideas. The student teachers involved in the PAF project told us that the structured nature of the enquiry and the expectations around such involvement afforded them the necessary 'permission' to develop greater levels of agency than might otherwise have been the case.

Professional knowledge base

Further, the PAF study highlighted the need for teachers to have the necessary systematic knowledge and understanding to be able to challenge, where appropriate, existing policies and practices and to be equipped to deal with change effectively as part of the ongoing process of continuing professional development. As noted above, a number of colleagues within our partner schools found it challenging to respond to the sudden removal of the previous National Curriculum levels and the requirement to create (or choose) a new assessment framework at short notice. We would argue that both Katherine and the student teachers who took part in the PAF study may have been better equipped to deal with such a challenge, since they had been required to draw on a range of perspectives in order to enable them to judge the validity and reliability of specific assessment approaches that they were undertaking in their classrooms. Thus teachers' work is seen as a 'professional endeavour' in which:

> their reflective abilities should bring together their own experience and the deliverances of research to enable them to determine both short and long-term courses of action.
>
> *Winch, Oancea & Orchard, 2015: pp. 210–211*

Likewise, Katherine was able to address the challenges of introducing a new assessment framework into her classroom practice because she was able to draw on a range of different theoretical perspectives before considering what might work within her specific context. Her reading of the wider assessment research literature and her analysis of existing frameworks enabled her both to develop an alternative set of assessment criteria (which would provide the data needed to satisfy the school's requirements for regular assessment updates) and to introduce key aspects of formative assessment into her classroom, particularly the use of pupil self-assessment.

Professional learning

In spite of calls for research to underpin teachers' practical work in the classroom, the extent to which teachers are able to engage both with and in research (BERA, 2014) does raise important questions in relation to Initial Teacher Education and ongoing professional development. One such question concerns how this 'research literacy' (BERA, 2014, p. 7) can be achieved. A key factor appears to be the involvement of specialist expertise (likely to be external to the school) which is able to illustrate innovative approaches, assist with the process of evaluation and scaffold the professional learning around these approaches (Cordingley, 2015). In both the studies examined in this chapter, there was external support in place, albeit from two different perspectives. In Katherine's case she was, as a Master's student, supported in her intervention research through regular discussion with and feedback from a university supervisor; in the case of the PAF project, the intervention was set up by the university, which provided both the initial grounding in the knowledge and understanding that might be required (delivered as part of the normal ITE programme) and ongoing support through individual monitoring by course tutors.

Similarly Cordingley (2015) identifies peer support as one of the key contributors to effective professional learning, through 'collaboration, especially reciprocal risk taking and professional dialogue' (2015: p. 240). The MFL interventions described here indicate both the strengths and the limitations of such collaboration. Although Katherine had the support of her colleagues in the school, the intervention was carried out very much within her own classroom and with little wider professional discussion. Colleagues had the opportunity to be involved but appeared to have little incentive to do so, in spite of the concerns that had been expressed collectively in relation to the schools' current practices for assessing and recording pupils' progress. Teachers may be sceptical about the value of educational research and not see its relevance to practice (Vanderlinde & van Braak, 2010), yet interventions of the sort that Katherine carried out are driven by a sense of immediacy and are carried out in real classrooms in which the teachers in question have a detailed understanding of the specific contextual factors involved. It may nevertheless still be the case that colleagues have insufficient interest in trialling innovative approaches and may prefer instead to implement approaches prescribed from elsewhere.

Where the PAF study differed was that it was deliberately set up in such a way as to require collaboration between a range of different research participants (university researchers, school-based mentors and student teachers). The fact that the interventions were being carried out on multiple sites enabled discussion to be focused on both the enquiry process and the emergent findings. The student teachers had a high level of responsibility for introducing innovative approaches, albeit within limited parameters, yet did have the necessary support structures in place to enable them to seek guidance where necessary, get feedback on the assessment tasks they were devising and share experiences of the intervention with others. We would therefore argue that the ambition to develop research literacy among teachers (BERA, 2014) is more likely to be realized if opportunities to do so are structured, rather than simply left to chance.

3. *What have we learnt about the interventions themselves?*

Scale and relevance

A further general issue raised by the studies reported in this chapter concerns their scope and their potential for wider impact. To what extent can such small-scale research produce knowledge with relevance beyond the specific classrooms and contexts in which it takes place? In both cases, it could be argued that there was real 'depth' of impact (albeit on a small scale). The interventions arguably led to a number of potentially beneficial outcomes related both to the participants' understanding and practice of assessment and to the pedagogical benefits of adopting new approaches to classroom-based assessment. The latter included a greater focus on the diagnostic aspects of assessment (Black & Wiliam, 2009) and the promotion of more pupil self-assessment in order both to enhance the learning process and to increase pupil motivation (Black et al., 2004). Readers may note that both our studies lack the measurement of pupil outcomes. However, this would have been difficult given that the focus of the studies was, precisely, the development of valid ways to measure pupil outcomes.

In terms of the assessment frameworks themselves, these were tested and, within the limitations of the individual interventions, judged to have some validity. Although these were small-scale, exploratory interventions, we would argue that they nonetheless represent a valuable first step in a wider process of the systematic, research-informed development of a new assessment framework. This process is particularly important in a context in which some schools may be feeling pressurized into making hurried innovations in their assessment practices, which risks the adoption of less principled frameworks or ones which are less appropriate in an MFL context.

However, the full impact of small-scale interventions as a first step can be realized only if their findings are available to other researchers and practitioners. Here we would note an imbalance in the possibilities for such dissemination between our two interventions. These possibilities tend to be more limited for classroom practitioners than for academic researchers, for whom publication and dissemination is already a professional expectation. We would therefore raise the question as to how the findings of such small-scale, mediated interventions might be disseminated more widely, given that many practitioners involved in such studies may produce interesting results, yet may not be in a position to communicate these beyond their immediate communities of practice.

Conclusions

The assessment frameworks trialled in our two interventions are attempts to develop subject-specific models of assessment which reflect research evidence concerning how languages are learnt, have positive washback on pedagogy and can play an effective formative role in guiding teaching and learning. Both frameworks were positively evaluated, at least within the limitations of these small-scale studies. These initial findings now invite further research to develop and evaluate the frameworks further, for the benefit of classroom practitioners. Thus, despite their exploratory nature and small scale, our studies represent potentially important early steps in a wider process of systematically developing and evaluating pedagogical innovations.

Beyond these specific findings, our studies also raise a number of broader issues relating to issues such as the relationship between research and practice; the potential impact of small-scale intervention studies; and the nature of teachers' professional learning. We address each of these points in turn.

First, we noted above that the relevance of educational research to classroom practice is sometimes viewed with scepticism (even hostility). However, both our studies illustrate how a research-informed approach can be effectively brought to bear on practical classroom problems. The immediate catalyst for the studies was the sudden shift in policy which removed the previous statutory assessment framework. However, the studies are also highly attuned to the specific concerns of the particular contexts in which they were conducted. This, we argue, reflects their 'mediated' nature. As we noted above, although this was achieved in different ways in the two studies, both were deeply rooted in both theoretical and practical perspectives, with practical concerns being mediated by research understandings, and vice versa.

Second, we would highlight that both of the studies reported in this chapter have had considerable impact in the immediate contexts (schools and ITE partnership) in which they were conducted. However, as with any research, the extent to which their findings can have wider impact depends on the effectiveness with which these are disseminated. Currently (notwithstanding this chapter), practitioner research has tended to have less easy pathways to dissemination than that conducted by 'academic' researchers (such as university lecturers). Our two case studies are no exception. We would therefore like to see increased possibilities for dissemination of practitioner research, such that this becomes normalized as part of the teacher's role as a 'research literate' professional. Of course, there may be differences in the methodological and theoretical rigour within this widened stock of published studies; however, this is something that individual teachers would continue to assess as part of their critical engagement with published research (Winch et al., 2015).

Finally, the contribution made by classroom interventions to teachers' wider professional learning should not be underestimated. Indeed, this may afford significant additional benefits alongside the new knowledge arising from the interventions themselves. For example, both Katherine and the student teachers involved in the PAF project developed rich and sophisticated understandings of the issues involved in assessing progress in MFL, and of the relationship between assessment on the one hand and teaching and learning on the other. Here we see a real 'depth' of impact of the studies – in terms of changes to teachers' beliefs and classroom practices – which contrasts with the more usual concern with 'breadth' of impact.

A question which then arises is to what extent these kinds of approaches to developing teachers' research-informed understanding of pedagogical issues are 'scalable'. Should all teachers have the opportunity to engage with and in research to the same depth as was achieved by Katherine through her Master's course and by our student teachers through their involvement in the collaborative research project? Echoing the ambition of the BERA/RSA (2014) inquiry, we would offer an affirmative answer to this question. Small-scale, appropriately mediated classroom interventions have the potential to play an important role in facilitating teachers' engagement with and in research.

Notes

1 http://educationendowmentfoundation.org.uk
2 The assessment framework for the National Curriculum in England, prior to the revisions in 2013, consisted of eight levels within each of one or more subject-specific attainment targets. For MFL there were four such attainment targets (speaking; listening and responding; writing; reading and responding).

3 Key Stage 3: students in their first three (sometimes two) years of secondary education, aged 11–14. Key Stage 4: students in the subsequent phase of education leading up to their compulsory national examinations, the GCSE (General Certificate in Secondary Education). Sixth form: two years of post-16 education leading to the Advanced Level (A Level) examination.

4 Student teachers had access to a range of exemplar assessment tasks that might facilitate the implementation of the PAF. They used their own judgement to modify and/or re-design these tasks to suit the work being undertaken in their own classrooms.

5 The nature of the previous National Curriculum descriptor for level 5 in writing included the requirement that pupils should 'refer to recent experiences or future plans, as well as to everyday activities'. This became interpreted by many teachers as being an indication that the pupils had to produce at least two different tenses within one assessed piece of work in order to attain a level 5.

References

Assessment and Qualifications Alliance (2014). *GCSE Specification Spanish*. Retrieved from: http://filestore.aqa.org.uk/subjects/AQA-4695-W-SP-14.PDF.

Assessment Reform Group (2002). *Assessment for Learning: 10 Principles*. Retrieved from: www.aaia.org.uk/content/uploads/2010/06/Assessment-for-Learning-10-principles.pdf.

Benson, P. (2010). Teacher education and teacher autonomy: Creating spaces for experimentation in secondary school English language teaching. *Language Teaching Research*, 14(3), 259–275.

BERA (2014). Research and the Teaching Profession: building the capacity for a self-improving education system. Final report of the BERA-RSA Inquiry into the role of research in teacher education. Retrieved from: www.bera.ac.uk/wp-content/uploads/2013/12/BERA-RSA-Research-Teaching-Profession-FULL-REPORT-for-web.pdf.

Black, P., Harrison, C., Lee, C., Marshall, B., & Wiliam, D. (2003). *Assessment for Learning: Putting it into practice*. Maidenhead: Open University Press.

Black, P., Harrison, C., Lee, C., Marshall, B., & Wiliam, D. (2004). Working inside the black box: Assessment for learning in the classroom. *Phi Delta Kappan*, 86(1), 8–21.

Black, P., & Jones, J. (2006). Formative assessment and the learning and teaching of MFL: sharing the language learning road map with the learners, *The Language Learning Journal*, 34, 4–9.

Black, P., & Wiliam, D. (1998). Assessment and classroom learning. *Assessment in Education: Principles, policy & practice*, 5(1), 7–74.

Black, P., & Wiliam, D. (2009). Developing the theory of formative assessment. *Educational Assessment, Evaluation and Accountability*, 21(1), 5.

Boers, F., & Lindstromberg, S. (2012). Experimental and intervention studies on formulaic sequences in a second language. *Annual Review of Applied Linguistics*, 32, 83–110.

Cohen, L., Manion, L., & Morrison, K. (2007). *Research Methods in Education*, 6th Edition, London: RoutledgeFalmer.

Coleman, J. (2009). Why the British do not learn languages: myths and motivation in the United Kingdom, *The Language Learning Journal*, 37 (1), 111–127.

Cordingley, P. (2015). The contribution of research to teachers' professional learning and development. *Oxford Review of Education*, 41 (2), 234–252.

Department for Children, Schools & Families (2007). *The Languages Ladder: Steps to Success*. Retrieved from: http://webarchive.nationalarchives.gov.uk/20130401151715/http://education.gov.uk/publications/eorderingdownload/dcsf-00811-2007.pdf.

Department for Education (DfE) (2013). National Curriculum. Retrieved from: www.gov. uk/government/collections/national-curriculum.

Department for Education and Science (DES)/Welsh Office (1991). *Modern Foreign Languages in the National Curriculum,* Department of Education and Science and the Welsh Office.

Edwards, A. & Talbot, R. (1997). *The hard-pressed researcher: a research handbook for the caring professions.* England: Addison Welsey Longman.

Elliot, J. (1991). *Action research for educational change.* Milton Keynes: Open University Press.

Fancourt, N., Edwards, A., & Menter, I. (2015). Reimagining a School–University Partnership: The Development of the Oxford Education Deanery Narrative. *Education Inquiry,* 6(3). 27724, DOI: 10.3402/edui.v6.27724.

Graham, S. & Macaro, E. (2008). 'Strategy Instruction in Listening for Lower-Intermediate Learners of French' in Language Learning, 58(4), 747–783.

Hassan, X., Macaro, E., Mason, D., Nye, G., Smith, P. & Vanderplank, R. (2005). *Strategy training in language learning – A systematic review of available research.* EPPI-Centre, Social Science Research Unit, Institute of Education, University of London, London. Retrieved from http://eppi.ioe.ac.uk/cms/Default.aspx?tabid=296.

Housen, A., & Kuiken, F. (2009). Complexity, accuracy, and fluency in second language acquisition. *Applied Linguistics,* 30(4), 461–473.

Johnstone, R. (2014). Languages over the past 40 years: Does history repeat itself? In P. Driscoll, E. Macaro, & A. Swarbrick (Eds.), *Debates in Modern Languages Education.* Abingdon: Routledge.

Lyster, R., Saito, K., & Sato, M. (2013). Oral corrective feedback in second language classrooms. *Language Teaching,* 46(1), 1–40.

Macaro, E., & Erler, L. (2008). Raising the Achievement of Young-beginner Readers of French through Strategy Instruction, *Applied Linguistics,* 29(1), 90–119.

Macaro, E., Graham, S., & Woore, R. (2015). *Improving Foreign Language Teaching: Towards a research-based curriculum and pedagogy.* London: Routledge.

McLaughlin, B. (1990). Restructuring. *Applied Linguistics,* 11(2), 113–128.

McNiff, J. (2002). *Action Research: Principles and Practice.* London: Routledge.

Mitchell, R. (2003). Rethinking the concept of progression in the National Curriculum for Modern Foreign Languages: a research perspective. *Language Learning Journal,* 27(1), 15–23.

Muijs, D., & Reynolds, D. (2010). *Effective Teaching: Evidence and practice.* London: Sage.

Oancea, A., & Pring, R. (2008). The importance of being thorough: On systematic accumulations of 'what works' in education research. *Journal of Philosophy of Education,* 42(1), 16–39.

Plonsky, L. (2011). The effectiveness of second language strategy instruction: a metaanalysis. *Language learning,* 61(4), 993–1038.

Professional Development Consortium in Modern Foreign Languages (PDC in MFL) (2013) *Alternative assessment framework for languages.* Retrieved from: https://pdcinmfl. com/alternative-assessment-framework-for-languages.

Qualifications and Curriculum Authority (2007). *Modern foreign languages: Programme of study for key stage 3 and attainment targets.* Retrieved from: http://webarchive.nationalarchives. gov.uk/20110223175304/http:/curriculum.qcda.gov.uk/uploads/QCA-07-3340-p_ MFL_KS3_tcm8-405.pdf.

Sadler, D. (1989). Formative assessment and the design of instructional systems, *Instructional Science,* 18, 119–144.

Saito, K. (2012). Effects of instruction on L2 pronunciation development: A synthesis of 15 quasiexperimental intervention studies. *TESOL Quarterly,* 46(4), 842–854.

Schmitt, N. (2008). Review article: Instructed second language vocabulary learning. *Language Teaching Research,* 12(3), 329–363.

Swaffield, S. (2011). Getting to the heart of authentic Assessment for Learning, *Assessment in Education: Principles, Policy & Practice*, 18(4), 433–449.

Tinsley, T., & Board, K. (2017). *Language Trends 2016/17: Language Teaching in Primary and Secondary Schools in England*. British Council.

Thomas, G. (2016). After the Gold Rush: Questioning the 'Gold Standard' and Reappraising the Status of Experiment and Randomized Controlled Trials in Education. *Harvard Educational Review*, 86(3), 390–411.

Vanderlinde, R., & van Braak, J. (2010). The gap between educational research and practice: views of teachers, school leaders, intermediaries and researchers. *British Educational Research Journal*, 36(2), 299–316.

Winch, C., Oancea, A., & Orchard, J. (2015). The contribution of educational research to teachers' professional learning: philosophical understandings. *Oxford Review of Education*, 41(2), 202–216.

Woore, R., Mutton, T., Molway, L., Macaro, E., & Savory, C. (in preparation). 'Towards a "Pedagogical Assessment Framework" in Modern Foreign Languages: an attempt to align language teaching, learning, assessment and research evidence.'

4

WHO IS DOING THE QUESTIONING?

A classroom intervention in secondary science classrooms to promote student questioning

Alexandra Haydon and Ann Childs

> Every other Jewish mother in Brooklyn would ask her child after school: 'So, what did you learn in school today?' But not my mother. 'Izzy,' she would say, 'did you ask a good question today?
>
> *Isidore Rabi (1898–1988), Nobel prize winner in Physics*[1]

> Those who ask questions – teachers, texts, tests, – are not seeking knowledge; those who would seek knowledge – students – do not ask questions.
>
> *Dillon, 1988, p. 197*

1. Introduction

This chapter describes an action research project, carried out by the first author with Year 9 students (13–14-year-olds) in England with the aim of promoting high-quality student questioning in science lessons. The motivation to carry out this research was initially prompted by the first author noticing a disparity in curiosity between her 4-year-old daughter and the students she taught. Her daughter attended a Montessori school, which embodies an approach to education where the children's learning is self-directed and curiosity celebrated, and that has shown to improve outcomes for school starters (Lillard, 2012). For example, two students at the particular Montessori school (aged four) were overheard discussing why Pluto was no longer a planet. Orbits of planets, moons and comets were discussed at length, with a level of scientific detail that the first author would be delighted to hear in her class of 14–16 year olds. This experience in collaboration with the second author, the first author's MSc supervisor, led to a process of the development of the action research described in this chapter.

The first part of the chapter looks at the key literature that argues for the value of student questioning to promote learning and considers strategies to promote student questioning in classrooms. The second part then describes the action research carried out by the first author with her secondary school students in England to promote high-quality student questioning. The chapter ends by considering implications for future work in schools and initial teacher education.

2. Students' questions in classrooms – what do we know?

This section reports on the key literature on student questioning that informed this study. Section 2.1 begins by looking at the educational benefits for students if they ask more questions in class. Section 2.2 then looks at literature which has analysed the nature and types of questions students ask. Section 2.3 looks at the literature which describes strategies classroom teachers have used to promote student questioning and, finally, section 2.4 considers the key barriers for students to ask questions and how these barriers might be overcome.

2.1 Why should students ask questions?

Whilst there is a large body of research on teacher questioning, empirical research on student questioning is harder to find (Chin and Osborne, 2008). However the research that has been carried out shows that students, from primary level through to university, ask few questions (Becker, 2000; Pearson and West, 1991; Dillon, 1988). For example, Becker (2000) notes that many primary students in the US have stopped asking questions and are not articulating a desire to discover, debate or challenge. Becker's research over 50 lessons in 25 elementary classrooms showed an average of only three questions from students each lesson, and a third of lessons having no questions from students at all. Dillon (1988) in his research in 27 US upper secondary school discussion classes found that the student body in a class on average asked only two information-seeking questions per hour, while the teacher was asking two per minute. Carr (1998), in a small UK-based study of six schools' science lessons found only five student questions per hour, but 22 questions from teachers in the same timeframe. Similar rates of student question asking were also found in US college classrooms (Pearson and West, 1991). In addition, few students spontaneously ask high-quality thinking or cognitive questions (White and Gunstone, 1992) with most questions being factual, procedural or closed in nature (Carr, 1998).

Why are students' questions important? First and foremost, questions from students indicate that they have been thinking about the ideas presented and have been trying to link them with other things they know (Chin and Osborne, 2008). By asking questions students reveal what they want to know, what they do know and what they do not know (Becker, 2000; Chin and Osborne, 2008). Secondly, student-generated questions are an important aspect of both self- and peer-assessment (Black et al., 2002). Thirdly, the skill of questioning is also important in problem-solving, decision making (Pizzini and Shepardson, 1991) and argumentation (Chin and Osborne, 2010). Furthermore, it has the potential to facilitate productive and higher order thinking, enhance creativity (Schodell, 1995; Bentley and Stylianides, 2017), and is also part of a scientific habit of mind (Chin and Osborne, 2008). Fourthly, Bentley and Stylianides (2017), in analysing students' questioning in mathematics, found that it allowed teachers to be better able to interpret students' 'knowledge types, personal example spaces (PESs), and areas of proximal development' which then allowed the teacher 'to design, for questioners, an additional and potentially more personalised follow-up task with higher specificity' (Bentley and Stylianides, 2017, p. 47) to further develop those students' learning of mathematics. Finally, teaching good questioning has been shown to improve critical thinking in university undergraduates (Hartford and Good, 1982; Watts and De Jesus, 2005), medical students (Loy et al., 2004) and parent involvement in education and patient activation in healthcare (Rothstein and Santana, 2011). Beyond school teaching if a student is able to ask good questions this has the potential to develop both a scientific habit of mind (Osborne, 2002) and a lifelong positive learning disposition (Claxton, 2008).

2.2 What are the nature and types of questions asked by students?

Students' questions, as part of the natural dialogue of classrooms, have been classified in many different ways. Some of the classification schemes are simple, for example classifying questions as 'procedural' (e.g. What do I do next?) and 'science content' (e.g. What is the symbol for Lithium?) (Carr, 1998). A more sophisticated classification scheme was developed by Chin and Brown (2002), who chose 'Basic – factual', 'Basic-procedural' and 'Wonderment'.

Pizzini and Shepardson (1991) developed the taxonomy of 'Input' (recalling information), 'Processing' (drawing relationships from data) and 'Output' (hypothesising, speculating, evaluating) to compare the quality and quantity of students' questions in problem-solving instruction versus teacher-directed laboratory instruction. Chin and Osborne (2008) criticise this taxonomy as not being sufficiently descriptive of the cognitive levels it purports to represent (Chin and Osborne, 2008). Ciardiello (1998), in his US-based action research, classified questions into the four levels presented in Table 4.1.

In our study we use Ciardiello's classification for two key reasons: (i) Ciardiello (1998) was a US high school vice principal and the only active teacher conducting action research that we have found apart from Carr (1998), and (ii) Ciardiello's four levels of questions were based on previous research by Gallagher and Aschner (1968).

2.3 What strategies can classroom teachers use to encourage students to ask questions?

Questions do not emerge spontaneously from students (Chin and Osborne, 2008); indeed, many students believe that questioning is the role of the teacher (Ciardiello, 1993). Research has shown that an explicit system of training is a requirement

TABLE 4.1 Asking good questions. Adapted from Ciardiello (1998)

Level	Description of question	Examples of question stems	Thought processes involved
1. Memory	Those whose answers are most likely to be found in a book, on a website.	Who ... What ... Where ... When ...	Naming, defining, identifying, and giving yes/no responses. Essentially they are closed.
2. Convergent thinking	Those which represent analysis and integration of given or remembered information, leading you to an expected end result.	Why ... How ... In what ways ...	Explaining, stating relationships and comparing and contrasting.
3. Divergent thinking	Those which represent intellectual operations wherein you are free to generate independently your own ideas.	Imagine ... Suppose ... Predict ... If ..., then ...	Predicting, hypothesising, inferring or reconstructing.
4. Evaluative thinking	Those which deal with matters of judgement, value and choice, characterised by their judgemental quality.	Defend ... Judge ... Justify ... What do you think about ...	Valuing, judging, defending or justifying choices.

for student generation of higher level questions (Ciardiello, 1993; Dillon, 1988; Chin and Osborne, 2008; Rothstein and Santana, 2011; Rosenshine et al., 1996), although in practice this is rare (Rothstein and Santana, 2011; Ciardiello, 1998). Research has shown that when students know how to ask their own questions they take greater ownership of their learning, deepen comprehension and make new connections and discoveries on their own (Bentley and Stylianides, 2017). Various strategies to encourage students to ask questions include:

- Teacher modelling for students how to ask questions (see for example Chin, 2004 and Chin and Osborne, 2008)
- Using question stems: teachers can encourage students to ask the generic 'W' questions such as Who? What? When? Why? (Watts and Pedrosa De Jesus, 2010).
- Question journals: Fensham (1989) suggested that students keep individual learning diaries in which to record their ideas, reactions and questions to activities in class.
- Questioning training models (Rosenshine et al., 1996): the two training models discussed by Rosenshine et al. have been used, with success, to train secondary

students to generate questions. (i) *Teachquest* by Ciardiello (1998) is an explicit instructional model to train students to raise questions at different cognitive levels of thinking using three sequential stages: identification, categorisation and construction of questions. The sequence of the strategy follows a similar progression for each of the four question types Ciardiello (1998) used (memory, convergent, divergent and evaluative). (ii) *Question Formulation Technique (QFT)*: described in a study by Rothstein and Santana (2011) where classroom teachers observed how the QFT process manages to develop students' divergent (brainstorming), convergent (categorising and prioritising) and metacognitive (reflective) thinking abilities in a very short time (this resonates well with Ciardiello's (1993) research).

2.4 What, if any, are the barriers to student questioning in the classroom and how can they be removed?

The literature identifies key factors/barriers which influence whether students ask questions in the classroom including the way teachers speak and ask questions, the gender of the student, and the need for a supportive and trusting classroom atmosphere.

First, Van Zee et al. (2001) identified different ways teachers speak in science classrooms and these can be classified into the five types shown in Table 4.2 below. Table 4.2 shows that only in three instances of teacher talk (guided discussion, student–generated inquiry discussion, and peer collaboration) would student questions be welcomed or occur frequently and spontaneously. Furthermore, the American educational researcher J.T. Dillon, in his research in elementary as well as secondary schools in the US (Dillon, 1979), found that the more teachers

TABLE 4.2 Teachers' speech and its influences on teacher and student questions

	Lecture	*Recitation*	*Guided discussion*	*Student-generated Inquiry discussion*	*Peer collaboration*
Mode of Teaching and Learning	Teacher transmits knowledge to students by telling	Teacher assesses knowledge of students by asking	Teachers construct knowledge with students by asking	Students construct knowledge with one another by asking and explaining	Students construct knowledge with one another by asking, explaining and doing
Teacher questions	Rhetorical	Test	Conceptual	Rare	None
Students' questions	Rare, or limited to end of class	Rare – maybe viewed as a threat	Welcomed	Occur frequently and spontaneously	Occur frequently and spontaneously

used questions, the shorter the students' responses and the less initiative students displayed.

Second, while there have been many studies into gender differences in the classroom, it has been difficult to find empirical research specifically focusing on the effects of gender on students' questions. The only research we found was based in a small number of college (university) classrooms in the US, and took place over twenty years ago. Specifically, Pearson and West (1991) found that male teachers received more questions than female teachers and that female students asked fewer questions than males students in courses taught by males. In addition, self-reported masculinity, which includes elements of independence, assertiveness, and a task-orientation, was associated with a greater likelihood of question asking.

Third, in getting students to ask more questions research has shown that students perceive that they could reveal their ignorance and lose status when asking a 'bad' question (Graesser and Person, 1994; Watts et al., 1997; Watts and Pedrosa De Jesus, 2010). It was also found that there are social barriers even when a 'good' question is asked, such as interrupting the teacher and changing the topic of conversation (Graesser and Person, 1994). Research has shown that classroom conditions are paramount in fostering or inhibiting a question-rich environment (Watts et al., 1997). Karabenick and Sharma's (1994) large study of US undergraduate classrooms is the only research we found dedicated to examining students' perceptions of their teachers' support of student questioning. Perceived teacher support affected the likelihood of student questions by influencing whether students asked questions and their level of inhibition.

2.5 Summary

In summary, the literature reviewed above has shown that although there is a significant literature on teacher questioning in science there is much less literature on student questioning. However, what literature there is seems to indicate that when students ask questions there are a number of significant benefits to their learning. The literature also suggests a number of strategies teachers can use to encourage more student questioning and it also suggests key challenges that have been shown to inhibit student questioning such as student confidence issues and gender issues. Informed by the literature and taking into account the concerns raised about the level of questioning in the first author's classroom the next section describes the research and development work carried out to promote student questioning.

3. The school-based practitioner research

This section describes the three phases of the practitioner research. We have taken the unusual step of describing each phase in full, the activities taking place, the research methodology and the results for each phase. We have adopted this structure so that the 'story' of how each phase influenced the development of the subsequent phase is provided in order to give a more coherent, chronological account of the research and development project as it unfolded.

Informed by the first author's original motivations and a review of the literature two key research questions were developed for the action research project:

1. What kinds of questions do Year 9 pupils ask in science lessons at the study school pre- and post-intervention?
2. What strategies can be used to train students to ask good[2] questions? What are the benefits to the learning and teaching of science of students asking good questions?

We carried out the action research in three phases, as mentioned above:

*   Phase 1: A baseline study to investigate what questions students were currently asking, their perceptions about the role of student questions in lessons, and the students' current questioning skills. The results from phase 1 were used to develop the intervention in phase 2.
*   Phase 2: An intervention in the first author's classroom to develop students' ability to ask good questions.
*   Phase 3: A follow-up investigation to see if any gains from the intervention were sustained over time.

All the participants in the study attended a fully inclusive state (public) secondary school (11–18 years). Students in Year 9 in a mixed attainment class taught by the first author were chosen for the student research sections of this study.

3.1 Phase 1: Gathering baseline data on student questioning in science lessons

Phase 1 covered three areas: (i) researching current practice to see what questions the teacher and students were asking; (ii) investigating student perceptions about asking questions in class; and (iii) investigating students' current questioning skills.

Beginning with the first area, in order to investigate current practice we audiorecorded one full hour lesson and analysed to find out:

i)   the number and type of students' questions;
ii) the number of students asking questions in the lesson; and
iii) the number of teacher questions.

Students were told that research was being conducted in the lesson before, but they were not told of the nature of the study so as to avoid artificially affecting the questioning in the lesson. We chose a lesson partway through a topic because research by both Van Zee and Minstrell (1997) and Pedrosa De Jesus et al. (2004)

TABLE 4.3 Questions asked by the teacher and students in class in pre-intervention recording

	Procedural questions	Science questions
Teacher	0	28
Students	1	8

showed that students will ask better questions when they know something about the topic being studied.

To analyse the recording we transcribed all questions before these were placed in a grid. Students' questions were categorised as 'procedural' (such as 'What page are we on?') or 'science content' (such as 'What is the symbol for Lithium?') (Carr, 1998) and then the latter category was re-categorised according to the schema outlined by Ciardiello (1998) into memory, convergent, divergent and evaluative questions (see Section 2.2).

This exercise was also repeated after the interventions had taken place (Section 3.3).

As shown in Table 4.3, during the pre-intervention lesson there were only eight science questions from students. Four of these questions were from one student and only four students in total asked questions during the lesson. Of the eight questions asked by students five were memory questions (e.g. what is an element? Is water an element? What is an electron?) and three were convergent questions (e.g. Why do metals lose electrons?). All eight questions were asked by boys. In addition, using Van Zee et al.'s (2001) classification of teaching talk the type of talk adopted in this lesson was resonant with the recitation style where teachers assess knowledge of students by asking questions, a style which was argued would not promote student questioning.

Although the intervention in phase 2 focused on one group of Year 9 students, a questionnaire was given to all students in Year 9 (270) to get a wider range of views on the importance of questioning in science (focus (ii) for phase1), the questioning environment in their science classroom, and the barriers they perceive to asking questions. A total of 189 students responded.

The findings showed that students agreed, although not strongly (average 2.2[3]), that asking questions was important in the learning of science. On average students neither agreed nor disagreed that they asked lots of questions in science but boys were shown to be more positive than girls (average of 2.8 compared to 3.3). Additionally teachers were perceived to ask more questions than students in class, although not strongly (average 2.6).

In the area of classroom environment in the response to the statement 'My teachers like me to ask questions' students gave an average score of 2.4 (not over-whelmingly positive). Students agreed (average score 2.1) that teachers could be trusted to take their questions seriously. On the questions related to barriers to asking questions in class, boys were more positive than girls (2.2 compared to 2.7). On average, students tended to disagree that they felt embarrassed asking questions but boys disagreed more strongly than girls (3.9 compared to 3.5). 78 out of 189 students responded to the open-ended question: 'The things that stop me from asking questions in science are…'. Of these 78 responses, 35 related to lack of confidence or fear of embarrassment. 71 per cent of these were from girls. Students tended to disagree, boys more strongly than girls (3.6 compared to 3.3), that they would ask more questions if the class was single sexed. Categorisation of the open questions from the questionnaire raised a number of other barriers such as lack of time for questions in class, poor relationships with the teacher, a lack of motivation or a lack of interest in science. Finally, a number of students perceived that that they did not need to ask questions, as one said:

> I understand everything. I do not need to ask questions.
>
> *Girl 143*

To complete our Phase 1 research, we conducted a baseline evaluation of students' question-posing abilities. Based on Dori and Herscovitz (1999), we gave the students in the study class a short piece of science text to read from a topic that was age and ability appropriate about white blood cells and immunity. The topic was chosen because students had just studied it and research has shown that students ask better questions when they know something about the topic (Van Zee et al., 2001; Pedrosa De Jesus et al., 2004). We gave students three minutes to read the text carefully and we then asked them to write down all the questions that they could think of underneath the text. We repeated this exercise after the intervention. The students' questions were then coded to be a memory, convergent, divergent or evaluative question (Ciardiello, 1998), as shown in Table 4.4.

Students in general did not ask many questions in response to the text, with fewer questions from girls than from boys. Question stems used were basic, e.g. 'Can …?' and there was no evident system or scaffolding of ideas.

In summary, the baseline study demonstrated a number of issues and challenges in students asking questions in science classrooms. Overall, they seem to ask much fewer questions than their teacher and these questions are generally low level. In addition, there does seem to be a gender issue in students' attitudes to ask questions in class with boys overall appearing to be more confident than girls.

TABLE 4.4 Analysis of questions written in response to a short piece of science text (pre-intervention)

We	Pre-intervention
Average number of questions written per student (all students)	2.9
Average number of questions written per student (male)	3.1
Average number of questions written per student (female)	2.7
Total number of divergent questions written	0
Total number of scripts showing organised hierarchical questioning	0

3.2 Phase 2: The intervention

The intervention took place over the course of a small topic (six lessons). A summary of those lessons is given below:

Lesson 1: Discussion of pre-intervention results and questioning training.
Lesson 2: 'Normal' lesson using the questioning techniques.
Lesson 3: 'Normal' lesson using questioning techniques with two observers.
Lesson 4: 'Normal' lesson using questioning techniques.
Lesson 5: 'Normal' lesson using questioning techniques – audio recorded.
Lesson 6: 'Normal' lesson using questioning techniques.

In Lesson 1 the initial results of the audio recording of the lesson (see Section 3.1) were shared with the Year 9 class by the first author, their teacher. The students were very surprised when they were confronted with the evidence that they did not ask many questions. This revelation was followed by an excellent discussion as to why questions are important in learning in general, learning in science and what they thought the features were of good questions. It was explained that they would be taught how to ask better questions and that the remainder of the topic would be taught using their questions as a basis for the lessons.

Students were then taken through the question training model *Teachquest* described by Ciardiello (1998). This training model was chosen for two reasons:

1. It was devised by a serving teacher and has been trialled in 'real' lessons with success.
2. It explicitly models questions of increasing levels of cognitive demand, and thus aims for the students to become increasingly metacognitive.

After the questioning training had been completed a small crib sheet was glued to the back of the students' books containing a summary of the question types and possible question stems that could be used. Students were encouraged to refer to this at all times. Students were informed that their exercise books would also be used as question logs, so that they would be able to see the progression in their questioning throughout the topic.

The remainder of the lessons in the topic were then taught with students' questions as a central focus. A detailed description of parts of these lessons can be found in Section 3.3. Data collection on the effectiveness of the intervention took place in lessons 3 and 5, and six weeks later. Lesson 3 was chosen as the observers were available; lesson 5 (audio recording) was chosen as it was in the same room, at the same time of day, as the original audio recording.

Three sources of data were collected. Firstly, lesson 3 was observed by two collaborating colleagues. The colleagues were asked to evaluate the lesson using the school proforma to evaluate learning and teaching and were not told about the exact nature of the lesson in advance. The colleagues concerned were highly experienced in using this proforma. In addition to completing the proforma, one of the observers spontaneously transcribed some of the questions students were asking without being asked to do so. The plenary discussion of the lesson was also audio recorded. Secondly, lesson 5 was audio recorded. This was a follow-up to the audio recording detailed in Section 3.2 and was carried out and analysed in an identical fashion. This allowed the nature and frequency of questions in the class pre- and post-intervention to be compared. Thirdly, the students' exercise books, which acted as question logs, were used as data and analysed.

3.3 Findings on the effectiveness of the intervention

3.3.1 Lesson 3

The lesson began with students being given a Qfocus (Rothstein and Santana, 2011) in the form of a statement – Reactions of metals with acids – and were given time to write as many memory questions in their books. Students then shared their questions and these formed the basis of a discussion with students answering each other's questions until all memory questions had been resolved. Students' spontaneous memory questions included: 'What is an acid?' and 'What different acids are there?' Students were then asked to compose some convergent questions, and they were prompted to use the stems in the back of their book. In pairs they were then asked to turn one of their convergent questions into a question suitable for investigation with the large variety of practical equipment that had been set out at the front of the laboratory. Investigation questions included: 'What happens when magnesium reacts with an acid?' and 'What happens to the temperature when magnesium reacts with an acid?' The two teachers observing the lesson commented:

> Students have raised questions to investigate rather than being told what to do – ALL [sic] students have actually raised an investigation question. They are not following a recipe but designing their own experiments. This increases curiosity.
>
> *Observer 1*

> Students were obviously thinking and some very good ideas were generated.
>
> *Observer 2*

Students then completed their preliminary investigations. Their findings led to further questions, some memory questions (e.g. What is the gas that is bubbling?), some convergent (e.g. Why is hydrogen coming out?) and some questions divergent in nature (e.g. If magnesium reacts like this, will zinc too?'). Further time was given for them to complete their investigations. Observer 2 commented at this stage that:

> Students were introduced to the chemical equations and possible gases being produced. They had to use information on the board to check which gas it might be. They were doing the thinking and working out for themselves.
>
> *Observer 2*

Class discussion revealed that, independently, all pairs had discovered:

a. that magnesium reacts with hydrochloric acid to produce hydrogen;
b. the gas test for hydrogen;
c. magnesium reacts in the same way with other acids to produce hydrogen;
d. that the reaction of magnesium with an acid causes a rise in temperature; and
e. that zinc reacts in the same way, also producing hydrogen, but not as quickly.

The ensuing discussion covered reactions of metals with acids producing hydrogen, why the temperature might rise, word equations, symbol equations, formation of salts, and reactivities of different metals. This discussion reached a depth not usually reached with this type of group in Year 9. In previous teaching this range of topics would 'normally' have taken up to three lessons to cover.

The sense of achievement in the room was witnessed and evidenced by the observers. For example, Observer 2 said:

> Students were pushed/coaxed to understanding the reaction equation at a much higher level. They were adopting the ideas and fighting for who was going to do the next step.

> *Observer 2*

In the plenary section of the lesson, a jar containing granules of calcium metal was placed obviously and silently on the front desk. The students were simply asked to write down a divergent question about the reactions of calcium with the same acid based on their own investigations. Students' questions varied around 'If magnesium reacts quite quickly, will calcium react quicker or slower?' This example shows students asking higher level divergent questions (Ciardiello, 1998), which were not apparent in the baseline lesson described in phase 1.

The final discussion was audio recorded and parts of this are discussed below. Six students are involved in this conversation: three boys (B1, B2, B3) and three girls (G1, G2, G3).

Teacher: Okay, before I do the reaction can we make a prediction – will it react quicker or slower?
[Silently points to periodic table on the wall.]
G1: Where is [the] calcium?
B1: It's there – in Group 2 (pointing).... Underneath magnesium...
G1: That means it's bigger than magnesium.
Teacher: I am going to ask a question. A memory question. When a metal atom gets bigger, as you go down the Group, does it get more or less reactive?

The teacher is modelling asking a question using the question conventions that the students have been taught. Student G1 has correctly identified an aspect of the atom of calcium and the teacher is directing the flow of conversation with the question.

B2: In Group 1, when you go down they get more explosive.
Teacher: So what is your prediction then?
G2: I think that it will be more bubbly, quicker.
B2: Yes, calcium will be more reactive.
Teacher: So your prediction is that calcium will be more reactive. Is everyone happy with that?

The teacher is using the reflective restatement (Dillon, 1988) to transfer the answering (and therefore thinking) responsibility back to the students. After the demonstration, the following discussion took place:

G3: Why? Why does calcium react so fast and magnesium not so fast?
Teacher: Excellent convergent question. Who can answer that question? Okay.
Who can start to answer the question?
[The teacher points to the Periodic Table.]
G1: It's bigger than magnesium, so it's easier for it to react.
Teacher: Easier for it to react…

In the excerpt above the teacher has confirmed the question type and is using pausing and the reflective restatement to allow students' ideas to develop. The teacher's practice here is resonant with orchestration practices advocated by Stein et al. (2008) to promote more productive mathematical discussions. In particular the teacher here seems to be attempting to account for the students' ideas while at the same time (by pointing to the Periodic Table) moving 'students collectively toward the development of a set of ideas and processes that are accountable to the discipline' (Stein et al., 2008, p. 332).

B1: Yes, because its things are further away.
Teacher: Things…
B3: Its electrons.
Teacher: Yes, and when a metal reacts it needs to …
B1: Give away its electrons
Teacher: So can we put this together? Calcium reacts faster than magnesium because?
B3: Because its electrons are further away and it is easier for them to get lost.
G2: It's like bags at a train station. If you have lots, it is easier for someone to steal one. If you only have one or two they will be closer to you and they won't get nicked.
Teacher: That (student's name) is a truly excellent analogy.

The students have used their questions to problem solve in this example with little direction from the teacher. The excerpt above demonstrates how students have explained a phenomenon using language and analogy at a far higher level than the first author, from her professional experience, would have expected from a mixed attainment Year 9 group. The two observers commented:

> Students are clearly developing their own ideas.
>
> *Observer 1*

> This Year 9 group are behaving like a top set but they are actually mixed ability. They are showing that they are thinking for themselves.
>
> *Observer 2*

3.3.2 Lesson 5

The findings from the audio recording of lesson 5 are shown in Table 4.5 and are compared to the findings from Phase 1.

Ten students participated in spontaneous question asking in the post-intervention lesson, in comparison to four pre-intervention recordings of the science lesson (see Table 4.3). Of these ten students six were boys and four were girls. In the the post-intervention lesson students asked seventeen science questions of which five were memory questions, eleven were convergent questions and there was one divergent question.

To illustrate in more detail how student questioning had developed after the intervention a transcribed extract from the start of Lesson 5 is shown below. However, what this extract also demonstrates is, firstly, the importance of the role of the teacher in encouraging much richer dialogue and reflection, particularly in using reflective statements and listening intently. Secondly, it also demonstrates students being able to engage in much more extensive and reflective dialogue with the teacher and amongst themselves including using skills of self-correcting.

The week before students had made copper sulfate solution from copper oxide and sulfuric acid and the solution had been left to evaporate on the window sill over the weekend. Six students are involved in this conversation, two girls and four boys.

Teacher: I want you to think of some questions using the strategies we have been using, about your experiment. Jot them down in the back of your book.

TABLE 4.5 A comparison of the types of questions asked in class by teachers and students in the pre- and post-intervention recording

Pre/post intervention	Procedural questions		Science questions	
	Pre	*Post*	*Pre*	*Post*
Teacher	1	3	28	14
Students	0	3	8	17

During the 2 minute and 22 second wait time after the teacher statement above, the teacher was circulating to ensure that all the students were writing questions. With the responsibility for the whole class to think of and write questions, the teacher is avoiding the main barrier (fear of embarrassment) identified in Section 2.2.

Teacher: Has anyone got a question?
B1: Why is there some black powder at the bottom?
Teacher: Why is there some black powder at the bottom? Mmm.

The teacher is using the reflective restatement and pausing to elicit further utterances from students. Both strategies seem to help the student to articulate his own ideas more clearly.

B2: The copper oxide was black wasn't it so maybe it is that.
Teacher: Mmm.
B1: Maybe I didn't filter it properly.
Teacher: So there was copper oxide mixed in with the copper sulfate solution.
G1: Yes, we have some too. I think we put too much in and it didn't dissolve.

In this lesson there was another example of the reflective restatement where the teacher is simply summarising what the students have said. In this example below no explanation is offered but the teacher is showing that she is listening intently to their answers.

Teacher: Didn't *dissolve?*…
G1: Didn't react with the hydrochloric acid.
B2: It wasn't hydrochloric acid, it was sulfuric. Because we made copper sulfate.

By repeating part of the students' answer with a rising intonation and inflection the teacher is drawing attention to part of the students' answer that may need further thought. In this case the teacher's question prompted an elaboration that clarified what the students meant and highlights how a teacher's question can influence student thinking.

B3: So if it takes longer to dry out then the crystals will be bigger.
B2: Miss, that is the same as lava in a volcano, isn't it? … the rocks that cool quickly have large crystals.
B4: No… small crystals.
B2: That's what I meant. Small crystals. And the ones that cool slowly have large crystals.
Teacher: Fabulous. Yes, that is right. A good link there to work you did last year.

In the previous excerpt we can see the students are self-correcting. This is an excellent example of the students both using their peers to scaffold their learning and activating prior knowledge. The next example shows that student questioning can sometimes be challenging for teachers:

Teacher: Right, any more questions about your evaporating dishes?
B5: Why is copper sulphate blue?
Teacher: Excellent question... I don't actually know.
  [Smiling]
  Maybe you can look that up tonight and I will too, we can talk about it tomorrow.

The question from B5 in the previous excerpt is potentially threatening to the teacher, as she had not thought about the question herself (Van Zee et al., 2001). However, the atmosphere created during this discussion was such that the teacher was able to respond by acknowledging that she did not know the answer and elicit further collaborative research. This serves another purpose: the students who asked questions and their classmates were learning that students can generate issues that teachers find interesting and that need further work (Van Zee et al., 2001).

The overriding feature of this entire conversation is that the students are the leaders as they enlarge the discussion and questioning in a specific area, whether they are the ones asking or responding to questions.

3.4 Phase 3: Post-intervention data collection

Phase 3 took place six weeks after the intervention and was designed in order to investigate whether students' questioning posing abilities had been sustained from the intervention and to get their more in-depth views of the intervention through the use of focus group interviews. As in the baseline study (Phase 1), students were given the same short piece of text to read as they were given at the start of the investigation (see Section 2.1). Again the students were asked to write down all the questions that they could think of on a sheet of paper. We analysed the data in the same way as in Phase 1 and the results compared to the baseline findings are shown in Figure 4.1.

Figure 4.1 shows that, by all measures, question posing capabilities has been sustained after the intervention. For the nineteen (out of a total of twenty) students who completed both pre- and post- intervention text response sheets showed an increase in the number of questions asked.

Post-intervention the scripts showed evidence of increased higher-order thinking. The complexity of the students' questions had increased with increased numbers of convergent and divergent questions asked (no divergent questions were asked pre-intervention). Examples of divergent questions were: 'If we have memory cells, why do we get the common cold more than once?' and 'What happens if our body does not react like this?'; these questions show a much deeper interaction with the

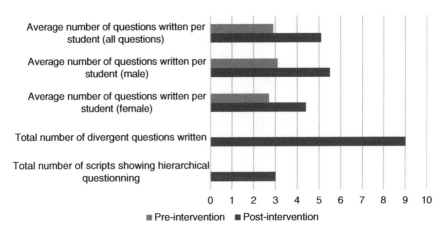

FIGURE 4.1 Pre-intervention (phase 1) and post-intervention (phase 3) text response analysis (n=19)

text. Pre-intervention most of the students' questions began with 'can…?'. Post-intervention a much wider variety of question stems was used. In addition, well-framed question asking post-intervention revealed misconceptions such as in the following question: 'If you are memory dyslexic are your white cells going to forget?'.

Finally a small focus group of four students (two boys and two girls) from the Year 9 group were asked about their views on why questions were important in science. They all agreed that questions were important and provided the following reasons:

> [Questions] help you answer your own questions. You start off with simple questions, get the answer, build a bridge almost… To understand harder questions.
>
> *G1*

Then students G1 and B2 discuss how questions from their peers help scaffold understanding:

> Other people's questions help you answer your own question… and my questions can help other people's answers.
>
> *G1*

> They help you make links… I like asking and answering questions. It helps because other people's questions can give you the answer to your question.
>
> *B2*

One student also spontaneously described how one of the main barriers to questioning had been removed by the exercises:

> When everyone has to ask questions you don't feel embarrassed because it is more embarrassing almost not to have one.
>
> *G2*

B1: Convergent questions

Teacher: What were they?

B1: Why? What were the ones that were if something then does that mean that …

G2: Those were the divergent ones.

B2: Sometimes the words convergent and divergent aren't very helpful.

Teacher: Can you think of better words?

G1: Complex and then like… compound (laughs) … no that wouldn't be right.

Teacher: So the hows and the whys… What other word would be better than convergent? I am asking for your help here as …

G2: It's bringing the ideas together. That's right isn't it?

B1: Can this do that …

B2: Well you get longer answers, so you could call them longer answer questions.

B1: Kind of like knowledge questions because you know that if you like know this from your knowledge, then you are asking what the next step is.

G1: Like building your knowledge questions.

B1: What about 'building questions'? That would be a good one.

FIGURE 4.2 Extract from focus group transcript

Students were asked what they had learnt about questions in recent lessons. All four students were involved in the ensuing discussion, working together to remind themselves of the different types of questions and their uses. Part of the conversation that took place is shown in Figure 4.2.

This extract is particularly interesting as the students are thinking about how the questions have helped them think and seem to be working in a metacognitive fashion to solve the problem of what a convergent question is.

The students were clear about the strategies that they had found useful.

> It is like reflecting. Having all the questions in our book means you can see how much you understand by the end because all the questions you have got at the beginning are all easy now.
>
> *B1*

Finally, students discussed if any of their questioning training was transferrable to other subjects. There was unanimous nodding. History, English and French were named.

> [History] and your arguments. [French] you have new stuff to learn and you don't know what you have to learn but it can help you work that bit out.
>
> *B1*

Overall these students were very positive about the experiences they had had in the lessons on questioning. They were able to talk at length about the benefits of learning how to question. They were able to verbalise, unprompted, many of the benefits of questioning discussed in the literature (see discussion) and expressed intentions to use their new skills across the curriculum.

4. Future work

In this section we will return to the original research questions and answer them in relation to the key literature.

4.1 What kinds of questions do Year 9 students ask in science lessons at the study school pre- and post intervention?

As in research by Dillon (1988), Carr (1998) and Becker (2000) the findings in Phase 1 of this study also showed that, pre-intervention, the Year 9 students asked very few questions in class. The baseline audio recording from Phase 1 also supports research by White and Gunstone (1992) showing that few students in our study asked high-quality thinking or cognitive questions spontaneously, with six out of the nine questions asked in the recorded lesson being procedural or of low order (memory questions). This was further supported by the questions students wrote in response to text where it was found that students did not ask many questions and only used basic question stems. The findings in Phase 1 also identified a number of barriers students perceived to their asking questions through their responses to the questionnaire. For example, some students said they lacked confidence and were fearful of embarrassment if they asked questions in class and more in this group were girls. In addition, there was a sizable proportion of the Year 9 students stating that they did not need to ask questions in science lessons, giving reasons on a theme of 'I know everything already' and this is resonant with Ciardiello's (1998) findings. An additional barrier identified was that students at the study school were not overwhelmingly positive about teachers' support for questions in class. Watts et al. (1997) found that classroom conditions were paramount in fostering or inhibiting a question rich environment and so this finding is something to consider in the future when encouraging students to feel comfortable to ask questions.

However, the findings from a range of data sources after the intervention show that specifically teaching students to ask questions did significantly increase both the number and complexity of questions they asked. This finding was reinforced by the student focus group where students described the scaffolding that had taken place during the lessons and how they were able to make links between the easy and difficult parts of the topic. In addition, analysis of classroom dialogue from Lessons 3 and 5, as well as showing much richer student questioning than pre-intervention, also identified other benefits to classroom talk such as students being able to engage in much more extensive and reflective dialogue both with the teacher and amongst themselves. Finally, one significant barrier identified by students, particularly girls, of the potential to feel inhibited or embarrassed to ask questions seemed to be removed post intervention, resonating with the research by Rothstein and Santana (2011).

4.2.1 What strategies are useful in teaching the students how to question?

In our research we found, just as Rothstein and Santana (2011) describe, that when students know how to ask their own questions they take greater ownership of their learning, deepen comprehension and make new connections and discoveries. The majority of the training was based on question stems and levels organised by Ciardiello (1998). The findings show that these proved to be readily accessible to the students who were able to recall the question types and associated meta-cognitive benefits with little prompting (evidenced in the student focus group). This study also corroborates three findings by Rothstein and Santana (2011):

1. That using techniques such as the Question Formulation Technique (QFT) process can help develop students' divergent, convergent and metacognitive thinking abilities.
2. That this development can happen in a short period of time.
3. That using techniques like QFT supports students to ask *scientific* questions and express those questions in an operational form.

In addition to the strategies described above, White and Gunstone (1992), Driver et al. (1994), Van Zee et al. (2001) also discuss the importance of overall lesson style for formative assessment as a strategy to facilitate students asking questions. This is where interaction between students, their peers and the teacher is key and the effect of lesson style on students' questions is clearly summarised by van Zee (2001) in Table 4.2 (see Section 2.4). Traditional teaching has often been based on the left (Van Zee et al., 2001) and the findings presented have demonstrated that the pre-intervention recording showed a lesson that would be described as a recitation. Post-intervention the mode of speaking had shifted to the right and the conversation was essentially a student-generated inquiry. This movement in the mode of speaking towards the right is essential, as van Zee (2001: 174) explains: 'we are interested not only in having our students generate insightful questions about science topics, but also in having them learn how to use questions to assist one another themselves, in coming to understand something through appropriate questioning.' In addition, as noted by one of the teachers, students' questions to the teacher were more likely to occur in one-to-one situations (Graesser and Person, 1994), which in turn are more likely to occur in a student-generated inquiry style lesson than a recitation.

4.2.2 What are the benefits of teaching question formation to the learning and teaching of science?

Firstly in terms of learning, Chin (2001) found that 'wonderment' questions stimulated the students to hypothesise, predict and generate explanations. In Chin's study students' questions were divided into two groups: basic/factual and wonderment. Ciardiello's (1993) convergent, divergent and evaluative questions would therefore have been classed as 'wonderment'. This stimulation was evident in the findings from our study. For example, in Section 3.3 a student asked a convergent question, 'Why does calcium react so fast and magnesium not so fast?' The findings show that this was followed by a series of utterances from the questioner's peers, a reflective restatement from the teacher and culminated in a scientific analogy of a highly complex process. The students seemed to be using their questions, as well as questions from their peers, to generate complex explanations from their observations and were learning through the formation and rearrangement of cognitive schemata (Chin and Osborne, 2008). It is unlikely that the deep-thinking would have been triggered if the questions had not been asked (Chin and Osborne, 2008), and this was acknowledged by the two observers in our study. The findings from the student interviews also showed that the students themselves agreed with this finding. They articulated how the different types of questions had made them reflect on how they were thinking. This was the intention of Ciardiello (1998) who described how an awareness of how you are learning, where your misconceptions lie and where your knowledge has gaps is key to building your understanding. Wood and Wood (1988) found that student initiative was far greater when question alternatives were used or teachers questioned less. The transcripts in Section 3.3 illustrate this well, where use of the reflective restatement, invitation to elaborate and pausing (question alternatives advocated by Dillon (1979)) elicit complex explanations and confirm the continued relevance of Dillon's research today.

The discussion reported in Section 3.3 was also far more advanced scientifically than the findings from phase 1 showed. The students were using their own questions and questions from others to scaffold their learning through stage 1 of the Zone of Proximal Development (Vygotsky, 1978) to facilitate the negotiation of meaning (Chin and Osborne, 2008). In the example in Section 3.3 five students asked and answered each other's questions, with each question taking their understanding further towards a developed explanation.

Secondly our intervention also shows benefits for students' own self-assessment. For example, we asked students to record their questions in their exercise books as they conducted tasks and these books then acted as question journals. The findings show that the students found these records useful, particularly for reflection at the end of the topic to show them how far they had improved their understanding. This relates to findings by Rothstein and Santana (2011) and Maskill and De Jesus (1997) who found that students' questions recorded in a journal provide a record of their conceptual levels and development of understanding over time. It also links with literature on formative assessment (see for example Black and Wiliam, 1998), which shows benefits for students when they self-assess. Watts and Pedrosa De Jesus (2010) describe questions as regulative actions, and thus if students are not asking questions it might mean that the existing conceptual framework, possibly faulty, will remain largely unaltered.

Thirdly, students being encouraged to ask questions in our study also showed benefits for their motivation as shown in Section 3.3 of the findings. There is a growing body of literature on the subject of motivation and much concentrates on a distinction between intrinsic and extrinsic factors that increase or decrease motivation (Dweck, 2000). The ability of the act of question-posing to arouse motivation and interest in the topic under study is only discussed briefly in the literature (Chin and Osborne, 2008; Chin and Kayalvizhi, 2002), but findings from this research do support findings from research by Wallace (1996) that students prefer investigating questions that they had composed themselves, and therefore had more control over their learning. The findings from our study also show that when students worked collaboratively to generate their own questions for investigation, design their investigations and generate new questions based on their observations, an unanticipated depth and breadth of science was covered independently by the small groups with little or no guidance from the teacher. Participation was high and behaviour good (as acknowledged by observers) and the students were curious and acting on their own curiosity. This corroborates reports from the 20-year study by Rothstein and Santana (2011) that formulating their own questions engages students in a new way, increases group participation and peer learning processes and improves classroom management.

5. Concluding remarks

In this section we want to reflect on our own learning during the course of the research. Initially, we brought different kinds of expertise to the research. The first author brought her deep contextual knowledge of the school and students she was working with and the second author her knowledge of key literature and research methods. These initial starting points resonate, to a certain extent, with the expertise that Hayward (1997) indicates mentors (experienced teachers) and University tutors bring to the education of beginning teachers. However, our purpose, initially at least, was the development of an experienced teacher's, i.e. the first author's, practice. However, over time as the collaboration developed, we both developed our understanding and expertise.

For the first author, conducting this research has resulted in deep reflection on her own classroom practice. Moving the mode of speaking towards student-guided discussions and student-generated inquiries in her classroom has had both striking and significant impact on student learning. This research supports the work of many researchers that teaching students to ask good questions has the potential to facilitate productive and higher order thinking and enhance the creativity of their ideas (Schodell, 1995). Asking questions is a scientific habit of mind (Chin and Osborne, 2008), but one that is often overlooked in the classroom as a skill that needs to be explicitly taught to students. For the second author, collaborating in this research resulted in her learning more about the important contextual classroom issues that need to be taken into account when developing students' ability to question effectively. This in turn raised a series of questions for author 2 in how to translate this learning, with an experienced teacher, to her work as a teacher educator with beginning teachers. In the first instance author 1 was invited by author 2 to share her findings in workshops with beginning teachers to begin this translation process and this led later to author 1 sharing this research with other science teacher educators.

Furthermore, author 1 has taken her work on considerably in her own school context. For example, in the following academic year, students' questions became the foundation of practical work and inquiry at Key stage 3 (lower secondary) at the study school. Author 1 has since moved on to another school where all students in Year 7 are taught question formulation as part of their Year 7 curriculum in science, and this is reiterated in Year 9. All the teachers in the science department have been introduced to question formulation and question boarding (simply writing down all the questions you can think of in relation to the topic on the white board) is used at the start of many topics. The question board is then photographed and can be used as a plenary, a progress check or as a basis for independent stretch and challenge, or a review at the end of the topic. Question cards with the stems on the reverse, were made by one of the teachers. In each science classroom there are enough cards for three for each of the largest class. These have been used in a number of ways:

1. As simple question stem prompts.
2. Giving three to each pupil. Each time the student asks a question they surrender a card – all three 'have to be' used up during the lesson. This is to encourage a student centered approach to questioning, and to equalise the question asking opportunities between the most shy and the more outspoken.
3. Giving one to each pupil. They are only allowed to ask one question in that phase of the lesson (this pushes the students to really think about how they construct their question for maximum gain).

The hope is that, as Rothstein and Santana (2011: 2) state 'as teachers see this [students' questions leading to deeper engagement, participation and improved classroom management] happening again and again they realise their traditional practice of welcoming questions is not the same as deliberately teaching the skill of question formation' and that this new practice becomes embedded. Overall, we would like to conclude that for both of us one of the most successful outcomes of the research is that it has given agency to students to ask the questions they want to so that, at the very least, they are able to answer a resounding 'yes' to Isadore Rabi's mother's question we included at the outset of this chapter.

Notes

1 As quoted in 'Great Minds Start With Questions' in *Parents Magazine* (September 1993).
2 By 'good' questions we mean those that are higher level such as convergent and divergent questions.
3 This was on a Likert scale of 1 being 'strongly agree', 2 'agree', 3 'neither agree or disagree', 4 'disagree' and 5 'strongly disagree'.

References

Becker, R. R. (2000) The critical role of students' questions in literacy development. *The Educational Forum*. Taylor & Francis, 261–271.

Bentley, J. & Stylianides, G.J. (2017) Drawing inferences from learners' examples and questions to inform task design and develop learners' spatial knowledge. *Journal of Mathematical Behaviour*, 47, 35–53

Black, P. J. & Wiliam, D. (1998) *Inside the Black Box: Raising standards through classroom assessment*. London: King's College London School of Education.

Black, P., Harrison, C., Lee, C., Marshall, B. & William, D. (2002) *Working Inside the Black Box-Assessment for Learning in the Classroom*. London: King's College London.

Carr, D. (1998) The art of asking questions in the teaching of science. *School Science Review*, 79, 47–50.

Chin, C. (2001) Learning in science: What do students' questions tell us about their thinking? *Education Journal*, 29, 85–103.

Chin, C. (2004) Students' questions: Fostering a culture of inquisitiveness in science classrooms. *School Science Review*, 86, 107–112.

Chin, C. & Brown, D. E. (2002) Student-generated questions: A meaningful aspect of learning in science. *International Journal of Science Education*, 24, 521–549.

Chin, C. & Kayalvizhi, G. (2002) Posing problems for open investigations: What questions do pupils ask? *Research in Science & Technological Education*, 20, 269–287.

Chin, C. & Osborne, J. (2008) Students' questions: a potential resource for teaching and learning science. *Studies in Science Education*, 44, 1–39.

Chin, C. & Osborne, J. (2010) Supporting argumentation through students' questions: Case studies in science classrooms. *The Journal of the Learning Sciences*, 19, 230–284.

Ciardiello, A.V. (1993) Training students to ask reflective questions. *The Clearing House*, 66, 312–314.

Ciardiello, A.V. (1998) 'Did you ask a good question today? Alternative cognitive and meta-cognitive strategies.' *Journal of Adolescent & Adult Literacy*, 42, 210–219.

Claxton, G. (2008) Cultivating positive learning dispositions. Daniels, H. et al., *Routledge Companion to Education*. London: Routledge.

Dillon, J.T. (1979) Alternatives to questioning. *High School Journal*, 62, 217–222.

Dillon, J. T. (1988) The remedial status of student questioning. *Journal of Curriculum studies*, 20, 197–210.

Dori, Y. J. & Herscovitz, O. (1999) Question-posing capability as an alternative evaluation method: Analysis of an environmental case study. *Journal of Research in Science Teaching*, 36, 11–430.

Driver, R., Leach, J., Scott, P. & Wood-Robinson, C. (1994) Young people's understanding of science concepts: Implications of cross-age studies for curriculum planning. *Studies in Science Education*, 24:1, 75–100.

Dweck, C. (2000) *Self-theories: Their role in motivation, personality, and development*. Psychology Press.

Fensham, P. J. (1989) Theory in practice: How to assist science teachers to teach constructively. *Adolescent Development and School Science*. New York: Routledge Falmer, 61–77.

Gallagher, J. J. & Aschner, M. J. (1968) 'A Preliminary Report on Analyses of Classroom Interaction,' *Teaching: Vantage Points for Study*, edited by Ronald T. Hyman. Philadelphia: J. B. Lippincott.

Graesser, A. C. & Person, N. K. (1994) Question asking during tutoring. *American Educational Research Journal*, 31, 104–137.

Hartford, F. & Good, R. (1982) Training chemistry students to ask research questions. *Journal of Research in Science Teaching*, 19, 559–570.

Hayward, G. (1997) Principles for school focused initial teacher education: some lessons from the Oxford Internship Scheme. In T. Allsop and A. Benson (Eds.) *Mentoring for Science Teachers* (pp. 11–26). Buckingham: Oxford University Press.

Karabenick, S. A. & Sharma, R. (1994) Perceived teacher support of student questioning in the college classroom: Its relation to student characteristics and role in the classroom questioning process. *Journal of Educational Psychology*, 86, 90–103.

Lillard, A. S. (2012) Preschool Children's Development in Classic Montessori, Supplemented Montessori and Conventional Programs. *Journal of School Pyschology*, 50, 379–401.

Loy, G. L., Gelula, M. H. & Vontver, L. A. (2004) Teaching students to question. *American Journal of Obstetrics and Gynaecology*, 191, 1752–1756.

Maskill, R. & De Jesus, H. P. (1997) Pupils' questions, alternative frameworks and the design of science teaching. *International Journal of Science Education*, 19, 781–799.

Osborne, J. (2002) Science without literacy: A ship without a sail? *Cambridge Journal of Education*, 32, 203–218.

Pearson, J. C. & West, R. (1991) An initial investigation of the effects of gender on student questions in the classroom: Developing a descriptive base. *Communication Education*, 40, 22–32.

Pedrosa De Jesus, H., Almeida, P. C. & Watts, M. (2004) Questioning styles and students' learning: Four case studies. *Educational Psychology*, 24, 531–548.

Pizzini, E. L. & Shepardson, D. P. (1991) Student questioning in the presence of the teacher during problem solving in science. *School Science and Mathematics*, 91, 348–352.

Rosenshine, B., Meister, C. & Chapman, S. (1996) Teaching students to generate questions: A review of the intervention studies. *Review of Educational Research*, 66, 181–221.

Rothstein, D. & Santana, L. (2011) *Teaching students to ask their own questions.* Harvard Education Newsletter, 27.

Schodell, M. (1995) The question-driven classroom. *The American Biology Teacher*, 57, 278–281.

Stein, M. K., Engle, R. A., Smith, M. S. & Hughes, E. K. (2008) Orchestrating productive mathematical discussion: five practices for helping teachers move beyond show and tell, *Mathematical Thinking and Learning*, 10, 323–340.

Van Zee, E. & Minstrell, J. (1997) Using questioning to guide student thinking. *The Journal of the Learning Sciences*, 6, 227–269.

Van Zee, E. H., Iwasyk, M., Kurose, A., Simpson, D. & Wild, J. (2001) Student and teacher questioning during conversations about science. *Journal of Research in Science Teaching*, 38, 159–190.

Vygotsky, L. S. (1978) *Mind in Society: The development of higher mental process.* Cambridge, MA: Harvard University Press.

Wallace, G. (1996) Engaging with learning. In: Ruddick, J. (ed.) *School Improvement: What can pupils tell us?* London: David Fulton.

Watts, M., Alsop, S., Gould, G. & Walsh, A. (1997) Prompting teachers' constructive reflection: Pupils' questions as critical incidents. *International Journal of Science Education*, 19, 1025–1037.

Watts, M. & De Jesus, H. P. (2005) The cause and affect of asking questions: Reflective case studies from undergraduate sciences. *Canadian Journal of Math, Science & Technology Education*, 5, 437–452.

Watts, M. & Pedrosa De Jesus, H. (2010) Questions and Science. In: Toplis, R. (Ed.) *How Science Works: Exploring effective pedagogy and practice.* Oxford: Routledge.

White, R. T. & Gunstone, R. F. (1992) *Probing Understanding*, London: The Falmer Press.

Wood, D. & Wood, H. (1988) Questioning versus student initiative. In J. T. Dillon (Ed.) *Questioning and Discussion.* Norwood, NJ: Ablex.

5

DEVELOPING SCIENCE EXPLANATIONS IN THE CLASSROOM

The role of the written narrative

Richard Taylor and Judith Hillier

Introduction

Explaining the world around us is at the heart of science (Solomon, 1986): science education enables students to develop those explanations (Millar & Osborne, 1998), and science teacher education supports science teachers as they refine their own explanations and consider how best to foster understanding in their students (Harlen, 2010). However, little research has been done on science teacher explanations or on how to support pre-service science teachers in the development of this part of their professional practice (Geelan, 2012). Moreover, as little is known about science teacher explanations, it follows that little research has been done in evaluating how successful their students are in understanding and taking ownership of these explanations in applying them to other contexts. If rich learning of science, where students have a deep understanding of scientific concepts and their interconnectedness, is to be nurtured, then more research is needed to understand how both science students and teachers learn this crucial skill of constructing explanations, and how teachers learn to foster this aspect of their students' development. Here, we are aligning ourselves with the work of Mortimer and Scott (2003) where they used constructivist ideas about alternative conceptions, but developed these further using socio-cultural perspectives to explore 'ways in which meanings are developed through language in the science classroom' (p. 4), in what they called a 'post-constructivist paradigm' (p. 4). The meanings in which we are interested are the explanations or 'stories' which 'tell how something or other comes about' (Ogborn et al., 1996, p. 9). This chapter looks at two interventions designed to support the development of learners' scientific explanations through the use of written narratives (Norris et al., 2005). Neither started as interventions but as ways of collecting data to reveal learners' understanding but the analyses revealed that the process had learning benefits and developed into interventions using written narratives.

The first intervention took place in a state-funded secondary school with Year 11 students (age 15 to 16) as they developed their understanding of forces and motion as part of their General Certificate in Secondary Education (GCSE) studies. GCSEs are an academic qualification awarded in specific subjects (e.g. English Literature, Science) taken by the majority of students in schools in England and Wales. In the past, GCSE examinations marked the end of a student's compulsory education. However, since 2015 all individuals are required to remain in some form of education until the age of 18. Students can choose some of the subjects they study at GCSE (e.g. geography, music); however, they are all required to study GCSE Science.

This intervention investigated how the process of writing explanations helped the development of students' ability to give scientific explanations of projectile motion at three points during the forces and motion topic – at the beginning, mid-point and end. In addition, the science teachers teaching this topic in the school collaborated to write a canonical explanation. Analysis of students' written explanations and the canonical explanation demonstrated that initially students and teachers identified very different mechanisms as the cause of the projectile motion. Moreover, this initial analysis indicated the importance of developing an understanding of technical terminology when constructing scientific explanations. Individual students' progress towards developing scientific explanations was measured by further analysis of each student's explanations written at the three different points during the topic. This analysis identified a range of progress, from students whose explanations were still markedly different from their science teachers' explanations at the end of the topic, to students who incorporated many aspects of their teachers' scientific explanation into their own explanations. Interviews suggested students whose explanations were more scientific had a better understanding of technical terminology. However, these students appeared to be reluctant to use these technical terms in their own written explanations.

The second intervention was conducted in the university as part of a teacher education programme with pre-service secondary science teachers as they developed their own explanations or *coherent internal accounts* (Hillier, 2013) of key concepts and phenomena in science. Data were collected by the use of narrative explanations of forces, electricity and transfer of heat during workshops. The tutor gave detailed written feedback on each individual explanation. Analysis of the written explanations provided by the pre-service teachers demonstrated that the intervention provided opportunities for consolidation and refinement of the pre-service teachers' subject knowledge. This was necessary as each had a degree specialising in one of the sciences (biology, chemistry, physics, earth science, engineering), but were preparing to teach across the whole science curriculum for students aged 11–14 years. Through the intervention, it became clear that this process of developing their own *coherent internal accounts* was a crucial, and explicit, step to be taken when transforming their knowledge of the subject into knowledge of how to teach that particular content: defined as pedagogical content knowledge (PCK) by Shulman (1986). Additionally Shulman (1986) also identified knowledge of student learning and conceptions as part of PCK. Interviews and questionnaires with the pre-service teachers showed that the intervention also impacted on their professional practice in the school classroom.

Although conducted in different contexts, with different learners, both these interventions required the participants to observe a scientific phenomenon and then write an explanation of what they had seen, to which they received written feedback. The two interventions will be described in turn: their methodology, the analysis of the data and the key findings, before discussing the insights yielded by each intervention, the similarities and differences between them, and the implications for further research and practice.

Written explanations in the school classroom

Methodology

The first intervention took place in a state-funded secondary school in a rural area of North Dorset. The participants were 55 Year 11 students (age 15 to 16 years) who were studying a Forces and Motion topic as part of their GCSE Additional Science qualification. The topic was chosen partially for pragmatic reasons of timing and convenience, but also as a great deal of Physics Education Research (PER) has looked at students' understanding of forces and motion concepts (e.g. Abrahams et al., 2015; Howe et al., 2016; Jarvis et al., 2003), which informed the design of the intervention and the data analysis. At the beginning of the topic, before teaching had introduced key forces and motion concepts, the students were shown a 'film-canister rocket pop'. This demonstration involved placing a vitamin tablet into a 35mm photographic film canister. The canister was then half filled with water and the lid was replaced. The water reacts with the vitamin tablet and produces a gas. The canister eventually 'pops' and launches into the air. A deliberately vague description of the motion of the rocket was given to the students (*When the film canister 'pops', it climbs into the air and then falls back down to the ground*). The students were then asked to write an explanation of this motion. By giving students a description of the motion, it was hoped they would focus their attention on explaining rather than describing what they had seen when the rocket popped. However, the description was left vague to provide an opportunity to assess whether a student chose to refine the description of the motion, e.g. they might decide to describe the canister as accelerating towards the ground rather than simply falling.

This process then comprised the main part of the intervention, with the written explanations produced by students also forming the data for analysis. The initial data collection was at the start of the topic, with further data collected, under the same conditions, at two later points during the topic: approximately midway though the topic, when key concepts and theories had been introduced to students (e.g. velocity, acceleration, Newton's laws); and then at the end of the topic, when students had been taught how these key concepts explain simple examples of motion (e.g. terminal velocity). Thus, students received their normal teaching;

the intervention aimed to use the process of writing explanations to help develop students' understanding further and also to capture their understanding at three distinct points in the six-week teaching sequence: beginning, middle and end.

Students worked informally during science lessons to write their explanations. It was stressed by the teachers that the exercise was for them to explore their initial thoughts about the Forces and Motion topic and to make these thoughts visible to themselves. It was made clear the exercise was not a formal assessment or test, as part of the ethical considerations of the intervention design. Hence, students were not prevented from sharing ideas with each other. However, students were encouraged to work individually so the ideas they explored were 'their ideas' rather than their 'neighbours', with the intention being that the written explanations would more closely reflect their own understanding.

Two experienced physics teachers taught the Forces and Motion topic. These physics teachers worked collaboratively, whilst referring to the course textbook, to write their own joint explanation of the motion of the film-canister rocket. This canonical explanation represented how the physics teachers hoped their students would explain the film-canister rocket pop after tuition. Therefore, this canonical explanation provided a benchmark to compare students' explanations and define their progress towards what might be thought of as a scientific explanation.

In addition, semi-structured interviews were used to further investigate and clarify, if necessary, selected students' explanations. It was hoped that interviews would highlight discrepancies between students' ability to talk about their ideas and their ability to write about them, and provide insight into the difficulties they faced when developing their written explanations. The systemic functional linguistic analysis of students' written explanations identified three groups of students who made different levels of progress towards developing scientific explanations (see next section). From each group, 10 students who were willing to give up some of their free time to participate were interviewed at the end of the topic. These students were interviewed in pairs to help them feel at ease and to encourage dialogue. Interviews were audio-recorded, with the students' permission, to allow for transcription and, therefore, a more detailed analysis.

Students' understanding of technical terms (e.g. force, acceleration, resultant, velocity) also became a focus for the interviews. This was because the analysis of students' written explanations suggested their understanding of these terms could play a crucial role in whether they were able to develop scientific explanations of the film canister's motion. A judgement about whether a student understood a technical term was made by whether they could use the term correctly or identify the correct use of the term (e.g. Cassels and Johnstone, 1985). To provide opportunities for these judgements to be made, students were shown a particular scenario during the interviews. Technical words were then used by the interviewer to describe the scenario or students were asked to correctly use technical words to provide their own description. For example, students were shown a falling lump of plasticine and asked to pay particular attention to when the plasticine hit the desk and stopped moving, and were then asked if the plasticine had accelerated. Students were also shown force diagrams and asked to identify the resultant force.

Data analysis

The analysis of the written explanations aimed to provide a robust and systematic characterisation, through Systemic Functional Linguistics (SFL) analysis (Halliday & Matthiessen, 2004) of these explanations to enable similarities and differences to be identified between individual students' explanations and the canonical teachers' explanation, and between individual students' explanations at the initial, mid and final testing points.

SFL was chosen because it aims to describe how individuals use language to make sense of their experience (Halliday & Matthiessen, 2004). In SFL, this function of language is called the ideational metafunction, which is split into two components: the experiential and logical functions. The experiential and logical functions explore how individuals use language to represent their experience by assuming individuals describe their experiences as a flow of events, for which they can then begin to provide an account. This flow of events is 'chunked into a series of figures' (Halliday & Matthiessen, 2004, p. 170), with each figure defining a discrete change or 'quantum of change' (Halliday & Matthiessen, 2004, p. 170). For instance, a student might identify the moment the rocket 'pops', and goes from being stationary to climbing into the air as an event. The same student might then see the rocket beginning to fall to ground, rather than continuing to rise, as a subsequent event. Hence, linking these two figures creates a flow of events that describes the motion of the film-canister rocket. Furthermore, this student might explain these events in terms of the build-up of pressure in the canister or gravity. The experiential and logical functions provide a framework to systematically analyse similarities and differences in the events students use to describe the motion of the film-canister rocket and how they explain these events.

The experiential function operates at a clause level and defines individual figures in terms of:

- a process unfolding through time;
- the participants involved in the process; and
- the circumstances associated with the process.

The grammar of events can be described with a transitive or an ergative model (Davidse, 1992): in the former, '[An] Actor is construed as bringing about the unfolding of a Process through time; and this unfolding is either confined in its outcome to the Actor or extended to another participant, the Goal' (Halliday & Matthiessen, 2004, p. 282). Hence, a transitive model is appropriate when a single participant is responsible for the events. To illustrate this point, Halliday & Matthiessen (2004, p. 283) use extracts of text from a retelling of the biblical story, Noah's Ark:

Noah and his sons went to the cypress forest to cut down the tallest trees of timber. For many days, they chopped and sawed.

In this extract, *Noah and his sons* are consistently responsible for events. This contrasts with a possible explanation of the film-canister motion.

The canister pops and climbs into the air. Then gravity pulls the canister down.

In the first clause, *the canister* is the actor but in the second clause, *gravity* is the actor and *the canister* is the goal. In contrast, in an ergative model *the canister* can be consistently identified as a medium – the medium through which the process is actualised (Halliday & Matthiessen, 2004, p. 284). Hence, the ergative model is better suited to describing events that are caused by many different external agents. This is often the case in scientific registers of text (Teich & Holtz, 2009). Therefore, an ergative model was used to analyse the clauses in the written explanations and is summarised in Table 5.1 using examples taken from students' written examples.

The logical function in SFL was used to analyse how the clauses within the written explanations, which define individual figures, were strung together or

TABLE 5.1 A summary of the ergative model used to analyse the events realised in clauses of written explanations

Examples of clauses that define figures		The ergative model				
		Process	Participants			Circumstantial Elements
			Medium	Agent	Range	
			Participant that makes the process possible	Participant responsible for the process	Additional participants	
Material Clause	The canister falls down	Falls	Canister			Down
	Gravity pulls the canister down	Pulls	Canister	Gravity		Down
Relational Clause	Gravity is greater than the drag	Greater than	Gravity		Drag	

TABLE 5.2 The logical functions identified within Systematic Functional Linguistics that connect clauses

Expansion		Explanation	Example
Elaboration		Provide further specification or description of a clause	Gas escapes from the canister **and** pushes against the ground.
Extension		Adds something new to a clause	The gas escaping from the canister generates a reaction force, **which** is greater than gravity.
Enhancing	Temporal	Qualifies a clause with reference to time	Gas escapes from the canister **when** it pops.
	Causal	Qualifies a clause with reference to cause	A resultant force acts on the canister. **Therefore**, it accelerates.
	Spatial	Qualifies a clause with reference to place	The film canister was stationary **and on** the floor.

expanded to form clause complexes that describe the motion of the film canister as flow of events and give account of this flow. The relevant logical functions, with examples taken from students' explanations, are identified in Table 5.2. The examples in Table 5.2 have been chosen for clarity. However, it is important to note that this expansion of clauses to form complexes is not always simply a linear process, where the first clause connects sequentially to the second clause. Clauses can also be embedded within others to express an unfolding of a series of events.

The ergative model, at a clause level, and logical connectives between clauses, define the experiential and logical functions of language that individuals use to describe the flow of events and the reasons for these events. Hence, if the film-canister rocket pop is viewed as a flow of events, SFL provides a comprehensive and powerful analytical tool for characterising and comparing the individual written explanations of students and the canonical explanation of their teachers. The results of this analysis are presented in the next section.

Results

Findings from the written explanations

Initial explanations

Figures 5.1 and 5.2 demonstrate the SFL analysis of two students' initial explanations of the rocket canister's motion.

Student A (group 3)

Explanation
The build up of pressure forces the film canister up into the air but then the mixture of friction and gravity forces the canister back to the ground.

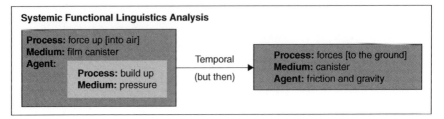

FIGURE 5.1 The systemic functional linguistic (SFL) analysis of Student A's initial explanation of the film canisters rockets motion at the start of the topic. Clauses are shown within boxes, temporal, spatial and extension logical connectives between clauses are shown horizontally from left to right and causal connectives are shown vertically from top to bottom. Note, group 3 students go on to develop a more scientific explanation of the motion of the film–canister rocket

Student B (group 3)

Explanation
The build up of pressure in the film canister pushes the film into the air, then air resistance causes the energy to transfer so it falls to the ground.

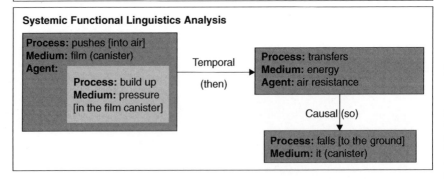

FIGURE 5.2 The systemic functional linguistic (SFL) analysis of Student B's initial explanation of the film canisters rockets motion at the start of the topic. Clauses are shown within boxes, temporal, spatial and extension logical connectives between clauses are shown horizontally from left to right and causal connectives are shown vertically from top to bottom. Note, group 3 students go on to develop a more scientific explanation of the motion of the film–canister rocket

These examples were chosen because they demonstrate the usage of SFL and also illustrate several features typical of all the students' initial explanations. These features are:

- Causal connections between events are specified within a process-medium-agent structure. Agents within this structure are typically pressure, gravity or friction, or simple processes, like the build-up of pressure.
- '*Forcing*' or '*pushing*' is often seen as a process rather than an agent that can affect the motion of an object. This is similar to the everyday use of *force*, as in forcing an individual to do something, rather than the force of gravitational attraction causing two massive objects, e.g. two stars, to move towards each other.
- The motion of the canister is often described quite simply, using everyday language rather than scientific vocabulary. For example, going down or up rather than accelerating.

The complexity in the canonical explanation compared with the examples given of students' initial explanations is noticeable – and, in the canonical explanation, it was decided to ignore more complicated aspects such as the friction between the canister and its lid. However, despite this, there are similarities in the structures of the canonical and student explanations, such as the frequent use of a simple ergative process-medium-agent structure to describe events at a clause level, which are then linked with logical connectives. However, it is clear that the teachers describe the motion of the film-canister rocket in terms of different events (e.g. the acceleration of the film canister in the direction of the resultant force), rather than simply re-stating the description provided to them (e.g. the canister 'climbs' or 'falls'). Moreover, the teachers identify different and more complex causes to account for these events (e.g. a resultant force acting on the canister) as opposed to simply *pressure* or *gravity*.

Mid-point explanations

The characterisation of the canonical explanation using SFL allowed students' responses to the mid-point assessment to be grouped according to their similarity with this explanation. In general, students' responses fell into three groups according to the number of features they shared with the canonical explanation:

- **Group 1** (24 students) – students did not include any features of the canonical scientific explanation.
- **Group 2** (15 students) – students used a mixture of everyday and scientific explanation by including some features of the canonical scientific explanation.
- **Group 3** (6 students) – students used many, but not all features, of the canonical scientific explanation.

A small number of students did not fit into these groups. Consequently, two further groups were defined:

- **Group 4** (2 students) – students chose to use scientific concepts other than force, for instance energy, in their explanations, which would tend to be more descriptive than explanatory in nature.

Canonical Explanation

Explanation

When the film canister pops, gas escapes from the canister and pushes against the ground. The force of the gas pushing against the ground generates a reaction force in the opposite direction and acting upon the canister. This reaction force or thrust is greater than the weight of the canister. Therefore, there is a resultant force acting upwards on the rocket. Consequently the rocket accelerates in the direction of this resultant force.

Systemic Functional Linguistics Analysis

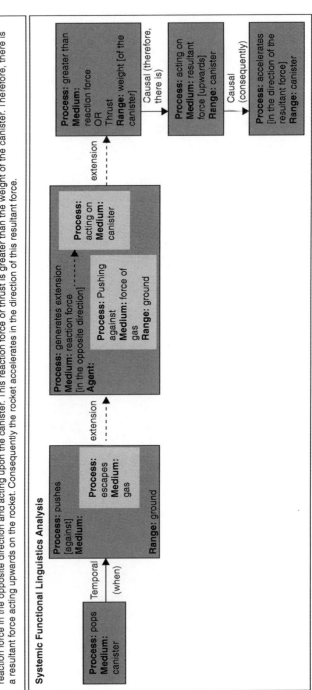

FIGURE 5.3 The systemic functional linguistic (SFL) analysis of a canonical explanation of the motion of the film canisters rocket. Note, clauses are shown within boxes, temporal, spatial and extension logical connectives between clauses are shown horizontally from left to right and causal connectives are shown vertically from top to bottom

- **Group 5** (9 students) – students' responses were a single word answer, for example: gravity, which is both underdeveloped as a response, and ambiguous.

Groups 1, 2 and 3 define the range of progress students have made towards developing scientific explanations. This range can therefore be used to chart the development of a scientific explanation. Typical examples of the explanations in each group, which illustrate this development, are shown in Table 5.3.

It is possible that the groups listed above could have emerged from an analysis that did not use SFL. However, the use of SFL made the categorisation of students' responses into the five groups more robust by making the differences between each group and the canonical answer more explicit, especially in the three groups that show progress towards a scientific explanation. For instance, the shift some students make between seeing *force* as a process, something that happens to an object, rather than a medium, something that can act on an object, is more apparent when using SFL. This change in an individual's ontological belief about the nature of a force is seen as necessary for the development of *force* as a scientific concept (Chi, 2005; Carey, 1978). Hence, this is an example of how a SFL analysis can identify important

TABLE 5.3 Typical examples of students' explanations in each group. Groups 1, 2 and 3 are defined by the number of features a student's explanation shares with a canonical teachers' explanation. Students' responses in each group illustrate the development from everyday to scientific explanation of the film-canister rocket's motion. Shared features in the explanations are shown in italics

Group	Example explanation	Typical features shared with the canonical answer
1	The build-up of pressure forces the film canister up into the air but then the mixture of friction and gravity forces the canister back to the ground.	No shared features.
2	When the *pressure builds up it overcomes the force of gravity* and climbs into the air. When there is no more force pushing it up, it falls down with gravity.	The idea of a resultant or 'overall' force causing motion, even if pressure is incorrectly identified as a force.
3	The pressure from the air trapped inside the canister increases, therefore *the force pushing the canister up is greater than the force keeping it down*, therefore *the canister positively accelerates*. When the canister starts to slow down, gravity pulls it down due to the decreasing pressure of the canister 'popping'.	The idea of a resultant or 'overall' force causing motion. AND Acceleration is correctly identified as the type of motion caused by a resultant force.

steps students take in the development of a scientific explanation of the motion of the rocket canister.

The change in how group 2 students and group 3 students describe motion, which can often be identified as a process in SFL, seems to be another important step. Group 2 students still typically describe the motion of the canister as 'climbing' or 'falling'. In contrast, group 3 students have begun to use the technical term, *accelerate*, to describe the canister's motion. In addition, group 3 students now recognise a resultant force as a cause of acceleration. However, these students did not use the technical term, *resultant*, to describe this force. Instead, they often relied on a full description of the forces acting on the canister (e.g. '*the force pushing the canister up is greater than the force keeping it down*'). Hence, the SFL analysis identified two instances when the use of technical terms seems to define steps in the development of a scientific explanation. Therefore, students' understanding of these terms was investigated more fully in the subsequent interviews, which took place at the end of the topic. Moreover, in recognition of the apparent importance of the technical terms, the physics teachers decided to place greater emphasis on developing their students' awareness and understanding of technical terminology throughout the remainder of the topic by explicitly discussing the meaning of these terms and encouraging students to use these terms.

Final explanations

It was intended to use the explanations students wrote at the end of the topic to extend and add detail to the picture this intervention was building of how students learn to explain scientifically. However, the goodwill of the students towards completing the written tasks had evaporated by the final assessment, due to the repetition of the question and their impending GCSE examinations. As a result, many of their responses were simple one-word answers or a single sentence. It was difficult to see how these answers would contribute to the developmental chart illustrated in Table 5.3. Hence, it was decided to exclude these explanations from the analysis. This was unfortunate, as students had not been given the opportunity to apply their knowledge of force to explaining several examples of motion, for instance, maximum speeds and terminal velocities. Moreover, analysis of these interviews might have revealed any effects of the intervention, after the teachers begun to focus more on the development of technical terms, had they been written with more care.

Interviews

After the analysis of the written explanations and after the Forces and Motion topic was completed, a sample of students from each group were interviewed to further investigate and clarify their explanations and check their understanding of technical terms (e.g. resultant force, acceleration). The opportunity to take part in an interview was offered to all the students who had written explanations. The final sample of two students from group 1, four from group 2 and four from group 3 were selected because they were willing to participate and could attend an interview at a time that suited both interviewee (student) and interviewer (teacher). These interviews showed the two interviewed students from group 1 had very poor understanding of the technical terms and often did not recognise these terms were associated with the topic. In contrast, the interviewed students from group 2 recognised these terms but often had a confused understanding of their meaning. For example, when asked what 'resultant force' means, one student replied:

> *Well isn't the resultant force when one is bigger than the other and you've got gravity pulling down but something else pulling him up.*

Here the student has correctly identified the conditions needs for a resultant force but cannot clearly state that this force is any force that is 'left over' when all the forces on the object are summed. Students in this group also misunderstand the term 'acceleration', associating it solely with the process of speeding up, rather than the process of changing speed (either increasing or decreasing). This lack of understanding is illustrated by students' response when asked if a lump of plasticine accelerates when it hits a desk and stops.

Student C: How's it accelerate when it hits the floor?
Interviewer: So that's the bit that doesn't make sense. What doesn't make sense about it?
Student D: Surely it would stop. Cos it's hit something.

Another student summarises the feelings of the previous two students in another interview.

Student E: I just don't get how it can accelerate when it's hit the floor because it wouldn't be moving.

The interviewed students from group 3 did not share this confusion – they were able to correctly identify and use technical terms as the following extract of dialogue illustrates. In this extract, the interviewer and student are discussing the motion of the film–canister rocket and drawing diagrams to aid the discussion.

Student F: It's accelerating here as it goes up (student uses the diagram to indicate the point when the canister leaves the floor – point A) then it slow down (pointing to when the canister is in the air just after it has left the floor – point B).
Interviewer: So it's accelerating there (indicating point A), but would you agree that it is accelerating there (indicating point B).
Student F: Yes.
Interviewer: How do you know it's accelerating there?

Student F: Because that arrow (pointing to an arrow representing a force) is bigger than that arrow (point to an arrow representing a force acting in the opposite direction).

Interviewer: Does it have a resultant force there?

Student F: Yeah.

However, why these students did not use these terms in their own explanations remained unclear.

Summary

As was stated in the introduction, asking students to write explanations of the film-canister's motion at an initial, mid and final point began as a method of data collection to assess the extent to which students adopt features of their teachers' explanation after instruction. SFL analysis provided a highly systematic tool for comparing students' explanations with their teachers', and, therefore, assessing each student's progress towards producing a scientific explanation. Moreover, this systematic analysis enabled students to be objectively and robustly grouped according to how successful they were in developing a scientific explanation by the mid-point of the topic. From the differences between these groups' explanations, it became increasingly clear that an understanding of technical terms (e.g. resultant, acceleration) might be an important requirement for students to develop scientific explanations. This led to specific action by the teachers to try to develop students' understanding of these technical terms in the remainder of the topic. Unfortunately, the lack of detail in students' final explanations meant that this hypothesis could not be fully tested. However, the interviews at the end of the topic suggested that students who understand technical terms make the most progress towards being able to write scientific explanations. The interviews also highlighted the differences between students' verbal and written explanations, suggesting that the process of writing narrative explanations is itself helpful in developing students' explanatory skills.

Written explanations with pre-service science teachers

This intervention was conducted in the context of a 1-year pre-service teacher education course for secondary science teachers at a university with three cohorts of participants and this section will focus more on the value of the intervention as perceived by the student teachers. These participants were all pre-service science teachers who were science graduates in biology, chemistry or physics (or related degrees) and were preparing to be science teachers in secondary schools, with a typical cohort size of 45. Part of the course comprised a series of workshops on key ideas in the school science curriculum. Each year, the intervention took place in four of these workshops in one term which covered the following aspects of the curriculum: the particle theory of matter, forces, electricity and energy. Each workshop had three aims: firstly, given the diverse backgrounds of the pre-service science teachers, the activities were designed to help develop their subject know-ledge, particularly if the topic was not part of their subject specialism. Secondly, the workshops introduced the pre-service science teachers to a range of ideas commonly held by children learning science which are different from the scientific view being taught as part of the curriculum. Thirdly, in each workshop, pre-service science teachers were presented with a range of teaching and learning activities and asked to critique these. The latter two aims can be thought of as helping to develop the pedagogical content knowledge (PCK) of the pre-service science teachers (Shulman, 1986). PCK is usually considered to comprise some understanding of the teaching and learning challenges for a particular topic or concept and knowledge of various pedagogical approaches for that topic/concept, hence the design of the workshop. The workshops were highly interactive in nature, with pre-service science teachers working in small groups (four to five) for much of the time. These groups were usually balanced in terms of gender and subject specialism.

During these workshops, common demonstrations were often shared by the tutor leading the workshop, to introduce the pre-service science teachers to some typical practical activities. These would usually be discussed and an explanation offered; however, this explanation was very much 'owned' by the tutor, the size of the group making it difficult to meaningfully co-construct explanations verbally. The tutor decided to ask the pre-service science teachers to write their own explanations of these demonstrations on blank sheets of A4 paper, and the tutor then provided individual written feedback. Copies were taken of these written explanations for analysis purposes, with the permission of the pre-service teachers. The analysis characterised the descriptions given and the mechanisms used to explain why the events occurred, including the extent to which these were complete, and whether these were at a macroscopic or microscopic level (e.g. Williamson et al. 2012), but this analysis will be presented elsewhere. These demonstrations are summarised in Table 5.4 below. The canonical explanations expected by the tutor for one of these demonstrations is presented in Table 5.5, together with the key features of the pre-service teachers' written explanations and a detailed description of the feedback is then given. Finally, the findings of the evaluations using written questionnaire and focus groups are discussed to identify the benefits of the intervention to the pre-service teachers and the insights yielded by this process of writing narrative explanations.

From Table 5.5, it can be seen that the canonical explanation for this apparently simple demonstration is quite complex, using a number of scientific ideas in a carefully organised way. This was also the case for all the other explanations and, in all cases, it is possible to provide an explanation using macroscopic ideas, e.g. about pressure or energy transfer or current. Indeed, the pre-service teachers often gave macroscopic explanations initially, as they were confident and secure with these concepts. Over the series of workshops, it could be seen that the pre-service science teachers learnt more about how to construct explanations using microscopic ideas which were understandable by younger secondary school students, and this was supported by the evaluation (discussed later). This is the first of the pedagogical insights yielded by this process of writing narrative explanations.

TABLE 5.4 The key theoretical ideas discussed in each of the four workshops, and the accompanying demonstration for which narrative explanations were written

Workshop	Demonstration	Key theoretical ideas
Particle theory of matter	Egg in a conical flask A small amount of boiling water (~150ml) from a kettle was poured into a conical flask, and then a peeled hard-boiled egg was placed on top. After a while, the egg moved into the flask. (A video of a similar demonstration can be seen here: https://youtu.be/uzJ0CqUD12I)	The particle theory of matter is used to explain the properties and behaviour of solids, liquids and gases, and underpins explanations of phenomena across the three sciences including rates of chemical reactions, osmosis and pressure.
Forces	Rocket balloon A number of rocket balloons were distributed around the room and pre-service science teachers were invited to inflate and then release the balloons which 'flew' about the room, emitting a loud noise, until they were deflated and fell to the floor. As an activity, this generally causes much hilarity, which can help to break down barriers about physics – often perceived as a dry and difficult subject.	Included a range of concepts taught at secondary school level: Newton's Laws of Motion, pressure, floating and sinking, terminal velocity, gravity, moments and friction.
Electricity	Burning pencil 24V is applied across a pencil sharpened at both ends, with due safety precautions taken. The pencil heats up, the wood starts to smoke, whilst the graphite core glows red. Then the wood bursts into flames, and splits open, leaving the glowing red graphite core intact. This is a highly memorable demonstration. (A similar video can be seen here: https://youtu.be/s9eE2jFoioM)	Voltage, current and resistance in series and parallel circuits, circuit symbols, analogies for electrical circuits.
Energy	Melting ice One ice cube is placed on a plastic chopping board, and another ice cube on a metal frying pan. Prior to this, learners are asked to touch the board and the pan and identify which felt warmer (the board), then asked to predict on which one would the ice melt faster (learners often say the board). The ice melts much faster on the metal pan, often to the surprise of the learners. (A similar demonstration can be seen here: https://youtu.be/yvB8Qd02oWk)	Energy, energy stores, transfer of energy between different stores, conservation of energy, renewable and non-renewable energy resources, generation of electricity and efficiency calculations.

TABLE 5.5 Explanation of egg in a conical flask and key features of the explanations provided by pre-service science teachers

Demonstration	Canonical explanation by tutor	Key features of explanations by pre-service teachers
Egg in a conical flask	The pressure of the gas mixture inside flask is reduced, as some of the warm gas escapes prior to the egg being placed on the flask, and as gas condenses on the sides of the flask as it cools. Both of these reduce the density of particles in the gas, reducing the number of collisions made by the gas particles on the lower side of the egg, and the reduction in temperature reduces the force of the collisions. This results in the external air pressure exceeding the pressure inside the flask and the egg is pushed into the flask by the air particles outside exerting a force on it by colliding with the upper side of the egg. It is possible to explain the phenomena using macroscopic ideas about pressure, but these are challenging to understand for learners unfamiliar with this concept, hence the need to use microscopic ideas about particles in order to construct a full explanation.	• Only one mechanism for reduction in particle density • Effect on pressure of gas cooling not included • Reduction in pressure stated not explained • Particle ideas not included (only macroscopic ideas about pressure and volume) • Explanation focused on volume reducing and egg being 'sucked' or 'pulled' into flask • Unclear language about forces and causal effects

Other common key features were for explanations to be incomplete, with one or more aspects missing, or for vocabulary to be used inaccurately. The strongest written narratives tended to use fewer key technical terms – only as many as were sufficient for the explanation to be coherent and complete. They also offered an explanation or definition for those key terms, rather than assuming understanding on the part of the reader. Many of the explanations included diagrams, but often these were sketches of the equipment, rather than scientific drawings, and in many cases lacked labels. Again, these aspects developed as the workshops progressed and the pre-service science teachers tried to give more complete explanations, to be more careful in their use of terminology and to consider their use of diagrams. These skills can be seen as consolidating their subject knowledge and helping them to start to transform it into PCK by showing them the sorts of explanations needed by teachers for learners. It can also be seen that they were starting to develop a more scientific voice in their explanations.

TABLE 5.6 Responses to the Evaluation Questionnaire (n = 49)

The four explanations tasks	Yes	No	Missing
Did these tasks help you to develop your subject knowledge? Please explain your answer.	77.6%	14.3%	8.1%
Did these tasks help you to think about how to explain concepts to students? Please explain your answer.	83.7%	6.1%	10.2%
Did you find the written feedback useful? Please explain your answer.	83.7%	8.1%	8.1%

Individual feedback was given for each explanation in the following areas: firstly, all the aspects of the pre-service science teachers' explanations which matched the canonical explanations were acknowledged and praised. Secondly, questions were asked where explanations were incomplete, or only used macroscopic ideas, with these being worded to hint at potential answers. Thirdly, incorrect statements or use of vocabulary were highlighted, and, again, questions asked to suggest how to improve the explanation. Finally, comments were also made on the extent to which the explanation was well organised, and whether good use had been made of diagrams to support the explanation. Interestingly, almost none of the explanations utilised equations. From the evaluations, it was clear that the pre-service science teachers found this written feedback helpful (Table 5.6), and it served to model how they could give feedback to their own students (in the interviews, discussed later).

Evaluation of the effectiveness of the intervention

Two evaluations were conducted to investigate the effect of writing these tasks and receiving written feedback on the development of the subject knowledge and PCK of the pre-service science teachers: written evaluations and focus group interviews. The pre-service science teachers on this course complete an evaluation form at the end of the first term on their experiences thus far. Three questions were added to the form and the overall responses to these can be found in Table 5.6. The questions were written in such a way as to yield yes or no answers, which could then be justified further, with the majority offering justification for their initial responses. These additional comments were analysed and the resulting categories can be seen in Table 5.7. The first column clearly shows that the process of writing narrative explanations and receiving written feedback helped these pre-service science teachers to develop their subject knowledge. The middle column also shows that the process had made them consider how they would explain to students – they had started to transform this subject knowledge into PCK.

Given the overwhelming positive response, it was decided to investigate why the pre-service science teachers had found it helpful to write these explanations by interviewing 10 of them in order to explore these questionnaire responses in more depth. Each focus group comprised two to four pre-service science teachers, with a

TABLE 5.7 Written comments about the process from the pre-service science teachers (numbers indicate number of responses in each category; some comments fell into more than one category, and not every response included a comment)

Positive comments about why it was helpful for subject knowledge	Positive comments about how it helped to think about explanations for students	Positive comments about the written feedback
Highlighted areas to revise (9)	Thought more about need for clarity and logical steps from basics (13)	Helped improve written explanation (11)
Made me think about how to explain (9)	Thought about explaining in a different way (5)	Useful (8)
Helped me deal with own misconceptions (5)	Thought more about careful use of language (4)	Helped improve subject knowledge (5)
Learnt new concepts (4)	Thought more about learners' perspectives (4)	Detailed (3)
Useful to have answer returned (2)	Showed what was missing from explanations (4)	Written was important rather than verbal (1)
Enjoyable – group aspect good (1)	Enjoyed the group discussions (2)	
	Thought more about cross topic links (1)	

Negative comments about why it was helpful for subject knowledge	Negative comments about how it helped to think about explanations for students	Negative comments about the written feedback
Needed more time (4)	Lack of subject knowledge limited effectiveness (4)	Wanted a model answer (4)
Confusing/hard (3)	Writing explanations is hard (3)	Too fussy (2)
Already knew it (2)	Not enough time (2)	Demoralising as still much to do (2)
	Task not clear (1)	Wanted a mark (1)
		Feedback confusing (1)
		Not enough time to make improvements (1)

mixture of genders and ages to reflect the cohort. One group had pre-service science teachers with a first degree in biology, another with chemistry degrees, and two mixed groups of physics or biology, and biology or chemistry. Pre-service science teachers were chosen from a group of volunteers, taking care to omit any whose high-stakes assessment on the course the tutor was directly involved with, to avoid undue pressure on the participants (Youens & McCarthy, 2007). Invitations were sent by e-mail, and the semi-structured group interviews took place at mutually convenient locations and times. The questions focused on the responses presented in

Table 5.6, and the participants were asked to what extent they agreed or disagreed with the statements, and then asked to explain their answers in more detail. They were also asked to comment on the usefulness of the demonstrations themselves and the extent to which they thought it was helpful for us to emphasise explanations and whether this was a helpful way of doing so. Suggestions for improvements were also sought. The pre-service science teachers' responses were transcribed and analysed carefully for further information about the benefits of this process.

The interviews confirmed the positive responses given in the questionnaire: firstly this process of writing narrative explanations had taught them the importance of:

> *organising your thoughts and thinking what do you need to discuss first in order for them [the pupils] to get to the point where they have that understanding*'; '*I would definitely try and think through the steps and the order*' and '*to check you can explain it beforehand.*

Significantly, the process had enabled the pre-service science teachers to realise that:

> *if you write it down yourself you might realise that you can't explain it ... unless you try and put it into words either on paper or spoken then you might not realise that what's in your head is not necessarily that ordered*', and that '*there is a difference between being able to quote a definition and being able to understand what the definition means.*

This was repeated across all four focus groups, clearly demonstrating that the pre-service science teachers had recognised their own need to have an explanation ready prior to teaching a lesson:

> *it made me just think about how I explained something in the way that you might want to hear how the explanation works rather than just a load of rambling nonsense which doesn't really get to the point or just kind of works its way around it, and then eventually within five minutes, whereas it could have only taken two minutes, you get to a place where they might understand.*

In the discussion it will be seen how the school-based intervention had a similar outcome, and the theoretical construct of a '*coherent internal account*' will be introduced (Hillier, 2013).

Secondly, it became evident that participating in this process had given the pre-service science teachers a better appreciation of learners' perspectives: '*it made me appreciate how students can struggle with concepts in the classroom because I was struggling with it*'. They realised that the discomfort expressed in some of the questionnaire responses about completing a task when your subject knowledge was unsure ('*I'm one of those people that doesn't want to write something down until I think I've got it right*') or when time was short was regularly experienced by school students: '*that's what we do to the kids all the time, and that's the challenge for them and you learn things from the challenge.'* The interviewees appeared to value these insights into learners' perspectives and could see how it helped them to be better teachers:*'you have to step back and think what do they know, what do these words mean to them?'*

Thirdly, the interviewees were positive about the written feedback, finding it *'encouraging'* and *'you were stretching us rather than being picky, it felt like being stretched'* and learning was never finished – *'you could always improve on something'*. They appreciated that the written feedback had modelled *'what a good teacher should do'*. When questioned about model answers, they recognised that they could always *'Google'* an answer without waiting for written feedback, and that *'a model explanation is really only in your words. And actually what we need to do is to develop the skills to put in our words. So actually* [a model answer] *wouldn't really have helped really probably'*, again pointing to the need for *coherent internal accounts*.

Finally, it appeared that the intervention had impacted on their classroom practice and on their PCK: the interviews occurred six weeks after the last workshop and the participants also talked about how they had applied what they had learnt to their planning and teaching in school. For example, one pre-service teacher said: *'I actually tried… I set them as homework to write an explanation.'* Several had used the questioning approach used in the written feedback in their own marking, whilst others had used the demonstrations in lessons, for example:

> they could tell me what was going to happen, but when it happened they couldn't believe it and they were really excited' and '[each demonstration is] quite exciting to watch but also because you haven't necessarily been taught it, they can come up with a range of explanations and then it's something to focus a lesson on.

Similarly, one pre-service teacher spoke about how they were *'really thinking about exactly how you're doing your explanation and keeping it as simple but as clear as possible'*, and another said *'I definitely taught a lesson whereby I was thinking … because I'd gone through that exercise … specific terms and careful use of language'*.

From all this, it can be seen that the intervention had not only impacted on their subject knowledge, but also on their PCK. The discussion will highlight the commonalities and differences between the two interventions.

Discussion

Development of a scientific voice and use of key technical terms

Across both interventions, the development of a scientific voice could be seen, and the use of key technical terms was vital in the writing of a narrative explanation. In the school-based intervention, it was clear that some students used technical terms, such as 'force', but not in a scientific way, e.g. 'the canister was forced back to the ground'. Other students used 'force' in a scientific way, but appeared to have confused understanding of concepts such as 'resultant force' and 'acceleration'. The final group used 'force' in a scientific way and could verbally articulate their understanding of 'resultant force' and 'acceleration', but did not use these technical terms in written explanations. As the students were asked to write several narrative explanations of the same phenomenon over a term, it was possible to see them develop a scientific explanation, and therefore 'voice', over time. It appeared that the students who had a shared understanding with their teachers of the meaning of key technical terms also had a better understanding of the scientific explanatory mechanism, and were able to articulate this better. However, the question of why students resist using key technical terms in their written explanations, when they are able to articulate them verbally, is not yet understood and requires further research.

Similarly, the university-based intervention was conducted over the course of a term, and the evaluation clearly shows that the pre-service science teachers felt it had helped them to develop a more explanatory scientific voice over time. In this case, the scientific voice took the form of being more aware of what is necessary for a scientific explanation, namely a clear and detailed explanation (not a description), built up from basic principles, rather than a descriptive, or incomplete explanation. Despite this increased awareness, the pre-service science teachers still struggled to consistently use microscopic ideas in their explanations, and subsequently the tutor has emphasised this much more in her teaching.

Together, it can be seen that these interventions seemed to be effective at developing the subject knowledge of learners in both school and university contexts.

Process of organising knowledge and constructing an argument – a coherent internal account

The second insight, common to both interventions, was the importance to both the school students and pre-service teachers of learning how to organise knowledge and construct an argument: in the school context this was for the purpose of demonstrating learning; in the university context this was in preparation for teaching. Described eloquently by the pre-service science teachers is this need for them, as learners, to develop their own explanation – a *coherent internal account* (Hillier, 2013). The school students were learning to produce organised explanations in their own words, and the systemic functional linguistic analysis revealed the extent to which students were able to link clauses together and to expand clauses to give more detailed and complete explanations. The pre-service science teachers were learning how to produce organised explanations in their own words which they could then use as the starting point for planning their teaching, and hence this is an explicit step to be taken by teachers in the transformation of subject knowledge into PCK.

Development of pre-service science teachers' PCK

The third insight is specific to the pre-service science teachers, and is the development of their PCK. The findings show that a better understanding of learners' perspectives had helped them to consider what language they used with their own students, and strategies they could use to build up scientific explanations in their classrooms. Given that PCK is recognised as a difficult concept for teachers to work with (Loughran, Berry & Mulhall, 2006), a process whereby pre-service science teachers are taught how to develop their PCK, and given an explicit step to take when transforming their subject knowledge into PCK, namely that of developing *coherent internal accounts*, is a valuable contribution to knowledge.

These findings reveal the impact these interventions had on the school students and on the pre-service science teachers. But what were the challenges and limitations of conducting these interventions?

Issues and challenges with carrying out an effective intervention

One challenge in the school-based intervention was that of repeatedly asking students to write the narrative explanations. This was avoided in the university-based intervention to some extent by asking the pre-service science teachers to write explanations of different phenomena, but still four was felt to be sufficient for the point to have been made. Another challenge was the giving of written feedback – crucial to the university-based intervention, but very time-consuming. Similarly, the analysis of the school students' explanations was important, but also took a long time.

In addition, it was difficult to explore the development of explanations over time, as the learners in both situations were also receiving a range of instruction in science and science education which could have impacted on their approach to writing narrative explanations. As this was exploratory research over time conducting the intervention and research using a quasi-experimental design would not have been appropriate.

Nature of collaboration

Both interventions were initially conducted separately and independently of each other, before connections and links were made, at which point the two researchers began to regularly discuss the interventions, analysis of the data and the implications of the findings. Very similar in nature, the school-based intervention aimed to support the development of explanations given by school students to be closer to the explanations given by their science teachers, whereas the university-based one could be thought of as supporting beginning science teachers to develop their explanations to be closer to those given by experienced science teachers. The two interventions both yielded a number of insights about these processes, and about how to develop the learning of both school students and beginning science teachers in order to nurture rich learning and teaching of science.

Conclusions and implications for the future

The interventions described here show that the process of constructing a written narrative can help learners to develop their use of language in science and to organise their ideas into a scientific explanation, both key skills for learning science. It also reveals gaps in learners' knowledge, which can be useful for learners, teachers and educators to use in a formative way to develop a deeper and more scientific understanding. The researchers have found this process to be useful, both in the school classroom and in the pre-service teacher education context. Crucially, for pre-service teachers, it is a way to make explicit the process of transforming subject knowledge into PCK. However, it must be emphasised that in both cases, this was conducted in a low-stakes assessment environment, where the formative nature of the task was made clear, rather than a high-stakes summative assessment environment. There are clear potential benefits for the science classroom and beyond, and we hope that others will find these approaches useful in their own practice.

In terms of future developments from these interventions the university-based intervention has become an established part of the course, and is now in its sixth year. The pre-service science teachers continue to value the process, and the researcher makes explicit what they are intended to learn from the process. As an intervention, it is one easily used and adapted by others running similar courses.

The school-based intervention is being developed into a new research project as part of a PhD. Moreover, the intervention has raised the awareness of the importance of technical terms and the benefits of requiring students to write in detail when learning scientific explanations. This has led to a focus on identifying and ensuring the meanings of key technical terms are taught by science teachers within the school. Similarly, assessment has been redesigned to provide students with the opportunity to write explanations and, therefore, for teachers to learn about their students' understanding from these explanations.

In terms of wider relevance beyond science education, although both these interventions were conducted in the context of science education in the UK, neither the process nor the benefits should be considered as being limited to science. Developing learners' use of key technical terms and an appropriate academic voice is necessary in many disciplines. Similarly, a process which teaches students to organise knowledge and construct a *coherent internal account* – their own logical argument – is valuable to teachers in a wide range of subjects, as is a mechanism for helping pre-service teachers to develop their PCK.

References

Abrahams, I., Homer, M., Sharpe, R. & Zhou, M. (2015). A comparative cross-cultural study of the prevalence and nature of misconceptions in physics amongst English and Chinese undergraduate students, *Research in Science & Technological Education*, 33(1), 111–130.

Carey, S. (1978). The child as a word learner. In M. Halle, J. Bresnan, & G. A. Miller (Eds.), *Linguistic Theory and Psychological Reality*. Cambridge, MA, USA: MIT Press

Cassels, J. & Johnstone, A. (1985). *Words that Matter in Science*, London, UK: Royal Society.

Chi, M. T. H. (2005). Commonsense conceptions of emergent processes: why some misconceptions are robust, *Journal of the Learning Sciences*, 14(2), 161–199.

Davidse, K. (1992). Transitivity/ergativity: the Janus-headed grammar of actions and events, in Davies, M. & Ravelli, L. (Eds.), *Advances in Systemic Linguistics,* London, UK and New York, USA: Pinter, pp. 105–135.

Geelan, D. (2012). Teacher Explanations. In B. J. Fraser & G. Kenneth (Eds.), *Second International Handbook of Science Education.* Dordrecht, Netherlands: Springer.

Halliday, M. A. K. & Matthiessen, C. M. (2004). *An Introduction to Functional Grammar* (3rd edition), London, UK: Hodder Education.

Harlen, W. (Ed.) (2010). *Principles and Big Ideas of Science Education,* Hatfield, UK: Association for Science Education.

Hillier, J. (2013). How Does That Work? Developing Pedagogical Content Knowledge From Subject Knowledge, *Teacher Education and Practice,* 26(2), Spring 2013, 321–338.

Howe, C., Tavares, J. T. & Devine, A. (2016). Recognition as support for reasoning about horizontal motion: a further resource for school science?, *Research in Science & Technological Education,* 34(3), 273–289.

Jarvis, T., Pell, A. & McKeon, F. (2003). Changes in primary teachers' science knowledge and understanding during a two year in-service programme, *Research in Science & Technological Education,* 21(1), 17–42.

Loughran, J. J., Berry, A. & Mulhall, P. (2006). *Understanding and Developing Science Teachers' Pedagogical Content Knowledge.* Rotterdam, Netherlands: Sense.

Millar, R. & Osborne, J. (Eds.) (1998). *Beyond 2000: Science education for the future,* London, UK: King's College London.

Mortimer, E. & Scott, P. (2003). *Meaning Making in Secondary Science Classrooms,* Maidenhead, UK: Open University Press.

Norris, S. P., Guilbert, S. M., Smith, M. L., Hakimelahi, S. & Phillips, L. M. (2005). A theoretical framework for narrative explanation in science, *Science Education,* 89(4,) 535–563.

Ogborn, J., Kress, G., Martins, I. & McGillicuddy, K. (1996). *Explaining Science in the Classroom,* Buckingham, UK: Open University Press.

Shulman, L. (1986). Those who understand: Knowledge growth in teaching, *Educational Researcher,* 15(2), 4–14.

Solomon, J. (1986). Children's explanations in science, *Oxford Review of Education,* 12(1), 41–51.

Teich, E. & Holtz, M. (2009). Scientific registers in contact: an exploration of the lexico-grammatical properties of interdisciplinary discourses, *International Journal of Corpus Linguistics,* 14(4), 524–548.

Williamson, V.M., Lane, S.M., Gilbreath, T., Tasker, R., Ashkenazi, G., Williamson, K.C. & Macfarlane, R.D. (2012). The effect of viewing order of macroscopic and particulate visualizations on students' particulate explanations, *Journal of Chemical Education,* 89(8), 979–987.

Youens, B., & McCarthy, S. (2007). Subject knowledge development by science student teachers: The role of university tutors and school-based subject mentors, *Research in Science and Technological Education,* 25(3), 293–306.

6

DEVELOPING TALK IN MATHEMATICS CLASSROOMS

Jenni Ingram, Nick Andrews, Jo Rudd and Andrea Pitt

Introduction

A feature of new mathematics curricula is the recognition of the important role talk plays in broadening a student's mathematical vocabulary, bringing increased lucidity to their explanations, and more generally developing and communicating their mathematical understanding. However, this recognition in turn raises the question of how teachers can provide opportunities for students to develop what we succinctly label *Talk in Mathematics (TiM)*.

In this chapter, we report on the collaboration between two teams of teachers from local secondary schools and three researchers over two years, who together have sought to address this question. Previous research has identified the way teachers initiate sequences of interactions, the emphasis on technical vocabulary and the use of silence as classroom-level factors that might influence the quality of TiM (e.g. Franke et al., 2009; Ingram & Elliott, 2016; Schleppegrell, 2007). In each cycle of the project we explored together one of these factors, affording teaching experiences and research findings to be blended by using each to interrogate the other. This has allowed us to exemplify different ways of realising effective strategies that support the development of TiM in a format that will be relevant to practising teachers wishing to explore these issues for themselves. The term *intervention* within this project refers to the identification of something that needs to be changed with decisions and actions that are intended to affect this change. In contrast to many other interventions, however, here the teachers identified what they felt need to change and took actions to affect this change. The project itself provided prompts and opportunities for the teachers to identify these changes and opportunities within their own practice for change.

While we constrain the discussion of our findings in the chapter to developing talk in mathematics, the research design and classroom strategies have applications beyond mathematics teaching. Furthermore, the discussion of the collaborative approach to working with teachers in order to develop practice, particularly the use of self-video and prompting tasks, contributes to the research on teacher education and professional development.

The 'Talk in Mathematics' Project (TiM)

A core principle of the TiM project was its collaborative nature, involving a group of mathematics teachers, teacher researchers, teacher educators and researchers, with the individuals taking on multiple roles. All those involved were established mathematics teachers with experience of working collaboratively to improve students' experiences of mathematics. Many have been involved in researching teacher practice, researching their own practice, and working with beginning and developing teachers. As we are all teachers, we will use teacher to refer to each member of the group, though this is just one of the roles each member had. All members of the group are referred to by their pseudonyms. The focus that brought us together was a desire to support students to develop their mathematical talk in lessons. Intrinsic to the collaboration was the differing expertise that each and every person brought to the project, enabling us to blend research and practice in a variety of ways.

Our approach to working collectively on TiM was to adopt a video club methodology. As a group we intended to meet six times across the year, though as is the way with collaborative projects of this size not all members were able to attend all meetings so the number at the meetings varied between six and eight people. Ahead of each meeting several teachers video recorded one of their lessons and one or two teachers chose a short clip from their video recording to share with the group as a whole. The choice of clip was down to the teacher of the lesson, but prompted by something about the talk within the clip that drew their attention. This clip was then used to form the basis of the discussions when we met as a group. Additionally, one other member of the group would bring a task to work on that focused on the same aspect of talk as the video. The group as individuals were focusing on different, though not unconnected, aspects of talk and the purpose of the task was to bring together these differences and make the connections explicit. The approach to intervention therefore was not to offer specific approaches for teachers in the group to enact, but rather to expand the range of choices that were available to them all through raising awareness of different features of classroom interaction. This approach to teacher development may be described as 'realistic' in the sense of Korthagen and Kessels (1999, p. 7) as teachers 'discover, in the specific situations occurring in everyday teaching' possible actions and strategies.

Reference has already been made to the video club methodology that was adopted, but there are further theoretical approaches that underpinned the ways in which we worked together. The collaboration was similar to what Jaworski (2006) referred to as a community of inquiry but also shares features with Nickerson and Moriarty's (2005) professional communities. The use of video and task design were shaped by Mason's discipline of noticing (2002), and bears similarities to

Coles' work (2012) with video in teacher professional development. The specific way in which we used video was new to this community, but the practice of co-observation, discussing practice and working collaboratively in this way were not new to the individual members. The way of working evolved over the project drawing on different practices as they became relevant and appropriate, becoming more aligned with Mason's discipline of noticing over time. The idea of attention became particularly apparent in the discussions of both the chosen video clip and the task when we met. In our discussion below we draw on these different ideas within the research as and when they become important in the illustration of the aspect of practice we are exploring.

In addition to the community's focus on teaching, there was also a research element. The data for the research was the videos of teaching and the recordings of the meetings and an ethnomethodological approach was taken to analysis. That is, the analysis of the data was driven by what the participants themselves paid attention to. In the case of the videos from the lessons, this was focused on how the teachers and students interacted with each other and what they drew attention to through their interactions. In the case of the meetings, the teachers who chose the video clips prompted the initial focus through their choice of clip, though this occasionally shifted as the video clip was watched and re-watched and discussed by the group.

Our focus in this chapter is on two specific areas that we worked on together: *pausing* and *developing meaning with mathematical language*. As we discuss each area we bring together the videos shared, the tasks we worked on, the discussions we had, and the research findings that were explored. Using illustrative examples we show the variety of opportunities that became available, whilst also revealing the challenge of combining the generality of research with the complexity of the classroom. Explicit references within the meetings to existing generalised research findings was increasingly found through the project to be unnecessary as different members of the group introduced ideas, strategies or issues from the contexts under discussion that are well documented in the research without necessarily being aware that this was the case. The emphasis was on exploring classroom practice, trying out new strategies and examining the perceived impact of these strategies. To emphasise this point, this chapter makes the connections between the existing research and the shared practices explicit, but it is to be remembered that these connections were not necessarily expressed in the meetings themselves.

Pausing

Background

One way in which the goal of students engaging in more mathematical talk in the classroom might be achieved is to focus on the opportunities they get to speak during periods of whole class teaching. Focusing on sequences of interactions between the teacher and a student is an opportunity to develop this talk as the teacher can choose both what to say and how to say it in a way that will affect students' responses. For example, what Ainley (1987) describes as a testing question such as 'What is 4 multiplied by 8?' is inviting a short response from the student, while choosing to ask more of a probing question such as 'What numbers multiply together to give 32?' is inviting a longer response, such as '1 and 32, 2 and 16, …', or a deeper response, such as 'factor pairs of 32'. Alternatively, should the student offer only '2 and 16' as a response to the question the teacher may choose to ask the same student 'are they the only numbers that multiply together to give 32?' In this way the teacher is perhaps embarking on a sequence of prompting questions that support the student in articulating a full response to the original question. A funnelling pattern such as this (after Bauersfeld, 1980; discussed further in Ingram, Andrews, & Pitt, 2017) may be subject to critique for the mathematical depth of the student's responses in such a sequence of interactions, however it does exemplify that, if we are seeking to develop student talk, our focus might also need to be on the nature of teacher talk. Furthermore, focusing on sequences of interactions between the teacher and a student that happen *during whole class teaching* is an opportunity for developing talk as students are sensitive to changes in the norms of interaction, learning that certain responses are being encouraged from what they observe being played out with others.

The examples of sequences of classroom interactions that have already been described above reflect the initiation-response-feedback (IRF) pattern (Sinclair & Coulthard, 1974). The prevalent use of this pattern of interaction has been criticised (e.g. Nystrand & Gamoran, 1991) for being too teacher-dominant, constraining meaningful student participation. But others have recognised the affordances of the IRF sequence for guiding a class of students towards a common goal (Lee, 2008; Mercer & Dawes, 2014; Nassaji & Wells, 2000), including variations within the overall structure such as using the third turn to prompt a fuller response from the same responder or a further response from another student. Drawing on the work of McHoul (1978) and ideas brought to a wider professional audience by Black and Wiliam (1998), the role of silences between turns is also worthy of attention. A silence during one speaker's turn is described in the literature as a *pause*, while a silence between two speakers' turns is described as a *gap* (see Ingram & Elliott, 2016 for further discussion of pauses, gaps and lapses). Table 6.1 sets out four typical turn-taking structures including silences that may occur in the classroom, coded for teacher turn (T), student turn (S), pause (P) and gap (G).

TABLE 6.1 Structure of turn-taking in formal whole class teaching, including silences

Sequence of turns	Code
Teacher initiates, there is a pause, teacher continues	TPT
Teacher initiates, there is a gap, student responds	TGS
Teacher initiates, student responds, there is a gap, teacher replies	TSGT
Teacher initiates, student responds, there is a pause, student continues	TSPS

The gap between the teacher's initiation and a student's response (TGS) is sometimes thought of as 'thinking time' and has also been described as 'wait time' (although in the literature, wait time is defined as a silence preceding a teacher turn, so only the pause in the TPT pattern or the gap in the TSGT pattern in Table 6.1). In some older research (e.g. Rowe, 1986) it was identified that frequently this gap is insufficient to achieve the purpose of allowing all students in the class to formulate a response. This finding has been brought to popular attention in recent years, and was known by some of the teachers involved in this project.

Our classroom experience and videos of mathematics lessons collected through research tells us that teachers can and do pause during whole class teaching but instances of students pausing are rare, often being treated as a sign of trouble in the interaction and prompting the teacher or another student to take over; the pause therefore is treated as a gap. But allowing a student to pause can provide an opportunity for a fuller response from the student. Further, variation to the TSGT pattern identified in Table 6.1 is possible if the teacher allows the gap to extend to a point of uncomfortableness (technically the point at which the gap turns into a *lapse*) since this can indicate to the student that there is trouble with their response and encourage a development of it. This highlights two distinct possible actions arising from research that are available to the teacher in order to encourage a fuller response from a student: either allowing students to pause (typically when the student is aware that they have not yet given a full response and have more to say); or extending a gap into a lapse (typically when the student might erroneously think they have already given a full response).

TiM collaboration

In a preliminary project meeting with one of the schools, the teachers decided that initially they would focus on the role of silences in whole class teaching. This became known in the group as a focus on 'pausing', but it should be noted that this did not limit the teachers to the technical meaning of the word discussed above and rather this became a catch-all term associated with providing greater opportunities for fuller student responses. The significance of this observation will be discussed in more detail below.

In advance of meeting again, three of the teachers video recorded a lesson each. A feature of the way this group worked at first was that another teacher was always present in the classroom when a lesson was being recorded, and so some informal discussions within the group had already taken place. At this early stage in the project, one member (Beth) presented a brief summary of the literature discussed above to the group. Then two other members (Charlie and Emma) shared short clips (2–3 minutes) from their own lessons.

For the short video clip associated with pausing that Charlie had selected, he was asked to identify a small excerpt that included a pause that he found particularly uncomfortable. The excerpt he chose featured a student (Adam) listing the factors of 32, the transcript of which is given in Table 6.2.

TABLE 6.2 Transcript of Charlie's video clip

Speaker	Talk
Charlie	one times (1.3)
Adam	one times (3.9) thirty-two (5.1)
Charlie	what did you do next (0.7)
Adam	umm (1.1) I did two (1.7) times (7.1) two times (2.5) sixteen (.)
Charlie	yep (4.2)
Adam	and then four times eight

Note: The values given in parentheses represent the length of a pause to the nearest tenth of a second. The symbol '(.)' denotes a pause of less than 0.3 seconds.

FIGURE 6.1 Charlie's representation of the sequence of interaction

Charlie was invited to represent part of this sequence of interaction using a supply of cards on which either the letter T, S or P was printed (see Figure 6.1 – here P was used to stand for either a pause or a gap). This starts with Charlie's question 'what did you do next?' Note that Charlie represented the 0.7 second pause after his question, the student's hesitation ('umm') and the 1.1 second pause that followed as a single pause. He also represented the student utterances 'I did two' and 'times', along with the 1.7 second pause in between them as a single turn.

Having represented the sequence of interaction in this way, Charlie drew particular attention to the pause that he had marked with a double P. He commented that this was a 'deathly pause' but continued:

> I was happy leaving that pause, although it was an uncomfortable pause, I pretty much knew there was going to be an end point.

The pauses following this were much shorter, with Charlie recalling that he was 'so relieved to get to the end' that he 'just cut [the student] off and moved on'.

Asking Charlie to represent the sequence of interaction in this way offered a way of analysing the excerpt together and to explore the extent of intentionality in the pauses that were left. His engagement with this task emphasised that the focus of his attention both in the meeting and during the lesson was less on deliberate positioning of pauses but rather on achieving an intended outcome of bringing a fuller response to articulation:

> I think yeah there was less focus on deliberate pauses from my perspective and more focus on allowing them to give an answer, giving them time to give an answer and not letting go so that he had to form that answer.

This was reiterated when speaking with another member of the group:

Charlie: I was more conscious of allowing the kids more time to speak and articulate what they wanted to say rather than where I placed pauses I wanted to make sure that I didn't talk over them rather than deliberately pausing in the middle of a question or at the end of an answer

Freya: so did you find yourself here thinking that I'm going to pause I'm going to wait now it was a conscious decision

Charlie: once he had started yes

What this reveals is that Charlie was not at this stage seeking to enact particular pre-determined strategies during his lessons but rather was acting in the moment, with these actions driven by a clear goal. However, his actions in this excerpt do align with allowing students to pause. In future meetings Charlie's attention seemed to shift to a different outcome and be increasingly focused on achieving a classroom environment that routinely afforded the use of pausing strategies. When introducing his video clip with the 'deathly' pause, Charlie had described the class as 'jumpy' and this was the dominant issue that he returned to in the follow-up meeting. This notion of jumpiness provides an interesting example of personal theorising within the collaborative project. In the lesson when he first began to include pausing within his whole class teaching, Charlie noticed a decrease in jumpiness that he attributed to 'slowing things down'. He felt that he himself was less 'jumpy' too – less inclined to adopt an energetic, rapid questioning style – and that this influenced the classroom atmosphere. But soon he noticed that managing sequences of interactions of the form TSPS was becoming problematic as students were more inclined to 'jump in', leading to a sequence of the form TS_1PS_2. He sought to account for this in the follow-up meeting, leading to a collaborative theorising that the initial impact of the strategy, the presence of an observer and the topic could all be factors in the differences he had experienced.

The 'jumpiness' that Charlie discussed was also negotiated by Emma in the clip that she shared with the group. She explained how this sort of response was unusual from the class, but she was taken by their enthusiastic participation in the whole class teaching and how they were 'buying into the maths in a big way'. Students had been working on a 'place value maze' where numbers in the maze were connected by operations such as 'multiply by 10' and 'divide by 100', and the excerpt she selected featured Billy offering a response to 7 divided by 100, the transcript of which is provided in Table 6.3.

Emma too was asked to try to represent her sequence of interaction using the same cards as Charlie, but the multiple speakers at first made this problematic. However, by focusing on her interaction with Billy, including the gestures that she used, it became clear how he was given time to reconsider his response. Figure 6.2 records how Emma ended up representing the sequence of interaction from Table 6.3, following a prolonged conversation with the rest of the group.

TABLE 6.3 Transcript of Emma's selected video clip excerpt

Speaker	Talk
Billy	is it 700 (3.3)
Emma	am I here Billy (.)
Billy	yeah (.)
Emma	am I going this way (.)
Billy	yeah (.)
Emma	so the calculation I'm trying to do is 7 divided by 100 (0.4)
Billy	seven divided (.)
Student 1	I know the answer (.)
Student 2	oh is it 7 (0.8)
Student 1	I know the answer (.)
Student 3	yeah (.)
Student 1	I know the answer (.)
Billy	Zero
Student 1	I know the answer (.)
Student 4	shh (.)
Billy	zero (0.9) point zero 7 (.)

Note: The values given in parentheses represent the length of a pause to the nearest tenth of a second. The symbol '(.)' denotes a pause of less than 0.3 seconds.

FIGURE 6.2 Emma's representation of the sequence of interaction

It was interesting to note how the sequence of interaction in the lesson developed from this point, and Table 6.4 provides a continuation of the talk from Table 6.3. Just as in the way Adam had been given an opportunity to give a fuller response in Charlie's lesson, so too had Billy through Emma's management of the interaction.

As with Charlie, Emma was not consciously attending in the lesson to where she was placing pauses but rather the outcome of having students enthusiastically trying to put forward and justify possible solutions was foregrounded.

In the follow-up meeting, Emma expressed how the focus on pausing had influenced her knowledge of students:

> *I do realise that some people take longer to formulate what they want to say, so I think some students in my class are really grateful that I'm doing it.*

In contrast to Charlie's experience, she found that 'jumpiness' had not continued to be a factor. Rather, encouraging students to talk more remained her goal and she particularly spoke about achieving what might be described as a discursive

TABLE 6.4 Transcript of Emma's video clip

Speaker	Talk
Emma	there's something really good about what you said there (.) can I write it on here because I do think these things help (.)
Student 2	zero zero point 7 (simultaneously with Billy's inaudible response) (0.8)
Emma	it's Billy's question (.) you can be thinking and you can be jotting something down and give yourself a little tick if you agree (0.9) Billy (0.6) I'm dividing by 100 tell me what to do (.)
Billy	so you have to (.) put the seven (0.9) across (0.8) to the hundredths because on the (0.7) what it's (0.4) cos on the one it's divide by 100 (.)
Emma	okay (0.5) so both in the units (1.0) to the hundredths column (.)
Billy	yeah (.)
Emma	okay (1.3)
Billy	and then you put the two zeros (.)
Student 5	no no no (.)
Emma	let him finish (1.0)
Billy	then you put zeros because you've gone past the tenths so you put a zero in (.)
Emma	tell me which columns to put a zero in (.)
Billy	(inaudible) one (.)
Emma	tell me the (.) tell me the title at the top of it
Students	(murmur)
Billy	tenths (0.7)
Emma	so you'd like a zero in the tenths column (0.8)
Billy	yeah and a zero in the units
Emma	and a zero in the units (.) Billy (0.5) are you happy with that (.)
Billy	yeah (0.6)
Student 2	I agree (.) actually yeah I agree

Note: The values given in parentheses represent the length of a pause to the nearest tenth of a second. The symbol '(.)' denotes a pause of less than 0.3 seconds.

atmosphere in her classroom, where students feel comfortable in expressing their thinking and are given space in which to do so:

> In the lesson that Charlie came to see I'd got four shapes on the board. I'd marked them up with their properties and I just wanted [the students] to tell me what they saw. I suppose it was more of an elicitation wasn't it really, but absolutely anything they wanted to tell me was okay... I'm trying to do everything I can to say no look just tell me anything.

While Emma was focused on this comfortableness as an outcome, Charlie described how the two of them had considered teacher actions that might help in achieving this:

We were talking about narrowing down the criteria of their responses weren't we or giving them some pointers for their responses I think so that there was a little bit more structure to what they were giving us.

This quotation has been included as it provided an insight into the interchangeable roles within the group, as Charlie was taking on a teacher educator role here.

Focus of attention during a period of change

From what was expressed in the meetings and observable from the video recording of lessons, particular attention was placed by the teachers in this project on outcomes. As we report here, both Charlie and Emma were initially concerned with allowing students the opportunity to provide a fuller repose to questions they were asked. Increasingly Charlie's attention was on reducing the 'jumpy' tendency of students in his class so that he might achieve an environment in which students were able to provide fuller responses without interruption. Conversely, Emma's attention was on encouraging students to 'say what they see' so that a discursive atmosphere might be achieved.

Less attention seemed to be focused on systematic experimentation with specific strategies – or changes in practice – that might help to achieve these goals. In the second meeting that focused on pausing, teacher actions were described in quite general terms. The teachers spoke of 'doing pausing' and even less specifically 'doing it', but there seemed to be a shared understanding amongst the group of this referring to a bundle of actions, some of which involved the use of silences as discussed in the literature, which were more likely to result in the sort of outcomes that were clearly valued. There were no examples of teachers explicitly taking up the technical distinctions between gaps and pauses when discussing these strategies, nor exploiting the effect of a gap that is stretched to the point of becoming a lapse. We conjecture that the design of the study in relation to pausing may be a factor in outcomes being foregrounded over changes in practice in what the teachers said in the meetings. The focus of the project overall is on developing student talk in the classroom, so from the outset attention is on outcomes.

Developing meaning with mathematical language

Background

Another key theme that was returned to several times across the project was the question of how to introduce new words or terminology to students and how to give students opportunities to use these new words or phrases. There is extensive research looking at the linguistic features of mathematics that can cause students difficulties (c.f. Pimm, 1987; Schleppegrell, 2007). One key distinction is the differences between everyday language, academic language and discipline-specific language. In the case of mathematics there is significant overlap between these categories with words that are used in everyday conversations also having mathematical meanings that may or may not be similar to those in everyday use, such as 'half', 'of', or 'function'. Similarly, there are words within academic language that students will encounter in a range of disciplines that may have similar or different uses in mathematics, e.g. 'factor', 'evaluate', 'translate'. Mathematics also has a lot of terminology that students will probably only encounter in the mathematics classrooms such as 'factorise', 'symmetry', or 'cumulative frequency'. In addition to this research, the group also reported that they felt students found process words such as solve, simplify or factorise harder to learn than object words such as equation, square or prime. One other concern frequently mentioned by the group was the recent changes to the curriculum, which changed the requirements in relation to understanding and using mathematical language. The teachers also had the impression that the new accompanying examinations would require students to express themselves in more mathematical ways in writing, whilst including less mathematical language in the questions so that students have to work out what is needed rather than being told what to do.

Research into the learning of vocabulary focuses on the importance of learning through authentic contexts (e.g. Nagy et al., 2012) and giving students opportunities to speak, hear, read and write the new vocabulary as part of the language of the context. Yet what does an authentic context for mathematical language look like? In this project, the focus was very much on offering students opportunities to speak mathematically, yet in many of the videos from the classrooms this speaking often consists of naming things in response to teachers' questions and students rarely use mathematical vocabulary within any form of sentence. Where it is given in a sentence, it usually forms some part of a definition that again the teacher has explicitly asked for. Knowing a word means not only knowing its form and meaning but also knowing how to use the word. In this project, the focus has been on students' spoken language use and ways of providing opportunities for students to use language, for a communicative purpose, and to improve the quality or nature of their spoken contributions in the classroom. As Laura put it:

> To be able to speak like a mathematician, to be a fluent mathematician I suppose they've got to be familiar with that language, so the more they're using it in their vocabulary must mean the more they understand what that word means. Not always but the listening is the balance with it because if they're listening to that word then hopefully they're hearing it in the right context as well. I don't think reading it has any impact other than them just being more aware of that word. If they're not hearing when it's being used, in what context, then they need to speak it themselves in that context.

TiM collaboration

The discussions in the group around how to introduce mathematical language initially focused on what experiences students should or could have before the new language is introduced. For example, using tasks that generate a need to make a distinction resulting in a new category that needs to be named, compared to giving a definition and then exploring examples and non-examples to give meaning to this definition. Many of the teachers reported that it was making the distinctions between examples or experiences that drove the way they introduced new language. For example, Keith and Freya both generated a meaning for expression by comparing and contrasting it to the meaning of equation and Laura contrasted the meaning of diagonal with the meaning of edge within the context of classifying quadrilaterals.

Yet the teachers also reported challenges to this approach in their discussions and other challenges were observed in the lessons they video recorded. One issue was the way in which students themselves were using mathematical words within the lessons. In Keith's lesson, which contrasted expressions and equations, students were able to offer definitions of both equations and expressions. However, 'one may know the definitions of the words *area* and *triangle*, for example, but may not know how to use these words together in a sentence in ways that would be considered meaningful within the discipline of mathematics' (Herbel-Eisenmann & Otten, 2011, p. 454) and in this lesson students only used the words equation and expression to give their definitions and these were not later used when they worked on tasks on solving equations and simplifying expressions. These definitions also varied considerably in focus and would not all be acceptable mathematically. In both lessons on expressions and equations the teachers and students both focused on the ability to solve equations but only simplify expressions (though not necessarily with mathematically acceptable meanings for solving and simplifying) as a way of making a distinction between equations and expressions. The discussions in both classes also focused on the role of numbers and the relationship with substitution within this distinction, for example in Keith's lesson questioning whether $2+2$ or $2x + 3x = 5x$ are expressions or equations, and if $x = 2$ does $2x + 3x$ become an equation?

Word learning is a process over time and students can recognise and use words when their mathematical meanings are only partially understood by them, and consequently teachers need to offer students many opportunities to both encounter and use a mathematical word in a variety of contexts in order for students to develop the mathematical meaning of this word. As a group we explored different ways of offering students these opportunities. Some of these questions and tasks used focused on offering students the opportunity to demonstrate that they had passive control over the words used, whilst others focused on opportunities for the words to naturally arise as students attempted to explain or argue in response to the prompt of the question or task. It is these foci that we explore in this section, using two contrasting examples, one where the task was felt to achieve the aims of the students using mathematical language in a mathematically meaningful way, and one where the teacher felt it was less successful.

The first example was chosen by Emma and focuses on the choice and use of tasks that generated the discussions Emma wanted from her students. A range of tasks were discussed, used and analysed, both from the classrooms in the project and from suggestions in the research, in order to identify the features of the task that provoked the discussions and this example illustrates a task that promotes a need for students to give mathematical reasoning. In this example, the task was taken from Nrich (http://nrich.maths.org/6962) and involves students picking a number between 1 and 25 and Emma saying whether she liked that number or not, using some sort of criteria related to the properties of that number, such as multiples of 3 or prime numbers. The students then had to work out what that criteria was from the numbers that Emma liked and the numbers that she did not like. In addition to this, Emma set up the task as a competition between two groups who were awarded points each time they offered a mathematical reason when they were asked what they thought the criteria was. The class had low prior attainment in mathematics and a diverse range of additional needs. Over the course of previous lessons, the students had been introduced to the words 'arrays', 'multiple', 'factor', 'square' and 'prime' and their definitions through the use of 'concrete' and 'pictorial' resources such as plastic counters, 100 square 'sieves' and 'factor bug' diagrams, but had not yet used these words themselves in a mathematically meaningful way.

At the beginning of this task the students and the teacher are using informal language to describe the properties of the numbers. Emma prompts the students to use the word multiple and the students begin to use the word multiple within their reasons, and both Emma and the students use multiple and times table interchangeably throughout the remainder of the lesson.

In some cases, as in the example above the mathematical word is naming something that the students can already describe effectively using more informal language. In the example both the students and the teacher switched between using language like 'belongs to the five times table' and 'multiple of five', or even 'belongs to the five and twenty multiple' (where the word multiple has been directly substituted for the word times table) throughout the lesson. Here the need to use the mathematical word does not arise from the need to name something, as the students already have a name for these numbers and their relationships. Instead the need arose from the teacher's task design where teams of students were awarded points for giving mathematical reasoning for their answers, which included using the mathematical language and words. This is not to say that learning the word multiple is akin to learning a new word that does the same thing as the word times-table. The word multiple is used in subtly grammatically different ways, as can be seen from the example of belongs to the five and twenty multiple, but also when its usage is extended within mathematics where it is appropriate to talk about a multiple of p, but not about the p times table.

In the group discussions the teachers gave examples from discussions with colleagues, but this was also observed in the videos from the group's lessons, where the naming of the category became a game of guess what's in the teacher's head, rather than a need to attach meaning to the new language. Students cannot guess the name of something if they have not met it before, and even where they have met a specific word before this does not necessarily mean that they can use it. New mathematical vocabulary needs to be introduced in a way that pays attention to the communicative purposes of that vocabulary within the mathematics classroom

TABLE 6.5 Transcript of Emma's video clip (2)

Speaker	Talk
Emma	boys, choose a number and I'll tell you whether I like it or I don't like it. alright?
Student	right, can I choose two?
Emma	no, just one at the moment.
((transcript omitted))	
Student	oh, six.
Emma	okay, I do like the number six. okay, Sam, do you have a reason why you think I might like number six?
Sam	it's in the ones, twos, threes and six times table.
Emma	'cause it's in the ones, twos, threes and six times table, okay, so all my numbers might be in the ones, the twos, the threes and six times table; that could be my reason. Sarah, you choose a number and i'll tell you whether I like it or not.
Sarah	I think you like the number five.
Emma	okay, and i'm afraid five isn't a number that I like.
Emma	do you, do you want to have a guess at why I might like six but not five?
Student	uh, 'cause you chose that.
Emma	oh, you think i'm just doing favourites; that's not the reason. can you think of a mathematical reason why I might like six but I don't like five?
((transcript omitted))	
Emma	okay. okay, so could it be that six is even? is five not even?
Students	no.
Emma	five is odd.
((transcript omitted))	
Emma	why don't you think I like nineteen?
Student	because you're siding with the boys.
Emma	[laughs] I promise you, it's a maths reason and not a –
((transcript omitted))	
Emma	you are giving me such good reasons. as well as thinking about times tables, can you think of the word multiples?
Student	yeah, multiples.
Emma	so, can we take some…? they are multiples of three, they are multiples of six. some of them are multiples of 12, number 24. you are so close to getting the answer.
Emma	what was my reason for liking those numbers?
Student	because… I don't know, they're special.
Student	because, because they're all –
Student	they're multiples of (six).
((transcript omitted))	
Emma	I do, I do like twenty and your reason was…? what was your reason for choosing twenty if I'm going to give you a stick?
Student	ten times two is twenty.
Emma	because ten times two is twenty.
Student	and it's in the five and the ten multiple as well.

(continued)

TABLE 6.5 (Cont.)

Speaker	Talk
Emma	yeah. now, you're right that twenty is ten times two. but I like Simon's reason. he said it was…?
Student	it's a multiple of five and ten.
Emma	it's a multiple of five and a multiple of ten.
Emma	but what I didn't say about this game is you are actually allowed to argue with each other about the maths. so, if you think that they said something that didn't make sense, I can actually give lollypop sticks for good maths reasoning. so, I think actually, I've had a good maths reason from the boys and I think I had a good maths reason from the girls why I might have chosen these numbers.

(Moschkovich, 2015). This also means that students need opportunities to use this vocabulary for these purposes, both receptively and productively.

The second example was chosen by Freya and arose in the discussions around the types of questions we could ask that would offer students opportunities to use key words in a meaningful way. The focus on the type of question was a theme that ran throughout the course of the project. This example was taken from a meeting two thirds of the way through the project but was specifically chosen by Freya because of the challenges that arose when using a question that was intended to encourage students to use mathematical vocabulary in a mathematically meaningful way. The extract comes from a shared video clip of previously low attaining students who had been asked to complete sentences with key words missing about a range of algebraic representations. The extract below is the discussion around $3a - 6 + 2b$. The students had met each of the words expression, identity and equation in a previous lesson, but also in previous years in school.

The students in this extract had successfully identified that $3a - 6 + 2b$ was an expression but it took the teacher several attempts to get a student to identify why it was an expression. This was done through prompting the students to compare the features of expressions with those of equations and identities. However, it is not until the sixth student that the students offer any explanation that includes mathematical language. This student also attends to the surface features of the expression and incorrectly classifies it as an equation on the grounds that it includes numbers. Another student then changes the direction of the discussion by focusing on what you can do with equations that you cannot do with expressions, i.e. whether they can be solved or not, yet the example later given by the student indicates that they are not clear about the distinction between expressions, equations and identities. So whilst this discussion did support the students in using the mathematical language that was the focus of the lesson, it did not result in the students using the language in a way that would be accepted mathematically.

TABLE 6.6 Transcript of Freya's video clip

Speaker	Talk
Freya	So can someone tell me how they know that that was an expression, not an identity or an equation?
Student	Is it…? I have no idea. I don't, I thought it was going to be, uh, I don't know.
Freya	Sam, why did you choose the word expression for that? What, what do you think makes it an expression?
Sam	Um, don't know. I guessed.
Freya	You guessed. Are there any that you knew it couldn't be, like could it have been an equation?
Sam	Oh, well they don't know.
Freya	Why couldn't it be an equation?
Student	It could be.
Freya	It could, so 3a take away 6 plus 2b, do we think that could be an equation?
Student	Yeah, no.
Student	Yeah, it can be an equation 'cause you add them all up and that's an equation. But an expression is…
Freya	So you think it could be an equation 'cause you could just add them all up and that would be an equation?
Student	Yeah, 'cause an equation's with numbers and sums in it, isn't it? And like pluses and equals.
Freya	Okay.
Student	Yeah, and an expression is with algebra.
Freya	So does an equation not have algebra?
Student	Oh, is it because you're not working it out?
Student	You don't need to work it out.
Freya	Okay, so with an equation, can you work it out?
Student	Yeah.
Freya	What do you work out with an equation?
Student	The sum of the numbers.
Freya	So can you give me an example of an equation?
Student	Uh, $4 + 4 + 2 = 10$.
Freya	Okay, can you write that on the board by you?
Student	Yeah, $4 + 4 + 2 = 10$.
Freya	Right, does anyone think that's not an equation and wants to say something else that is an equation? Or do we all agree that is an equation?
((transcript omitted))	
Student	I think both.
Freya	What do you mean? It's an equation and it's an expression?
Student	Mm.
Freya	Okay.
Student	I know what expression means, like, in like not maths, but –
Freya	I know, but we need it in maths.
Student	Why shouldn't …?

(continued)

TABLE 6.6 (Cont.)

Speaker	Talk
Freya	Terry?
Terry	Uh, we don't know what the answer is.
Freya	Okay, but does that mean it's an expression because you can't work it out?
Student	[Inaudible words]
Freya	Yeah, so if someone came along and said a is 2 and b is 3, then you could substitute into the expression, yeah?
Student	It's —
Freya	But that wouldn't stop it being an expression, so just because you know what the letters are worth doesn't stop it being an expression, because you can substitute the values into the expression

Individual words are part of wider conceptual networks that include understanding relationships with other related ideas (Lemke, 1990). This was not an idea explicitly discussed by the group but was observable in all the lessons they video recorded. In the second example above, expressions were explored alongside and in contrast to equations and identities. In addition, knowing how to use a word also means knowing what other words are typically used alongside it. Again in the example of expressions and equations, Freya explicitly worked on the meaning of expression and equation through their relationship to the processes of solving, substituting and simplifying.

The discussions around expressions and equations led to one further level of complexity to students' use of these words. Students often used these terms alongside the words 'is' or 'has' but in two different ways. These words can be used to describe either an attributive relationship or an identifying relationship but only the latter can function as definitions. For example, 'an expression is with algebra', 'one has the answer', 'if it was just like 3 + 4 or ... so once you've written ... so that's an expression, then once you've written down 7 it becomes an equation.' None of these statements from the students functions as a definition, with the first two describing an attributive relationship and the last one as an identifying relationship. As Moschkovich (1999) has shown, this can lead to students and teachers talking about features from different perspectives, one as a defining property and the other as an attribute which adds to the complexity of students developing an understanding of the role of definitions in mathematics, including what counts as a definition.

Conclusion

In this chapter we have detailed an approach to synthesising teachers' classroom experiences, discussions and decisions around practice, and relevant research. Whilst many interventions involving teachers feature the explicit dissemination of research findings or conjectures and hypotheses around potentially effective teaching strategies, the aim of this project was to draw on the teachers' awareness of potential actions or interventions within their own practice.

Whilst videos are widely used in professional development, these are often videos of exemplary practice, problematic situations, or illustrate a particular feature that the professional development is focused on. In this project the teachers videoed themselves and chose short clips to share with the group, which enabled them to also choose the focus of the meetings and the areas they wished to work with. This way of working brings together reflective practice and action research (Mason, 2012), which other research has shown to have a more sustained impact on practice (e.g. Mason, 2016; Sherin & Dyer, 2017). This way of working and using video is relevant to teacher development and growth in general, though it has been researched thoroughly within the field of mathematics education.

The group came together with the explicit aim of improving both the quantity and quality of students talk in mathematics (TiM). On many occasions the discussions between teachers in the group naturally drew attention to features of their lessons, to aspects of their decision making, to their aims and goals which resonate with themes from prior research. Yet the teachers themselves were not aware of this research knowledge nor was it necessary for the research to be shared explicitly in the discussions. In the case of considering pauses, the distinctions made in the research literature between different types of pauses were however shared explicitly and the teachers may have drawn upon this in their future decision making, but consequences of pausing for students' learning were emphasised more than the deliberate use of pauses themselves.

These findings bring to the fore the relationships between those involved in collaboration and their respective expertise, and the complexities of connections between classroom practice and research. We would suggest truly collaborative research draws upon the teachers' own expertise and works with this in a 'realistic' way (Korthagen & Kessels, 1999), rather than an approach of telling teachers about research or providing research informed professional development in the hope it will change their practice. Whilst some members of the group, particularly the researchers, have knowledge about research findings that may be relevant to the discussions, these are not made explicit. The nature of teacher development is about teachers theorising their own practice and in the case of the TiM project, teachers often made conjectures and decisions that resonated with the existing research whilst not being aware at the time of this. Thus we are collaboratively building on teachers' existing expertise and professionalism to improve and develop practice.

References

Ainley, J. (1987). Telling questions. *Mathematics Teaching*, 118, 24–26.

Bauersfeld, H. (1980). Hidden dimensions in the so-called reality of a mathematics classroom. *Educational Studies in Mathematics*, 11, 23–41.

Black, B. P., & Wiliam, D. (1998). *Inside the Black Box: Raising Standards Through Classroom Assessment*. London: King's College London School of Education.

Coles, A. (2012). Using video for professional development: the role of the discussion facilitator. *Journal of Mathematics Teacher Education*, 16(3), 165–184. https://doi.org/10.1007/s10857-012-9225-0

Franke, M. L., Webb, N. M., Chan, A. G., Ing, M., Freund, D., & Battey, D. (2009). Teacher questioning to elicit students' mathematical thinking in elementary school classrooms. *Journal of Teacher Education*, 60(4), 380–392. https://doi.org/10.1177/0022487109339906

Herbel-Eisenmann, B. A., & Otten, S. (2011). Mapping mathematics in classroom discourse. *Journal for Research in Mathematics Education*, 42(5), 451–485. https://doi.org/10.5951/jresematheduc.42.5.0451

Ingram, J., Andrews, N., & Pitt, A. (2017). Revisiting the roles of interactional patterns in mathematics classroom interaction. In *Proceedings of the 10th Congress of Research in Mathematics Education*. Dublin.

Ingram, J., & Elliott, V. (2016). A critical analysis of the role of wait time in classroom interactions and the effects on student and teacher interactional behaviours. *Cambridge Journal of Education*, 46(1), 1–17. https://doi.org/10.1080/0305764X.2015.1009365

Jaworski, B. (2006). Theory and practice in mathematics teaching development: Critical inquiry as a mode of learning in teaching. *Journal of Mathematics Teacher Education*, 9(2), 187–211.

Korthagen, F. A. J., & Kessels, J. P. A. M. (1999). Linking theory and practice: Changing the pedagogy of teacher education. *Educational Researcher*, 28(4), 4–17. https://doi.org/10.3102/0013189X028004004

Lee, Y.-A. (2008). Yes–No Questions in the Third-Turn Position: Pedagogical Discourse Processes. *Discourse Processes*, 45(3), 237–262. https://doi.org/10.1080/01638530701739215

Lemke, J. L. (1990). *Talking Science: Language, learning, and values*. Norwood, NJ: Ablex.

Mason, J. (2002). *Researching Your Own Practice: The discipline of noticing*. Abingdon: Routledge.

Mason, J. (2012). Noticing: Roots and branches. In M. G. Sherin, V. R. Jacobs, & R. A. Philipp (Eds.), *Mathematics teacher noticing: Seeing through teachers' eyes* (pp. 35–50). Mahwah, New Jersey: Erlbaum. https://doi.org/10.1080/00107530.1986.10746139

Mason, J. (2016). Perception, interpretation and decision making: understanding gaps between competence and performance—a commentary. *ZDM – Mathematics Education*, 48(1–2), 219–226. https://doi.org/10.1007/s11858-016-0764-1

Mchoul, A. (1978). The organization of turns at formal talk in the classroom. *Language in Society*, 7(2), 183–213.

Mercer, N., & Dawes, L. (2014). The study of talk between teachers and students, from the 1970s until the 2010s. *Oxford Review of Education*, 40(4), 430–445. https://doi.org/10.1080/03054985.2014.934087

Moschkovich, J. N. (1999). Supporting the participation of English language learners in mathematical discussions. *For the Learning of Mathematics*, 19(1), 11–19.

Moschkovich, J. N. (2015). Scaffolding student participation in mathematical practices. *ZDM – Mathematics Education*, 47(7). https://doi.org/10.1007/s11858-015-0730-3

Nagy, W., Townsend, D., Lesaux, N., & Schmitt, N. (2012). Words as tools: Learning academic vocabulary as language acquisition. *Reading Research Quarterly*, 47(1), 91–108. https://doi.org/10.1002/RRQ.011

Nassaji, H., & Wells, G. (2000). What's the use of 'triadic dialogue'?: an investigation of teacher-student interaction. *Applied Linguistics*, 21(3), 376–406.

Nickerson, S. D., & Moriarty, G. (2005). Professional communities in the context of teachers' professional lives: A case of mathematics specialists. *Journal of Mathematics Teacher Education*, 8(2), 113–140. https://doi.org/10.1007/s10857-005-4795-8

Nystrand, M., & Gamoran, A. (1991). Student engagement: When recitation becomes conversation. In H. Waxman & H. Walberg (Eds.), *Contemporary Research on Teaching for the National Society for the Study of Education* (pp. 257–276). McCutchan Publishing. Retrieved from www.eric.ed.gov/ERICWebPortal/recordDetail?accno=ED323581

Pimm, D. (1987). *Speaking mathematically: Communication in mathematics classrooms.* London: Routledge.

Rowe, M. B. (1986). Wait Time: Slowing Down May Be A Way of Speeding Up! *Journal of Teacher Education*, 37(1), 43–50. https://doi.org/10.1177/002248718603700110

Schleppegrell, M. (2007). The linguistic challenges of mathematics teaching and learning: A research review. *Reading & Writing Quarterly*, 23(2), 139–159. https://doi.org/10.1080/10573560601158461

Sherin, M. G., & Dyer, E. B. (2017). Mathematics teachers' self-captured video and opportunities for learning. *Journal of Mathematics Teacher Education*, 20(5), 1–19. https://doi.org/10.1007/s10857-017-9383-1

Sinclair, J., & Coulthard, M. (1975). *Towards an analysis of discourse: The English used by teachers and pupils.* London: Oxford University Press.

7

THE ROLE OF PRACTITIONER RESEARCH AND PUBLICATION IN DEVELOPING A CUMULATIVE AND CRITICAL TRADITION OF RESEARCH IN CLASSROOM-BASED INTERVENTIONS IN HISTORY EDUCATION

Katharine Burn, Jaya Carrier and Anna Fielding

Introduction

The relative dearth of large-scale systematic research in history education

Although proposals for curriculum reform in history education tend to generate considerable political debate and passionate media coverage, much of the discussion and many of the proposals advanced by policy-makers in England tend to be ideologically driven, rooted in arguments about the purposes of history education, with comparatively little reference to research. While there is no guarantee that the availability of extensive, high-quality empirical research would make any difference to the debate, there is very little such evidence on which to draw. A review of history education research in England over the past 25 years reveals few substantial studies.

Among those studies that have been conducted, the one that generated the widest range of publications was Project CHATA, or 'Concepts of History and Teaching Approaches', funded by the Economic and Social Research Council (ESRC); a project devoted to exploring and mapping levels of progression in children's understanding in relation to a series of concepts generally recognised as defining the nature of history (see, for example, Ashby, Lee & Dickinson, 1997; Lee, Ashby & Dickinson, 1996). These are concepts such as change and continuity, cause and consequence, significance, evidence and interpretations that structure the kinds of questions asked within the discipline and the means by which historical knowledge is constructed. They are explicitly characterised as 'second-order concepts' within the most recent national criteria for GCSE (public examinations at 16+) (DFE, 2014, p. 6) and were referred to in previous iterations of the National Curriculum as 'key concepts' (QCA, 2007).[1] Although the title of the project promised potential 'Teaching Approaches', the published work essentially focused on children's conceptual understanding, proposing models of progression in relation to different concepts, identifying some of the inter-relationships between them and highlighting important and deep-rooted misconceptions that impede the development of more powerful knowledge. The one notable exception to a characterisation of the research as 'all CHA and no TA' was Lee's (2005) chapter 'Turning principles into practice', which built on the CHATA findings, but this was actually supported by, and published as part of, a large-scale US research synthesis *How Students Learn* (Donovan & Bransford, 2005). Even here the principles were very broad, emphasising the importance of developing students' understanding of the nature of history, with significant implications for curriculum design but much more difficult to translate into specific, small-scale classroom interventions.

Funding from the ESRC was also secured for the Usable Historical Pasts (UHP) project (Foster et al., 2008), based, like Project CHATA, at the Institute of Education, University of London. Again the focus was on examining students' *existing* understandings, exploring the extent to which those who had studied history up to the age of 16 were capable of drawing their knowledge together to construct a framework that they could use as the basis for informed speculation about possible or plausible future developments. The results revealed how difficult students of that age found it to make meaningful connections between their study of the past and the present (or future), and how unlikely they were to draw on their formal study of the past in constructing their own identities. These problems were attributed to young people's fragmented view of the past and to their restricted conception of change as an event rather than a process. Again, however, the essential conclusion drawn was that solving the problems in equipping young people with 'usable' understandings of the past would require significant changes to the structure of the history *curriculum*, rather than specific pedagogical interventions. Moreover, despite the fact that concerns about students' fragmented view of the past had long been proclaimed by politicians, most famously in Gordon Marsden's critique of 'Yo!-Sushi' history (Hinsliff, 2005), and explicitly highlighted in successive subject reports by the inspectorate (Ofsted 2007, 2011), attempts to secure further funding to explore the impact of alternative curriculum models achieved only limited success (Blow, Rogers & Shemilt, 2008). Findings from a funded pilot study were published (Blow, 2011; Blow, Lee & Shemilt, 2012), but development thereafter was essentially only undertaken in small-scale interventions by committed teachers (such as Rogers 2008, 2016; Nuttall, 2013).

The obvious exception to claims about a lack of funded research in history education in England is the significant investment made by the Department of Education and the Pears Foundation through the UCL Centre for Holocaust Education, although it is important to acknowledge that this research and professional development project also encompasses citizenship and religious education. It began with an extensive survey that mapped *teachers'* substantive knowledge of the Holocaust as well as aspects of their teaching practice and their pedagogical concerns (Pettigrew et al., 2009) and was followed by a similarly wide-ranging study of students' knowledge and understanding (Foster et al., 2015). So far this detailed, authoritative, national portrait has provided a secure foundation for a range of professional development programmes delivered through face-to face training over one or two days; through an online Master's level module; and through a more recent 'Beacon Schools' peer-to-peer support model, based on an intensive residential programme for lead teachers. Obviously this can be classed as a form of classroom intervention, but the rigorous evaluation of the Beacon Schools programme that is being undertaken has yet to be reported.

It is clear that within England at least, more attention has so far been paid to identifying problems in history education than to generating and testing possible solutions through specific classroom interventions. There have been no recent programmes of research comparable to the quasi-experimental control trials conducted in the US by Stanford University as part of the 'Reading like a Historian' project (Reisman, 2012), or the range of experimental studies undertaken by researchers in the Netherlands into ways of improving different aspects of students' historical thinking – such as the process of contextualising sources (van Boxtel & van Drie, 2012). Where interventions have been proposed in England, they have tended to focus less on teaching approaches and more on the nature of the curriculum and how it is structured.

A curricular approach may be an entirely appropriate response, if the problems uncovered are genuinely such that they can only be tackled in the construction of the curriculum, rather than at the level of day-to-day classroom teaching. (Indeed, while the Stanford 'Reading like a Historian' project offers teachers plans and resources for individual lessons to be used as stand-alone 'supplements', the materials that have been developed by the project are presented as a coherent scheme of work and it is as a six-month curriculum programme that they have been evaluated.) But before consideration can be given either to this suggestion or to other hypotheses, such as the suggestion that the problem lies in an inadequate theorisation of classroom phenomena, or that there has been ineffective sharing of meaning between researchers and practitioners, it is important to acknowledge what *has* been happening in history education research in England, given the lack of significant investment in it. For it is certainly not true that there has been no history education research.

The response of the history education community: teacher research

The studies that academic researchers have been able to conduct, usually with small grants from charitable foundations, have not tended to focus in detail on classroom practice. Husbands, Kitson and Pendry (2003), for example, relied mainly on interviews in their case studies of experienced heads of department, particularly to delineate the range of knowledge bases on which they drew. Others have studied young people's *experience* of school history, looking variously at their enjoyment of the subject, the value that they attribute to it and the kinds of personal connections, if any, that they identify in relation to what they are studying (Harris & Haydn, 2010; Harris & Reynolds, 2014). While the Historical Association has sought to monitor the ways in which history is being taught, to inform both its professional development programmes and its representation of teachers' views in response to government policies, its limited budget extends only to an annual survey of history teachers (see, for example, Harris & Burn, 2012; Burn & Harris, 2016), mapping their current concerns and development priorities and tracking shifts in the allocation of curriculum time to the subject and patterns of uptake at 14+ and 16+ (when the study of history is no longer compulsory). In terms of focusing on specific approaches to promote effective learning, it seems that almost as much attention has been paid within doctoral research to strategies that promote *history teachers'* learning as to those that support *young people's* learning of history (see, for example, Burn, 2007; Harris, 2012).

That is not to say that academics engaged in history education have been unconcerned about young people's learning of history, or that they have failed to focus on the exploration and development of strategies by which to address the specific challenges that young people face. The ways in which they have sought to do so, however, tend not to be through the conduct of classroom intervention studies, but through the promotion of teachers' own classroom-based research. This represents both a pragmatic response to the lack of funding for a subject that was removed from the 'core' of the English National Curriculum to 'foundation status' before it was ever implemented and the expression of a profound commitment to practitioner research within the tradition long associated with Lawrence Stenhouse (Elliott, 2016).

Evidence of this commitment can be seen in the professional journal *Teaching History*, published by the Historical Association since 1970, and edited almost continuously since 1998 by Christine Counsell (who was until 2016 a Senior Lecturer at the University of Cambridge), initially working alone and then in collaboration with various co-editors, including history education researchers and practising teachers. The importance of the journal, not merely in promoting the dissemination of teachers' work, but in creating a genuine professional discourse, in which teachers engage both with 'academic' research and with the work of other practitioners (as well as with historical scholarship) is demonstrated by two articles that map the output of the journal in different ways. The first was written by Counsell herself, in response to the Education Secretary's announcement, in 2010, of plans to revise the National Curriculum. Counsell (2011a) insisted that any review of the history curriculum should pay serious attention to the achievements of teachers themselves in giving effective pedagogic form to the disciplinary objectives embedded within the original and subsequent versions. Her argument, which is essentially an attack on various forms of 'genericism', is built on an analysis of history teachers' own efforts to 'address complex problems of uniting content and concept and of motivating lower-attaining or marginalised students whom others (variously) claim can be helped only by narrow narratives or by giving up on disciplinary rigour altogether' (Counsell, 2011a, p. 201) and is illustrated in relation to four specific aspects of history teaching.

The first is in combating reductive and dry approaches to the use of evidence through the development of enquiry-based teaching in which sources are used critically as evidence to answer questions about the past (rather than the reductive teaching of source work, compounded by the formulaic nature of GCSE examination questions, that risked conceptual confusion by conflating 'source' and 'evidence'. A second contribution that Counsell (2011a) claims teacher-researchers have made is by clarifying the *analytical* demands of questions related to other second-order concepts such as change and continuity and historical significance and identifying the essential role played by *linguistic* development in devising strategies to enhance students' causal explanations. A third important contribution is their effective blending of overview and depth – based on identification of an essential interplay between the two – that has made it possible to develop more coherent historical 'frameworks' in which students' substantive knowledge is sufficiently secure for them to be able to construct meaningful 'big pictures' of the past, and thus to discern the patterns and trends necessary to their own orientation in time. Finally, Counsell (2011a) suggests that teacher-researchers have also found ways of enlivening the curricular construct 'interpretations of history' enabling students not merely to appreciate the distinctions between scholarly and popular history but to explain how and why accounts of the past are constructed and employed in particular ways.

Counsell (2011a) does not refer explicitly to the role of the journal itself in sustaining a community of professional enquiry among history teachers, but the range of examples of practitioners' published work on which she draws reveals the critical role that it played in making teachers' work visible to others, in an accessible, yet rigorous form. Articles by practising teachers account for 35 per cent of the references within the paper (37 out of 106 references). In relation to each of the four aspects of practice discussed, Counsell could illustrate the ways in which teachers were responding to problems identified by academic history educators and building on one another's work not only to elucidate the problems within current practice but also to develop practical ways of promoting more effective learning.

While the journal itself was incidental to Counsell's argument about the importance of teachers' work, Fordham (one of the journal's co-editors from 2010 to 2016) set out to map the nature of its articles more systematically by carrying out a citation analysis over a 10-year period between 2004 and 2013. His intention was to determine whether teachers' own writings could be said to constitute a professional discourse, thereby allowing the research reported within them to transcend some of the limitations and conventional critiques made of practitioner enquiries (Fordham, 2015). He was interested not merely in how many teachers had written for the journal, but in the relationships between the work of different teachers and in the nature and range of the sources on which they drew. In conducting this analysis, he chose to include both practising teachers and those who had recently left the classroom (to become advisers or teacher educators), which resulted in a collection of 171 articles. Altogether these articles include 1,696 citations of 929 different publications, with the mean number of citations made by each author being 9.9 [SD=6.3]. By constructing social network graphs around the 16 most frequently cited publications (of which 12 were by teacher-researchers) he could examine both the extent of the connections and the particular focus of connected discussion, where it existed.

One of these networks, for example, centred on an article by Kitson (2003) that encouraged more explicit emphasis on the purpose of reading in the classroom, arguing that teachers needed to make clear to A-level students (studying for public examinations at 18+) the ways in which reading could contribute to progression in learning history. Bellinger (2008) built on this idea by introducing historical scholarship into her A-level lessons, prompting Howells (2011) – who cited both Bellinger and Kitson – to suggest that students would need to learn how to 'read historically' and to explore what this might look like in practice. Laffin (2012) – drawing on ideas advanced by all three previous authors – identified a number of different features of historical writing that students would need to learn about in order to become 'historically literate'. Other connections were made within the network. Croft (2005), for example, took up Kitson's ideas with much younger students, encouraging them to use a particular historian's work as a model for the construction of their arguments, while Ward (2006) encouraged her A-level students to notice and exploit the particular 'devices' employed by the historian Eamon Duffy. The work of both Croft and Ward was cited as an influence by Howells. McCrory (2013), a newly appointed teacher educator who had only recently left the classroom, provided another kind of link (and a new stimulus for teacher research) by noting that both Kitson and Bellinger who were dealing with historical texts that focus on historical diversity (the extent of similarity and difference between individuals and groups) 'only hint' at the difficulty of expressing analytical judgements effectively at both levels. As this brief description has illustrated, in most cases the teacher publications that cite Kitson's work also draw on one another, suggesting a rich and well-integrated dialogue.

The history teacher-researchers did not only draw on one another's work in *integrated* ways; they also did so *extensively*, as Fordham's further analysis reveals. Of the 929 citations in the history teachers' published work, 28 per cent are of articles by other practising teachers and a further 14 per cent are of works by teachers who had only recently left the classroom and who were reporting on their work with a 'teacher voice' (rather than from the perspective of academic research). Even if the latter are discounted, the proportion of references to teacher-researchers is a third higher than the proportion of references to empirical research in history education conducted by academics (which account for 21 per cent of the citations). It is also considerably higher than the proportion of references to more generic works of education, defined by Fordham (2015, p. 144) as 'research based on the philosophical, psychological or sociological studies of education', which was only 9 per cent. More important than such generic studies are works of scholarship by academic historians, which account for 22 per cent of the references. While Fordham acknowledges that generic work about education may be less *accessible* to practising teachers than work within their subject discipline or professional education community, he suggests that history teacher-researchers actually tended to find little to interest them within it, at least as a contribution to their published discourse. His argument is that history-specific sources are extremely important in the construction of history teachers' professional knowledge bases and that in building their own research tradition they essentially draw on the research of other history teachers, in conjunction with the (relatively) few wider studies that there have been into how children learn history, and on works of historical scholarship, particularly those that deal with the nature of history as a discipline. Given the comparative dearth of empirical research in history education conducted by academics, history teachers have effectively sought to conduct their own, drawing on their disciplinary background and on the practitioner research and reflections of their colleagues.

Exemplifications of history teacher-researchers' ongoing professional discourse

The following section of this chapter uses two specific examples to illustrate and examine this kind of practitioner research, rooted in the subject discipline and drawing as much on enquiries published by other history teachers as on more academic investigations. The two examples, each presented here by the individual teacher who carried out the study (the second and third authors of the chapter), correspond very closely to the kind of discourse analysed by Fordham, and both have been published in more detail in *Teaching History* (Fielding, 2015; Carrier, 2015). In each case the research was undertaken as the final stage within a part-time Masters' degree that allowed a high degree of subject-specialisation within a broader programme. In both cases the teachers designed classroom interventions to tackle specific weaknesses in their students' approach to particular kinds of historical question. They were both problems that the teachers regarded as highly significant in relation to the demands of public examinations, although each teacher addressed them on different timescales. In summarising their research, they focus specifically on the nature of the difficulty and on the classroom intervention that they developed in seeking to address it, particularly highlighting the sources that they used to analyse the issue and to hypothesise about possible solutions. The other dimension to which they pay particular attention is related to the distinctive strength of small-scale practitioner research (but can also be seen as its most restrictive limitation) — its responsiveness to highly specific contextual factors.

In examining their practical interventions and the recommendations that they generate, we will also pick up on Fordham's (2015) main finding about the *focus* of history teachers' published research. This is his discovery that history teacher-researchers tended to engage much less in the generation and validation of particular practical strategies (though they did devise and test some of these), and much more in the fundamental process of *curriculum theorising*, of precisely the kind envisaged by Stenhouse (1975).

Case study 1 – Jaya Carrier: Developing students' capacity to conduct an independent historical enquiry

The nature of the problem

The impetus behind my intervention was the difficulty that Year 13 students (aged 17–18) encountered in producing an independent piece of coursework. They struggled with many aspects of this process, but particularly with framing meaningful historical questions and understanding the processes by which they might begin to investigate them. Across the school, concerns had been raised by teachers in different subjects about A-level students' apparent inability to engage effectively in independent learning. The school had only recently expanded to include a sixth-form (for students aged 16–18), which meant that there had been little previous thought about developmental approaches for establishing the kind of self-regulation and awareness of appropriate learning strategies required at this level. A final facet of the problem, as I understood it, were the beliefs about independent learning held by colleagues and Teaching Assistants (TAs) within my department. Several of the history teachers assumed that a more independent approach would only be feasible for the highest attaining students, while the TAs considered that many of the students whom they supported (often with moderate or severe learning difficulties) would simply lack the confidence required to pose and begin to answer their own historical questions.

In these circumstances my response was to experiment with incorporating an early experience of more independent learning within our curriculum for Year 7 (the first year of secondary education, for students aged 11–12) in order to begin cultivating some of the dispositions and practical skills that would ultimately be required for tackling history coursework in Year 13 (at the age of 17–18). I also wanted to explore whether we could create structures or devise specific strategies that would enable all students, regardless of their current levels of attainment, to undertake some aspects, at least, of independent historical enquiry, and whether successful engagement in that enquiry might influence their own and their teachers' conceptions of the process of independent learning itself and of their capacity to engage in it.

The range of research and evidence on which the intervention was based

Although I found a range of practical suggestions and teachers' analysis of their effectiveness on which to draw in designing the intervention, very few of the strategies promoted had been substantiated beyond small-scale classroom interventions by practising or former history teachers. In several cases, the teacher-researchers whose work I followed were themselves drawing on previous articles from *Teaching History*. The broad challenge that I was seeking to address and the lack of a systematic programme of research into students' conduct of their own independent enquiries also meant that I was necessarily ranging quite widely in seeking potential strategies to test. Most prominent amongst the strategies and principles I made use of were ideas from Burnham (2007), Conway (2011) and Hammond (2011), all practising teachers reporting on their own exploratory work. Burnham's initial dilemma was similar to my own: her A-level students' struggle to frame appropriate research questions for their independent coursework. Her response – a particular focus on using stimulating visual sources with Year 7 students to encourage them to generate a variety of questions and then to work on distinguishing between 'big' and 'little' questions – was not one that I specifically adopted. It did, however, prompt my own decision to look at developing the independent learning processes required by A-level students from the very beginning of secondary education.

The work of Conway (2011) and Hammond (2011), focused on student owner-ship of their learning, also influenced the design of my enquiry. In both cases, their decisions to increase the amount of choice given to students (sometimes in relation to the specific questions to be tackled, sometimes in the format of their answers) resulted in a heightened level of student engagement and enjoyment. I sought to emulate this emphasis on increasing student choice while retaining important struc-tural support by framing a common question that students would tackle through a series of independently chosen case studies.

I was also guided by Dawson's (2009) influential enquiry model, which involved generating an initial hypothesis in response to a limited range of evidence and then testing and reformulating it in the light of additional sources. I therefore began by advancing an historical claim, that 'the main cause of success in war is always superior weaponry'. The students were asked to investigate this claim with refer-ence to a conflict of their choice, using sources that they had identified, and to refine it in light of the evidence that their sources provided. The design of the enquiry was also influenced by Counsell's (2000) work on planning for evidential understanding, insofar as I also encouraged students to evaluate the usefulness of the sources that they had chosen in relation to the particular question that they were seeking to address. Obviously being able to assess the relevance of the source to the hypothesis was a crucial first step in determining whether they could address the central question and with what degree of confidence.

Finally, since a particular aim within my investigation was to explore how students' misconceptions and fears about independent learning might be tackled, generic work on self-regulation, resilience and student motivation were important in my consideration of the problem. The work of Claxton (2002) and of Stipek (2001) informed my understanding of students' perspectives, particularly as to why lower-attaining students or those with low self-esteem might struggle with an inde-pendent learning project, although it did not contribute specifically to the design of the enquiry.

Contextual factors that influenced the nature of the intervention

Certain contextual factors – the school's developing focus on its new sixth form and a recent inspection report – were favourable. Stimulated by Ofsted's critique of the school's current practice, senior managers were keen to support teacher interventions across all subjects that adopted a developmental approach to independent learning. This found formal expression in a contribution from school funds towards the fees for my Master's degree, provided that I undertook to disseminate my findings to the wider staff body. Nonetheless, pressures on curriculum time meant that I could afford to allocate only six lessons to the enquiry, in order not to detract from the focus on other specific topics that we needed to address during the course of Year 7.

Changing interpretation of the problem through adopting an action research orientation

The fact that I was undertaking the intervention as a form of action research (rather than formally testing a pre-determined intervention) meant that I was alert to new understandings of students' difficulties as the enquiry advanced. Ongoing evaluation at each stage quickly alerted me to the fact that a distinction I had drawn for students between historical sources (primary sources) and accounts (historians' subsequent interpretations), which I thought would provide a useful structure for the enquiry, proved to be of little value in developing their capacity to select and use materials effectively to answer the central question. The distinction was too coarse-grained and did not focus specifically on the *causal* nature of the question, which required them to pay attention to the content of the source, as much as to its nature. I realised that focusing on the use of evidence was essentially inadequate without prior emphasis on helping students to unpack the demands of the other second-order concept embedded in the question posed: causation. My understanding of the problem of how to encourage students to conduct independent historical enquiries was therefore significantly altered, prompting a substantial adaptation in the structure of the enquiry before we taught it again the following year. Rather than asking students to find different types of sources related to one general hypothesis, we began by generating a range of hypotheses about the decisive causes of victory (encompassing tactics and leadership as well as weapons) and paid much more attention to the kinds of sources that would be likely to deal with each of those elements.

I also learned much more about how students interpret an injunction to 'search' for sources; for example, by using key words within an internet search engine without any prior filtering in light of the particular question posed. This discovery prompted us to model the process much more carefully, deliberately constructing a trial search undertaken together, in which we included particular keywords that we knew would generate a range of 'red herrings'. The students could be encouraged to test each of the resulting suggestions in relation to the central question, thereby alerting them to the need for different kinds of approaches and prior filtering. Our deliberate inclusion of these red herrings drew again on Counsell's (2000) suggestions about the value of adding obstacles while working on shared tasks to sharpen students' appreciation of what is actually required of them when working independently.

Other findings

The adaptations reported above relate specifically to securing effective independent work in *history*, reflecting what we learned about students' understanding of the research process within historical enquiry and about the interplay of different historical concepts. We also gained valuable insights into students' attitudes towards and assumptions about independent enquiry – insights with implications for independent learning in other subjects:

- The power of independent learning to generate enthusiasm, particularly where students' sense of ownership was strong.
- The capacity of a focused research project to change students' views about the value and purpose of homework – and (for a minority) a transformation in their views of research and ability to use historical sources.
- The need to uncover and transform notions widely held by students of independent learning as a solitary activity in which collaboration with others (or requests for help) are deemed inappropriate.
- The challenges of moving beyond students' recognition of the value of being resilient to the development of such resilience in the face of challenges.
- The scope of a successful intervention, structured with careful regard for teachers' and TAs' concerns, to overcome potentially limiting assumptions and develop a rather more inclusive and empowering view of students' capacities.

The status of these findings is necessarily tentative, rooted as they are in the context of one particular school, with claims of impact based only on teachers' reports of students' responses along with the students' enquiry outcomes and their changing perceptions (reported in questionnaires and interviews) about the nature and demands of independent learning. While they echo several of the claims in the history teacher research and wider educational literature on which I drew, they also offer further insights for history teachers into the interplay between different second-order concepts in students' developing understanding of the enquiry process. In so doing, they point less obviously to the value of specific short-term teaching strategies and more to the need for longer-term considerations of curriculum structure and the sequencing of students' learning.

Case study 2 – Anna Fielding: Developing students' capacity to write analytical descriptions of the process of change

The nature of the problem

My intervention was driven by a very specific concern that our students were underperforming on one particular part of their GCSE history exam: a unit which required them to analyse patterns of change and continuity across a wide-ranging period of study (in our case a span of Chinese history from 1900 to 1989). A detailed breakdown of the results achieved by students across the department in preceding years suggested that significant numbers were achieving lower marks for this particular question than for other kinds of historical analysis. Diagnostic tasks set at the end of previous modules revealed a tendency among some students to equate change with the occurrence of specific events, which they merely listed when asked to describe change. While others were able to construct a reasonable narrative, this too fell far short of the analysis required.

The range of research and evidence on which the intervention was based

As Counsell (2011b) noted, the analysis of patterns of change and continuity had received rather less attention in the published literature than questions relating to historical causation. This is despite the fact that the experimental Schools Council History Project (SCHP), established in 1972, specifically included a developmental study of change over time as one of its original examination modules, detailing the need for students to be able to analyse the pace, extent and direction of change in relation to the module's central theme. The relative neglect of change and continuity persisted despite the research findings of the Frameworks Group, which built on the original evaluation of SCHP (Shemilt, 1980) to map out a progression model in students' understandings of change and explore the relationship between students' appreciation of change and their grasp of key principles associated with chronology and time (Blow et al., 2008).

While my work was profoundly influenced by the findings of Project CHATA, the most useful ideas for intervention actually came from the work of Foster (2009, 2013), who had sought to address the problems faced by her own students at different stages; those in Year 9 (aged 13–14) seeking to explain patterns of change achieved by the Civil Rights movement as well as those in Year 13 tackling similar issues within their final 'synoptic unit'. Inspired by Foster's careful analysis of the range of demands implied by questions about patterns of change – an analysis informed by thoughtful reflection on the work of historians such as Fairclough (2002) and Tuck (2010) – I borrowed extensively from the teaching strategies that she had adopted, notably the use of metaphors as tools to help students visualise the different dimensions of change. Another teacher-researcher on whose work I drew was Woodcock (2005), for his focus on the power of equipping students with analytical vocabulary, allowing 'the linguistic to release the conceptual' in students' thinking. A third teacher-researcher whose work I used was Nuttall (2013). Nuttall had built on the work of the UHP research group and the initial Frameworks project (Blow et al., 2008) by choosing to preface each new period study with a highly schematic framework, mapping out distinct developmental stages in the particular 'story' that the students would be tracking over time.

The importance of contextual factors

The nature of the problem and the specific series of measures that I adopted in a small number of lessons, conducted with two classes of Year 11 students (aged 15–16) both reflect the particular circumstances of my school. As an independent, selective upper school, that receives students at the age of 13 from a wide variety of educational backgrounds (including a range of overseas contexts), we have very little time before embarking on formal examination courses to develop students' conceptual understanding of the nature of the discipline. The fact that students' previous experience of history usually involves highly focused preparation for the Common Entrance examination means that many regard history purely as a matter of mastering substantive content and are reluctant to engage in any kind of experimental reasoning or hypothesising, particularly if it does not seem to be directly linked to examination demands or to mirror the format of examination questions.

I was therefore obliged to conduct my classroom intervention within a very short time-span as their GCSEs loomed ever closer. Three strategies involved the use of images and while the students could readily see the value of the first – a visual timeline with images carefully chosen to provide a clear representation of different phases – they needed considerable persuasion and a strong rationale before they would engage in the second: constructing a visual metaphor to capture the rate of change (such as the reading generated by a pedometer measuring the accelerations and decelerations of a runner on an exercise treadmill). The students were subsequently more amenable to creating and comparing a series of 'living graphs' for different groups in society over time, allowing them to see how the same developments affected different people in different ways. Their warmest response was to the final work that we did, developing appropriate vocabulary with which to represent the kinds of patterns that we had discerned.

Changing interpretation of the problem through adopting an action research orientation

Although the specific interventions occurred in only three lessons (at intervals during the final unit), the fact that I was undertaking the research as a practitioner enquiry allowed me to reflect on the students' difficulties as the sequence unfolded, refining my understanding of the problem as well as the strategies that I was implementing. The most significant developments related to my own appreciation of the complexity of the problem. While I recognised students' basic misconception in equating change with discrete events, I had not initially taken on board the range of dimensions that they would need to consider in order to characterise a process that impacts on the lives of different people in different ways and on different timescales. I also became much more aware of how my students' prior learning experiences shaped their expectations of me as a teacher and their conceptions of productive learning activities, thus restricting the range of pedagogical strategies actually available to me.

Findings

The intervention appeared to be highly effective in relation to its specific aim. This was reflected both in the changing nature of the analytic descriptions of change that the students wrote at different stages during the scheme of work and in their examination results, which were significantly better than those achieved by their peers in comparable groups within the school. My colleagues and I were sufficiently persuaded of the power of two short-term strategies – the use of visual metaphors or analogies to characterise change and the provision of pictorial timelines at the beginning of any sustained period of study (both taken directly from other history teachers' research) – to incorporate them immediately into our routine practice. On a longer-term basis we are much more aware of the need to ensure that students *learn* to engage in a wider variety of tasks and problem-solving strategies (that do not merely mirror the demands of particular mark-schemes) in order to ensure that those strategies will be available to us in responding to particular conceptual demands. We have also been alerted to the value of planning much more systematically for students' learning over the course of several years, rather than seeking to make quick fixes later on. While specific targeted interventions undoubtedly offer some useful steps forward, they are not an effective substitute for sustained curricular theorising on a longer time-scale.

Discussion and implications

Set in the specific context of a relative dearth of academic educational research and a significant tradition of practitioner research, these examples allow us to reconsider some of the general questions with which this book is concerned from the specific perspective of history education.

1. Is history teachers' own research an appropriate or effective means of generating and testing classroom interventions?

This first question invites us to consider whether teacher-research can be regarded as an appropriate or effective means of stimulating the development and establishing a secure warrant for the use of particular interventions intended to overcome specific challenges associated with teaching and learning history. The very fact that teachers' intervention studies are conducted in their own classrooms obviously increases the likelihood that the results of their research will be directly applicable to practice. The fact that many teachers, like those in the studies reported here, carry out their first practitioner enquiries in the context of Master's programmes, supervised by subject specialists, also offers scope for effective collaboration between practitioners and researchers. Foster (2013), for example, was supervised in her research by Counsell, who had drawn attention to the nature and extent of the problems that she was seeking to address (Counsell, 2011b), even if she was not directly involved in researching those problems or potential responses to them. Obviously it would be better if teachers' research endeavours could be tied into more securely funded, wide-reaching initiatives: if, for example, Nuttall's (2013) work could have been undertaken as part of an extensive network of teachers systematically experimenting with different approaches to securing usable frameworks, with the support and guidance of the original UHP project team. But in the absence of such projects, it remains invaluable for teachers at least to be able to read and reflect on the experiences of Nuttall's students, alongside those of Rogers (2008), who was also involved in the pilot work undertaken by the Frameworks Group (Blow et al. 2008), and those of Fielding (2015) whose small-scale investigations were inspired by it.

Obviously the testing to which individual teachers can subject particular interventions is of a very limited and particular kind, with a tendency for teacher-researchers to rely on qualitative data that mainly provides insights into students' perceptions of, and responses to, their experience of particular interventions. While this can certainly illuminate the range of factors that may affect the operation of any given intervention, thus enabling readers to consider its likely applicability in their own context, such data rarely allows teachers to isolate and track the impact of the interventions on particular outcomes. It should be noted, however, that the lack of standardised measures for assessing progress specifically in history means that the scope for such tracking is more limited in history than in 'core' or STEM subjects. Were substantial funding ever to be made available for large-scale trials of specific classroom interventions in history, considerable effort would need to be invested even by academic researchers in developing and validating appropriate research instruments.

The publication of teacher-researchers' work, as Fordham (2015) has demonstrated through his citation analysis, not only permits scrutiny and critique of teachers' methods and findings; it also serves to make accessible to other practitioners the implications of work conducted by academic history education researchers. In reflecting on the sources that underpinned her study, Fielding, for example, stressed the importance of Foster's (2013) work in helping her to make sense of the original findings of the Frameworks Group (Blow, 2011; Blow et al., 2012).

Thus, while it is far from being the perfect solution to the generation of more successful classroom interventions in history, teacher-research of the kind reported here and regularly disseminated through *Teaching History* plays a crucial role in ensuring the generation and testing of potential classroom interventions. In the absence of more extensive funding it is perhaps the only viable way forward.

2. What is involved in adapting effective classroom-based interventions for use in different contexts?

Even the two case studies presented here, serve to illustrate just how significant an issue the question of adaptation is. While some of the issues associated with transferring interventions from one context to another were clearly recognised by the teachers, others – such as Fielding's students' resistance to unfamiliar kinds of teaching strategies – took them by surprise, prompting the abandonment of particular elements almost immediately. If teachers themselves are unaware of some of the distinctive contextual factors that may shape what is actually possible, it is likely that outside researchers may also struggle to appreciate them. The latter certainly need to work hard to understand teachers' own interpretation of the problems that they are trying to address and to pay careful heed to their perceptions of the barriers and obstacles that they will encounter. Carrier's acute awareness of her colleagues' assumptions and concerns allowed her to pre-empt them in some ways, acknowledging the challenges inherent in what she was asking of them and working with the TAs to provide structured resources that could be used as a fall-back if necessary, thereby removing much of the fear and enabling them to take risks that they would not previously have considered.

The distinctive features of every context, some of which only become apparent as an intervention gets underway, mean that any attempt to implement a suggested innovation will depend on careful negotiation. It is likely to require careful definition of the minimum standards – the core elements from which there can be no deviation in order for the intervention to retain its identity – as well as the permitted degrees of variation and scope for interpretation that remain.

3. Is it possible to design classroom-based interventions of short duration that could help to alleviate significant problems of students' learning?

While Fielding was confident in her conclusion that two of the specific strategies that she had used made an appreciable difference to students' learning, the implications of much of her work as well as the findings from Carrier's intervention, point to the inadequacies of separating particular teaching or learning strategies from questions of curriculum design or structure. Experimentation with any specific element of history education quickly seems to reveal its interconnections to other aspects of students' learning within the subject, and thus to raise questions about the order in which particular issues are addressed or about how one kind of approach is related to the use of another in building, or layering, the development of students' understanding.

Fordham's unequivocal conclusion from his investigation of ten years of history teacher-research – at least in its published form – was that it was primarily concerned with *curricular* questions – and that in asking such questions, history teachers were actually fulfilling and *extending* Stenhouse's (1975) vision of the 'teacher as researcher' by producing 'a sustained and coherent research tradition that extends the boundaries of particular contexts, and, as such, represents a coherent and codified form of professional knowledge' (Fordham, 2015, p. 147). In making this claim, Fordham acknowledges Stenhouse's opposition to any kind of curricular prescription, but argues that the imposition of a National Curriculum – as a common curriculum framework that 'represents the "recontextualisation" of the academic discipline as a school subject' (p. 147) – has actually facilitated teachers' endeavours and enabled them to transfer professional knowledge more easily from one context to another.

Elliott (2016), reflecting on a much smaller collection of history-teachers' published research, reached a similar conclusion about the way in which history teachers' attempts to wrestle with specific issues of students' learning in history essentially prompted their engagement with *curricular* theorising, leading to the fulfilment of Stenhouse's vision. It thus appears unhelpful to suggest that researchers' failure to generate more successful classroom interventions may reflect an unproductive emphasis on issues of learning or curriculum. Instead it would appear that the development of specific teaching strategies simply cannot be separated from wider issues of curriculum construction. Acknowledgement of this interplay makes it clear just how important it is for teachers and researchers to be able to collaborate in large-scale endeavours, in which it is possible to track specific interventions (such as students' framing of their own enquiry questions, or the identification of their own sources for particular enquiries, or the production of particular kinds of advance framing) through from the beginning to the end of secondary education.

It is interesting to note that the one *large-scale* collaboration between teachers and researchers currently being undertaken in history education in England (through the UCL Centre for Holocaust Education), which is specifically designed to respond to the problems in children's learning uncovered by a large national survey, has chosen very deliberately not to focus on small-scale pre-determined classroom interventions. Its emphasis, instead, is on the development of teachers' historical knowledge (through a residential education programme incorporating specific site visits and archival research) followed by focused support in the design and evaluation of new schemes of work: curricular rather than pedagogical interventions. While teachers who have engaged in the programme (as well as those running it) have shared their developing practice and research findings through *Teaching History* (see, for example, Leyman and Harris, 2013), they have also been required to serve as a 'beacon' for other schools, providing more direct access to the schemes of work that they develop through face-to-face meetings and opportunities for observation. The model simultaneously acknowledges the limitations of providing neatly designed packages for delivery by teachers and the value for teachers of being able to envisage exactly what a particular idea looked like in practice – not so that they could copy it, but so they could work out what elements might be feasible or worthwhile in their own context and what elements would need to be adapted in order to achieve their intended purpose.

Note

1 The adjective 'second-order' is used to distinguish these concepts from the substantive or 'first-order' concepts that relate to the content that historians study; concepts such as 'peasant' or 'parliament'.

References

Ashby, R., Lee, P. & Dickinson, A. (1997). How children explain the 'why' of history: The CHATA research project on teaching history. *Social Education*, 61(1), 17–21.

Bellinger, L. (2008). Cultivating curiosity about complexity: What happens when Year 12 start to read Orlando Figes' The Whisperers? *Teaching History*, 132, 5–13.

Blow, F. (2011). 'Everything flows and nothing stays': How students make sense of the historical concepts of change, continuity and development. *Teaching History*, 145, 47–56.

Blow, F., Lee, P. & Shemilt, D. (2012). Time and chronology: Conjoined twins or distant cousins. *Teaching History*, 147, 26–36.

Blow, F. Rogers, R. & Shemilt, D. (2008). 'Framework working group report'. Unpublished report of a QCDA-funded research and development group established at the Institute of Education, University of London.

Burn, K. (2007). Professional knowledge and identity in a contested discipline: Challenges for student teachers and teacher educators. *Oxford Review of Education*, 33(4), 445–467.

Burn, K. & Harris, R. (2016). Why do you keep asking the same questions? Tracking the health of history in England's secondary schools. *Teaching History*, 163, pp. 49–56.

Burnham, S. (2007). Getting Year 7 to set their own questions about the Islamic Empire, 600–1600. *Teaching History*, 128, 11–17.

Carrier, J. (2015). Taking the plunge: Developing independent learning with Year 7. *Teaching History*, 161, 30–36.

Claxton, G. (2002). *Building Learning Power: Helping young people become better learners*. Bristol: TLO.

Conway, R. (2011). Owning their learning: Using 'Assessment for Learning' to help students assume responsibility for planning, (some) teaching and evaluation. *Teaching History*, 144, 51–57.

Counsell, C. (2000). 'Didn't we do that in Year 7?' Planning for progression in evidential understanding. *Teaching History*, 99, 36–41.

Counsell, C. (2011a). Disciplinary knowledge for all, the secondary history curriculum and history teachers' achievement. *Curriculum Journal*, 22(2), 201–225.

Counsell, C. (2011b). What do we want students to do with historical change and continuity? In I. Davies (Ed.) *Debates in History Teaching* (pp. 109–123). Abingdon: Routledge.

Croft, M. (2005). The Tudor monarchy in crisis: Using a historian's account to stretch the most able students in Year 8. *Teaching History*, 119, 15–21.

Dawson, I. (2009). *Developing Enquiry Skills*. Retrieved from http://thinkinghistory.co.uk/EnquirySkill/index.htm

DFE (2014). *GCSE subject content criteria, April 2014,* Retrieved from www.gov.uk/government/collections/gcse-subject-content

Donovan, M. & Bransford, J. (Eds.) (2005). *How Students Learn: History in the Classroom*. Washington, DC: National Academy of Sciences.

Elliott, J. (2016). Teaching for historical understanding: Thematic continuities with the work of Lawrence Stenhouse. In C. Counsell, K. Burn, & A. Chapman, A. (Eds.) *Masterclass in History Education: Transforming teaching and learning* (pp. 173–184). London: Bloomsbury.

Fairclough, A. (2002). *Better Day Coming: Blacks and equality 1890–2000*. New York & London: Penguin.

Fielding, A. (2015). Transforming Year 11's conceptual understanding of change. *Teaching History*, 159, 28–37.

Fordham, M. (2015). Realising and extending Stenhouse's vision of teacher research: The case of British history teachers. *British Educational Research Journal*, 42(1), 135–150.

Foster, R. (2008). Speed cameras, dead ends, drivers and diversions: Year 9 use a 'road map' to problematise change and continuity. *Teaching History*, 131, 4–8.

Foster, R. (2013). The more things change, the more they stay the same: developing students' thinking about change and continuity. *Teaching History*, 151, 8–17.

Foster, S., Ashby, R., Lee, P. & Howson, J. (2008). Usable Historical Pasts: A study of students' frameworks of the past. ESRC End of Award Report, RES-000-22-1676. Swindon: ESRC.

Foster, S., Pettigrew, A., Pearce, A., Hale, R., Burgess, A., Salmons, P. & Lenga, R. (2015). *What do students know and understand about the Holocaust? Evidence from English secondary schools*. London: UCL Centre for Holocaust Education.

Hammond, K. (2011). Student-led historical enquiry: what might this actually be? *Teaching History*, 144, 44–50.

Harris, R. (2012). 'Purpose' as a way of helping white trainee history teachers engage with diversity issues. *Education Sciences*, 2(4), 218–241.

Harris, R. & Burn, K. (2012). Curriculum theory, curriculum policy and the problem of ill-disciplined thinking. *Journal of Education Policy*, 26(2), 245–261.

Harris, R. & Reynolds, R. (2014). The history curriculum and its personal connection to students from minority ethnic backgrounds. *Journal of Curriculum Studies*, 46(4), 464–486.

Haydn, T. & Harris, R. (2010). Pupil perspectives on the purposes and benefits of studying history in high school: A view from the UK. *Journal of Curriculum Studies*, 42(2), 241–261.

Hinsliff, G. (2005, December 18). Schools blasted for Yo! Sushi take on history. *The Observer*. Retrieved from www.theguardian.com/uk/2005/dec/18/politics.secondworldwar

Howells, G. (2011). Why was Pitt not a mince pie? Enjoying argument without end: creating confident historical readers at A-level. *Teaching History*, 143, 4–14.

Husbands, C., Kitson, A. & Pendry, A. (2003). *Understanding History Teaching*. Buckingham: Open University Press.

Kitson, A. (2003). Reading and enquiring in Years 12 and 13: A case study of women in the Third Reich. *Teaching History*, 111, 13–19.

Laffin, D. (2012). Marr: magpie or marsh harrier? The quest for the common characteristics of the genus 'historian' with 16-to-19-year-olds. *Teaching History*, 149, 18–25.

Lee, P. (2005). Putting principles into practice: understanding history. In Donovan, M. and Bransford, J. (Eds.) *How Students Learn History in the Classroom* (pp. 79–178). Washington, DC: National Academy of Sciences.

Lee, P., Ashby, R. & Dickinson, A. (1996). Progression in children's ideas about history. In M. Hughes (Ed.) *Progression in Learning. BERA Dialogues 11* (pp. 50–81). Clevedon: Multilingual Matters.

Leyman, T. & Harris, R. (2013). Connecting the dots: helping Year 9 to debate the purposes of Holocaust and genocide education. *Teaching History*, 153, 4–10.

McCrory, C. (2013). How many people does it take to make an Essex man? Year 9 face up to historical difference. *Teaching History*, 152, 8–19.

Nuttall, D. (2013). Possible futures: using frameworks of knowledge to help Year 9 connect past, present and future. *Teaching History*, 151, 33–44.

Ofsted (2007). *History in the Balance*. London: Ofsted

Ofsted (2011). *History for all: History in English schools 2007–10*. Retrieved from www.gov.uk/government/uploads/system/uploads/attachment_data/file/413714/History_for_all.pdf

Pettigrew, A., Foster, S., Howson, J., Salmons, P., Lenga, R.A. & Andrews, K. (2009). *Teaching about the Holocaust in English Secondary Schools: An empirical study of national trends, perspectives and practice*. London: Institute of Education. Available online at www.holocausteducation.org.uk/wp-content/uploads/Final-Report-Master-Document-19-October-2009-_HIMONIDES_.pdf

QCA (2007). *History programme of study key stage 3*. Retrieved from http://webarchive.nationalarchives.gov.uk/20130802151252/www.education.gov.uk/schools/teachingandlearning/curriculum/secondary/b00199545/history

Reisman, A. (2012). Reading like a Historian: A document-based history curriculum intervention in urban high schools. *Cognition and Instruction*, 30(1), 86–112.

Rogers, R. (2008). Raising the bar: Developing meaningful historical consciousness at Key Stage 3. *Teaching History,* 133, 24–31.

Rogers, R. (2016). Frameworks for big history: Teaching history at its lower resolutions. In C. Counsell, K. Burn & A. Chapman (Eds.) *Masterclass in History Education: Transforming teaching and learning* (pp. 59–76). London: Bloomsbury.

Shemilt, D. (1980). *History 13–16: Evaluation study.* Edinburgh: Holmes McDougall.

Stenhouse, L. (1975). *An Introduction to Curriculum Research and Development,* London: Heinemann.

Stipek, D. (2001). *Motivation to Learn: Integrating theory and practice.* London: Pearson.

Tuck, S. (2010). *We ain't what we ought to be: The black freedom struggle from emancipation to Obama.* Cambridge, Mass: Harvard University Press.

van Boxtel, C. & van Drie, J. (2012). 'That's in the time of the Romans!' Knowledge and strategies students use to contextualize historical images and documents. *Cognition and Instruction*, 30(2), 113–145.

Ward, R. (2006). Duffy's devices: Teaching Year 13 to read and write. *Teaching History,* 124, 9–15.

Woodcock, J. (2005). Does the linguistic release the conceptual? Helping Year 10 to improve their causal reasoning. *Teaching History*, 119, 5–14.

8

'MAPPING-OUT' THE INFERENTIAL RELATIONS OF THE SUBJECT CONTENT OF GEOGRAPHY LESSONS

A planning intervention for pre-service teachers to inform teaching and learning

Roger Firth and Alexandra Strutt

Introduction

How secondary school students can access and engage with the curriculum subject disciplines, develop a deeper understanding of that subject knowledge,[1] and of the world in which they live, and what the role of the subject specialist teacher might be – are important educational questions. Enabling pre-service teachers to understand the interplay between teaching, learning and subject knowledge and support students' conceptual development is likely to be a central purpose of subject-specific pre-service teacher education. There are, however, tensions which exist in schools between established teaching and learning practices and the possibility of meaningful conversations for pre-service teachers, which adequately account for disciplinary forms of subject knowledge and how such knowledge should be conceptualised and used.

Mitchell and Lambert (2015) have expressed concern about the conceptualisation of subject knowledge development in the preparation of new secondary school teachers. They call attention to the taken-for-grantedness of subject knowledge in schools and address the ways in which subject knowledge has been marginalised. They stress the importance for 'new geography teachers [to] address the nature of geographical knowledge and develop a sound conceptual framework in the subject to inform curriculum [and pedagogic] thinking and practice' (p. 373; emphasis added). This should be built on 'a new disciplinarity in which the subject discipline becomes an overarching structure informing the teacher's thinking and an essential part of a coherent body of educational knowledge' (p. 367).

An analysis of the current state of geography education has also been offered by Morgan (2017). He draws attention to the way in which in schools subject knowledge has been downplayed (or at least simply assumed) in favour of more generic teaching skills (p. 529), how 'the trajectory of geography teacher education over the past three decades has moved away from a focus on geographical content and the complexities of knowledge' (ibid.) and 'how geography teacher education would benefit from a renewed focus on developing teachers' capacity to deal with the complexities of geographical knowledge and theory' (p. 531). The concerns of Mitchell and Lambert and Morgan are in relation to a progressive case for subjects in a school curriculum for the twenty-first century. Geography is their case in point, as it is here, though as Mitchell and Lambert point out, 'the questions raised about the opportunities and preparedness of teachers[2] to engage with disciplinarity translate to other subject specialist communities' (Mitchell and Lambert, 2015: 365).

'Geography is a well-established school subject which is present in most education jurisdictions around the world' (Lambert and Solem, 2017: 8). In England, as elsewhere, 'it has nevertheless faced recurring questions about its purpose and even its place in the school curriculum' (ibid.). Consequently, 'even in circumstances that seem to support a resurgence of "knowledge-led" curricula, such as is the case in England' (ibid.)[3] it is necessary to be very clear about the grounds on which to promote geography as a worthwhile school subject. Debates about the purpose and place of knowledge in education are inevitably also about how knowledge is conceptualised.

Debates about knowledge in geography education have recently taken on significance encouraged by consideration of a broadly based collective of social realist theorists in the sociology of education (Muller, 2000; Young, 2008; Wheelahan, 2010; Moore, 2009, 2013; Maton, 2014; Rata, 2017; among others). Social realism has emphasised the way education has had difficulties with the very idea of knowledge and 'is highly critical of the "educational dilemma" posed by the alternatives of traditionalism and instrumentalism in curriculum policy and their "progressive" postmodern critics' (Firth, 2011: 292). An essential part of the social realist argument is that *all* young people have a pedagogic right to 'powerful' disciplinary knowledge (Young, 2008).

Social realism is concerned with understanding bodies of specialised knowledge and how over time they are structured and built and can be theorised for use in educational settings. It seeks to recover knowledge as a real object with its own 'structured and structuring structure' (Maton, 2010: 42) and draws attention to the possibilities for and constraints on recontextualising disciplinary knowledge for educational purposes within schools. Social realism can assist subject teachers to focus on the relations within knowledge itself: its epistemic and social relations – and provides a theoretical and methodological framework to unpack the structures of disciplinary meaning-making and knowledge development. It has also drawn the theorising more directly in relation to curriculum and the conceptualisation of what has been termed 'powerful knowledge'. Researchers in the geography education community have taken up these arguments (for example, see Firth, 2011, 2014, 2015; Maude, 2018, 2016; Morgan, 2017)[4].

The pedagogic challenge remains, however, in terms of how far it is possible to make explicit these relations within knowledge so that students understand 'the systematic conceptual elements of a subject and the relationships between them and also the procedures required to gain and validate knowledge' (Young and Muller, 2016: 170). It is here that Robert Brandom's work (1994, 2000) on inferential reasoning could be particularly helpful. As Young and Muller state, an inferential account 'helpfully draws attention to the joined-up nature of concepts and the social basis of this joined-upness' (p. 171) 'that binds concepts into a knowledge structure' (p. 170). Brandom's position can be aligned with the perspectives of social realism insofar as he is concerned with the normative and social conditions within which knowledge is produced (Luckett, 2016: 1007). Both provide a basis for developing a more explicit subject pedagogy that makes the requirements of the various disciplines clear and could better support students' conceptual development and better understanding of geography. Both underpin the 'subject knowledge work' of the pre-service teachers (see below).

This chapter reports on intervention research[5] that links directly to debates about subject knowledge. It took place within the University of Oxford's Secondary Postgraduate Certificate in Education (PGCE) course, more commonly known as the Oxford Internship Scheme. It explored pre-service teachers use of an inferentialist epistemology and concept mapping to plan and teach a sequence of lessons and their perceptions of how it can harness students' conceptual development and better understanding of geography.

A working assumption of the PGCE Geography course has been the need to address the arguments around knowledge that have developed in the educational field in recent times and to extend the opportunities and preparedness of pre-service teachers to engage in pedagogical thinking in relation to subject knowledge. This is the purpose of the subject knowledge work that all pre-service geography teachers undertake during the course of the PGCE year. It focuses on theories of knowledge (constructivism and social realism) and the different understandings of how knowledge is constituted and how they are implicated in differences in teaching, learning, assessment and the purpose that education serves in modern society (Rata, 2017: 1003). The contextual factors which make the consideration of subject knowledge problematic within schools are also given attention. 'How subject knowledge is progressively conceptualised as the pre-service teacher (known as 'trainee' in England) makes the adjustment through 'training' from their own academic study of a curriculum subject within a university degree to a more pedagogically oriented conception of that subject for teaching in schools' (Brown et al., 2016: 492) is an important foundation for 1-year postgraduate pre-service courses in England.

In what follows the intervention research is introduced in the first section; the second section outlines the semantic theory of inferentialism and seeks to show its implications for school education; this is followed by a third section which addresses the policy settings of schools and pre-service teacher education and their bearing on the situational context within which pre-service teachers learn to teach in secondary schools, drawing attention to the influential discourses of constructivism and performativity; the fourth section presents and discusses the findings through the use of the pre-service teachers' own accounts. The chapter concludes with some thoughts on what inferentialism has to offer pre-service teachers pedagogic practice and more broadly teacher education and professional knowledge.

The intervention research

The research was small-scale and exploratory. It involved three pre-service geography teachers (one of which is the second author) and their university tutor (first author). The names used are pseudonyms. The sites of the research were the partnership schools of their second placement and in each case involved the planning and teaching of a short sequence of six lessons to a Year 8 class (students aged 12–13 years).[6] The pre-service teachers used an inferentialist epistemology and concept mapping to map-out the inferential relations of the conceptual content of the lessons to be taught. Inferentialism was introduced prior to the intervention study through a workshop session as part of the pre-service teachers' subject knowledge work. Previously taught lessons were scrutinised using lesson plans, the learning task-subject content pairings (McCrory, 2017), learning materials, students' work and lesson evaluations. Attention was especially given to the 'game of giving and asking for reasons' (see later) and what this means for conceptual reasoning, based on ideas from McCrory (2015), including the 'if… then reasoning' sitting beneath what we say and think, and that 'all concepts function with a referential and an inferential guise' (p. 40). The use of concept mapping as a learning strategy was familiar to the preservice teachers before the intervention study, but not its use as a planning tool.

It drew on an adaptation of a lesson study approach to classroom research (Fernandez et al., 2003; Lewis, 2009; Lewis et al., 2006). An inductive strategy was used for the purpose of extracting patterns and explanations from the data and these are presented as the accounts of the pre-service teachers. The main source of data were the meetings that took place between the university tutor and each pre-service teacher; an initial planning meeting before the start of teaching, a discussion of a lesson observation based on stimulated recall (Lyle, 2010) and a final meeting at the end of the sequence of teaching. The meetings involved the university tutor and a single pre-service teacher each time. They enabled critical reflection and ongoing refinement of the pre-service teachers' perceptions of their pedagogic practice and thinking. The meetings were audio-recorded and transcribed. A presentation by the pre-service teachers to the PGCE Geography cohort was also used; the pre-service teachers shared their experiences and professional learning and this was video-recorded and transcribed. Documentary data (lesson plans, concept maps, lesson evaluations) was also used.

The methodological approach for the intervention was to use recent developments in philosophy that are concerned with meaning, language, thought and conceptual development and their relationship to the world, namely the work of Robert Brandom. The theoretical reach of his work, however, is much wider, including knowledge. Derry (2008, 2013, 2017) has been at the leading edge in examining the educational implications of Brandom's work on inferentialism.

Inferentialism changes the common conception of learning evident in the practice of teaching. Although 'not a learning theory or a pedagogical approach' (Bakker and Hußmann, 2017: 2) McCrory (2017), in reference to Derry's work, emphasises that 'the work of Brandom… gives us a new language and a new perspective to scrutinise approaches to instructional design' (p. 39). She advances 'the argument that teachers cannot work to develop students' conceptual development to full effect if they overlook the relationship between representation and its content (ibid.) and that 'asking what it is for a concept to have meaning affords new ways of framing both instructional design and explanations of variation in student learning' (p. 29). These ideas and arguments form the basis of this chapter as they did the intervention. The intervention research study was framed by the following considerations:

1) Each pre-service teacher's instructional design choices (lesson planning and teaching).
2) Each pre-service teacher's perceptions of how it supported the development of students' reasoning practices and conceptual development.

The pre-service teachers' experience of teaching geography in their placement schools had amplified the recognition of the need for a more well-defined understanding of the nature of subject knowledge itself and what that might mean for their pedagogic practice and student progress. They came to recognise the cogency of current practice in schools and the prevalent symbolic order guiding such practice and its relationship to subject knowledge. The research intervention study was seen as a space that offered a potential distancing from the reductive discourses around subject knowledge and an opportunity to assert some ownership over their professional development.

Inferentialism

Inferentialism stands in distinction to the more traditional orthodoxy *representationalism* (also known as *referentialism*) in philosophical work concerned with linguistic meaning and mental content (what we say and think) and their relationship to the world. With a degree of oversimplification Brandom argues that to understand how we come to know and develop understanding we need to reverse the conventional order of explanation, to prioritise inference over representation (or reference).

According to representational approaches the meaning of our linguistic expressions and mental content are primarily to be explained in terms of the (broadly) referential relations they bear to things in the world (objects, events, states of affairs or whatever they represent).

The basic idea is 'we are confronted with things in the world and somehow make our words and thoughts stand for them' (Peregrin, 2012, p. 1). Representationalist theories start with notions of reference to things. We use our linguistic expressions and mental content as we do because of what they denote or stand for. The idea at the heart of representationalism is the world is independent of mind and language and made meaningful by the constructions placed on it (Derry, 2013, p. 32). The prioritisation of representation arises from a misunderstanding about its nature – that initial meaning arises solely from its relation to its object and that only once this is grasped can inferences be made.

Instead, Brandom takes inference as explanatorily basic – he gives priority to the system of inferences in which the object is disclosed. Bransen (2002) describes the idea thus:

> The fact that a statement means something, that it has intentional import, that it says something about something, that it employs conceptual content is a fact we should not try to understand in terms of referential relations between the statement and some state of affairs [in the world] but in terms of inferential relations between the statement and other statements'.
>
> *p. 374*

This is to say our linguistic expressions and thoughts depend for their meaning on the system of inferences within which they are disclosed; they are governed by the regularities or rules of inferential use and notions such as reference are explained as a by-product of them. Put simply, the key idea of inferentialism is that our linguistic expressions and thoughts are accorded meaning in terms of their inferential connections, by being situated within a network of inferential relations. Instead of considering how we come to know and develop understanding to be based on linguistic and mental (object-like) representations, which are assumed to be more or less correct representations of objects in the world, it is primarily an ability, the practical ability to master inferential relations – that is reasoning practices (Noorloos et al., 2014: 321).

Brandom often illustrates his ideas by comparing the responsiveness of a human knower to that of a mechanical instrument such as a thermostat. While a thermostat is responsive to a temperature increase or decrease, which would cause a switch on a boiler to be turned off or on, it cannot be said to understand the environmental conditions. The knower, however, has the practical *know how* to situate their response in a network of inferential relations (reasons) – to know what follows from something being hot or cold, what would be the evidence for it, what would be incompatible with it, and so on. For the knower, taking the temperature to be hot or cold 'is making a move in the game of giving and asking for reasons – a move that can justify other moves, be justified by still other moves, and that closes off or precludes still other moves' (Brandom, 2000: 162). The difference between the thermostat and the knower lies in the experience that the knower brings to the situation. While humans understand why they turn the heating on or off, a thermostat does not. Crucially, humans are responsive not only to external stimuli (the world), but also to reasons. This, as Taylor et al. (2017) emphasise, 'describes one of inferentialism's key concepts – the game of giving and asking for reasons – a participatory practice which consists of the intersubjective making, disputing and ratifying of [knowledge] claims' (p. 744). They 'propose that the game of giving and asking for reasons is the inferentialist concept most *pertinent for an account* of *learning activity; that is, for the dynamics of learning'* (p. 775; emphasis added).

For Brandom, the distinguishing feature of a human knower is their responsiveness to reasons rather than simply to causes. For Brandom, humans act and communicate inferentially. They take up a stance in an inferentially articulated space. In making a claim to know we are not as commonly thought giving a description of an object or idea but placing the claim about it in a *space of reasons* (Sellars, 1956). Here again Taylor et al. are helpful in identifying a second key concept of inferentialism. This 'complementary concept is pertinent for an account of the [subject] *content of what is taught* (p. 775; emphasis added). As Taylor et al. explain (we have added our interpretation of this account):

> In other words, the space of reasons is the space in which (rational) commitments are made and are justified [the nature of the subject discipline] as following from previously established commitments [what students already know]. In participating in the game and trying out different claims and the reasons for them, this space is explored and—at least partly—mapped out [the subject discipline and progression]. Humans are inducted into this space in the course of both their cognitive and social development [aims of a subject based curriculum]. An inferentialist perspective on the content of learning, therefore, characterises learning dynamics in terms of the navigation of an established part of the space of reasons or the exploration of a new area within the space of reasons [continuity and progression]. It is worth emphasising that in this way any talk of the possession of concepts must on the inferentialist view be equated to the ability to use them and to reason with them; that is, to make inferences with these concepts [key concepts and conceptual development].
>
> *Ibid.*

In relation to the teaching of geography in school classrooms it is the space mapped out by the teacher based on students' previous learning and' by reconnecting with the 'intellectual traditions' of the discipline (Mitchell and Lambert, 2015: 377).

In summary, context not simply conscious intention imparts understanding and reason and our experience of the world, through our senses, is already conceptual. That is to say, inferentialism lays out our understanding of the world not in terms of what our words and thoughts refer to in the world, but in relation to networks of inferences that drive the need to know. Inferentialism emphasises the role of reasoning (i.e. inference-making). Knowledge and understanding (conceptual development) in this account is that which can be offered and stands in need of reasons (Young and Muller, 2016: 199).

In educational terms it informs us that really grasping subject knowledge 'involves knowing *how to do something with it* – knowing how to apply a concept or concepts to it and how to articulate the inferential reasoning and consequences entailed in using a concept or concepts' (Luckett, 2016: 1007). And as Luckett emphasises, 'this implies a form of "practical mastery that can be made explicit"' (ibid.) – through pedagogy. As McCrory (2017) asks, 'what would instructional design (and the resultant students' progress) and teachers' preparatory courses look like if they were modelled on a theory of meaning which required "referent resonance" constituted by "relevant inferential reasoning" rather than a simple word to world correspondence' (p. 31).

Learning to teach: influential discourses and subject knowledge

The policy settings of schools and pre-service teacher education have a direct bearing on the situational context within which pre-service teachers learn to teach in secondary schools. They call attention to 'the prevalent symbolic order guiding current teacher practice' (Brown et al., 2016: 492) and particularly the 'specific discourses that shape the way in which teaching is understood and the interaction with subject knowledge' (Ibid.). In doing so, we highlight the significance of two influential discourses that are likely to shape pre-service teachers thinking and interactions with subject knowledge: namely *constructivism* and its lack of clarity surrounding the delineation of knowledge; and *performativity*, with emphasis on increased government control and an all-pervasive instrumentalism, whereby teachers and teacher educators have become more directly accountable derived from standards or competencies. It should also be mentioned that a substantial part of University-led courses of teacher preparation now take place in schools (24 of the 36 weeks). 'The latest initiative in England... has made the symbolic move towards "training" being school-led as well as school-based and has affected university influence on training' (Brown et al., 2016: 492).

Constructivism

In recent decades constructivism[7] has emerged as a very powerful discourse for explaining the development of human knowledge and how students learn and remains so today. The influence of constructivism and its conception of mind and world pervades both the general education literature (McPhail, 2016) and geography education (Lambert, 2011; Firth, 2015). As a theory it has epistemological, psychological and pedagogical dimensions; though as Stemhagen et al. (2013) suggest, 'it is likely that some trouble with the term stems from misunderstandings as to which form of constructivism is at play' (p. 57).

The influence of constructivism as a reform-oriented theory grew strongly through the 1990s–2000s, as did the body of literature. Former government policy, in particular the National Strategies, encouraged teachers to direct their professional efforts into pedagogy. The National Strategies played a significant role in the take-up of constructivist ideas at this time, being presented to teachers as the foundation for reforming teaching and learning. The National Strategies, which 'represent one of the most ambitious change management programmes in education' (DfE, 2011: 2), were 'a systematic attempt at a national level to drive improvements... in the way that subjects were taught in classrooms' (ibid.). The discourses of constructivism that reached schools through the National Strategies, however, often bore little relation to the theoretical implications of their parent theories.

In the development of its tenets in geography education the psychological and pedagogical dimensions of constructivism have been most influential. The focus has been on the learner and the learning process and the idea that students are active 'constructors' of knowledge. 'Crediting learners with the ability not just to learn through constructing their own meaning, but to make new knowledge... is coupled to particular epistemological assumptions' (Derry, 2013: 49). It leads to 'a one-sided emphasis on an active constructive aspect of knowledge that by implication avoids consideration of knowledge beyond individual construction... which diverts attention from a focus on knowledge per se' (ibid.).

The argument here is that pre-service teachers need to move beyond a one-sided emphasis on an active constructive approach to knowledge, which by implication avoids consideration of disciplinary knowledge itself. To help teachers become more aware of the discipline and its approach to knowledge emphasis can be given to the idea of *disciplinary constraint* (Stemhagen et al., 2013). Stemhagen et al (2013) provide a critique of over-simplified applications of constructivism to teaching 'by illustrating the way constructivist methods are constrained to differing degrees in the classrooms of the [subject] disciplines' (p. 55; emphasis added).

Disciplinary constraint is based on *disciplined judgment*, a term 'designed to help educators become more aware of their discipline and its unique approach to knowledge, and how to help students learn to employ the conceptual tools provided by these disciplines' (p. 58) in secondary school classrooms. They argue 'that constructivist classrooms must balance the individual judgments that students apply during the course of their work with the normalising tools of judgment as employed within the particular discipline in question' (ibid.). In choosing to emphasise the disciplinary facets of student learning by introducing disciplinary constraint to the pedagogical process the argument is that a stronger conception of knowledge is necessary.

Performativity

In England, as elsewhere, the introduction of the various apparatus of performativity has created a culture that encourages compliance in teaching and teacher education (Brown et al., 2016; Hardy, 2018). Here, we are concerned with standards driven compliance and draw attention to the constitutive role of Teaching Standards in the practice of the teacher and its impact on subject knowledge.

The education sector has seen the creation of lists of statutory competencies or Teachers' Standards (DfE, 2012), which are used in schools in England and pre-service teacher education. Introduced in 1997, and most recently revised in 2011, they define the minimum level of professional practice and conduct expected of all teachers from the point of qualification. They are part of the attempt to construe consensus around teachers' professional knowledge, values and practice leading to consistency of teacher performance as well as teacher education provision and teacher assessment (Oancea, 2014: 512).

Achieving the Teachers' Standards is a requirement of gaining Qualified Teacher Status (QTS), which is a prerequisite for all qualified teachers in England. The Teachers' Standards 'are lists of auditable performances' (Connell, 2009: 218) and present teaching as a technical activity that involves the 'acquisition of trainable expertise' (Beck, 2009: 8). They are 'predicated on the belief that all knowledge required for teaching can be acquired through experience' (Amos, 2014: 24). Beauchamp et al. (2013) describe the current Standards as 'regulatory rather than developmental in intent' (p. 5). They are underpinned by what McNamara & Murray (2013) state is:

> an understanding of teaching as a) essentially a craft rather than an intellectual activity; b) an apprenticeship model of teacher training that can be located entirely in the workplace; and c) the related assumption that more time spent in schools inevitably – and unproblematically – leads to better and 'more relevant' learning.
>
> *p. 14*

The Standards, as would be expected, are almost silent on knowledge itself, being focused on what the teacher can do and in demonstrating 'strong' and 'secure' knowledge of the subject that is kept up-to-date. They circumvent any emphasis 'on developing teachers' capacity to deal with the complexities of geographical knowledge and theory' (Morgan, 2017: 531). They betray a static view of knowledge which can be readily 'audited'. A question can therefore be raised as to whether preservice teachers thinking and practice is being *standardised* in particular ways. The Standards privilege performativity and 'practical' and experiential knowledge over theoretical, pedagogical and subject knowledge (ibid.). 'The concept of "performative professionalism" is evident to some extent in all the various Standards currently in use across the UK but is demonstrated most clearly in England' (Beauchamp et al., 2013: 5). They reflect a policy tendency not only in the UK but elsewhere (Menter, 2017: 2).

The ethnographic study by Puttick (2018) of pre-service teachers' positionalities as knowers within school geography departments illustrates the complexities and identity politics that pre-service teachers negotiate (p. 39) in relation to subject knowledge and is illustrative of aspects of this 'standardisation' process. He uses the social realist concept of knowledge–knower structures (Maton, 2014) to explore the kinds of knowers accepted as legitimate in these departments. 'A dichotomous view of teachers as knowers was found, being positioned as knowing or not-knowing particular areas of subject knowledge' (p. 25) arguing that 'this binary view is related to the language of the Teachers' Standards' (ibid.). He draws attention to how the preservice teachers in the study negotiate the tensions around the need to be judged as having 'strong' and 'secure' subject knowledge by drawing heavily on a binary conception of knowing/not-knowing particular aspects of their subject (p. 39). He 'argues that these departments only offer "fleeting and serendipitous" opportunities to discuss subject knowledge, and even these opportunities can be problematic for pre-service teachers to access because of the ways in which judgements are made about the strength and security of their subject knowledge' (p. 39).

In conclusion Puttick stresses 'the need for developing more expansive discourses around subject knowledge' (p. 25). The study emphasises the importance of subject departments as the primary unit of organisation within secondary schools, but how 'opportunities for professional discussions in departments are limited and are often dominated by immediate practical concerns' (p. 25). This presents a challenge for pre-service teachers, teacher mentors and university tutors alike across university-school partnerships, who might 'seek to construct alternative, more sophisticated discourses that reject simplistic audit and gap-filling approaches towards subject knowledge' (p. 40).

At the same time teacher preparatory courses themselves have been subject to inspection and external definition of what they should contain as governments have sought to gain central control over the training and development of teachers. A recent research study by Brown et al. (2016) has reported on the experience of university teacher educators adjusting to new academic and operational conditions and how the conditions are reconfiguring and reprioritising the manner in which the area of subject knowledge is addressed within preparatory teacher courses – in line with the market-led terminology that governs current practices. In consequence the teacher educator is likely to have made adjustments to university-based provision to support pre-service teachers as they become immersed in to the school's preferred mode of practice, including the extent to which they are presenting subject knowledge in the established way.

Findings and discussion

As previously stated the intervention sought to extend the opportunities and preparedness of pre-service teachers to engage in instructional decision making in relation to subject knowledge. An inferentialist epistemology and concept mapping were used and data was collected from a number of meetings as well as documents. We now consider the pre-service teachers' instructional design choices (lesson planning and teaching) and their perceptions of how it supported the development of students' reasoning practices and conceptual development. Their accounts appear in italics throughout.

Lesson planning and teaching

The pre-service teachers used concept mapping as a diagrammatic tool to categorise, link and organise concepts, and as a result they thought that lesson planning became more time efficient. Their construction of the concept maps took place in conjunction with planning lessons rather than completing the mapping prior to writing their plans. Eventually Laura came to use a concept map as a replacement for her lesson plans; she found this far more useful. Nicole didn't always use concept mapping.

There was similarity in the level of detail, though Laura produced the most comprehensive concept maps. She constructed her concept maps around what she called *'the big question of the lesson'* (e.g. how can humans live with tornadoes?), whereas Charlotte and Nicole used the theme of the lesson to construct their mappings (e.g. the social, economic and environmental consequences of tourism in Antarctica). A number of key concepts underpinned the previous National Curriculum programme of study for geography (QCA, 2007)[8] and Laura consistently used these in her planning during the intervention study. The relevant key concepts were used to frame the relationships between the subsidiary concepts and supporting details to be taught. For example, her lesson on how humans live with tornadoes used the key concepts of physical and human processes, place and interdependence in relation to *'tornado formation and location'*, *'the impacts of tornadoes'* and *'living with tornadoes'*. She did this to emphasise to herself and to her students within lessons how these *'big ideas'* structurally and systematically recur and underpin the study of geography; *'students need these key concepts to deepen and broaden their knowledge, understanding and skills. They are central to the mastery of the subject'*. She described the concepts as *'threshold concepts'* (referencing Meyer and Land, 2003), emphasising *'their troublesome but transformative nature'*. Laura explained her use of the key concepts as giving:

> *A holistic understanding of the dynamic and fluid nature of geography [which] will allow learners to think about the world with far more meaning and reason, ultimately gifting them with far more agency as adults.*
>
> Laura

Two of the pre-service teachers stated that concept mapping using an inferential framework had been *'significantly helpful'* in improving their planning and teaching. Laura stated, *'I can't imagine how it could be more helpful for PGCE students'*. Similarly, Charlotte pointed out, *'I imagine I will use this going forward next year… I think it* [inferentialism] *should be in the PGCE training next year'*.

Laura, in particular, was very positive about the intervention: *'I think absolutely that the intervention improves my planning and teaching.* More insightfully, she commented

> *Once I started inferential concept mapping, I felt that I was tapping into a way of thinking, geographical thinking, that had always underpinned my planning process; and the concept map served to make that thinking more tangible and explicit.*
>
> Laura

The emphasis on geographical thinking was explained in terms of her undergraduate course and her understanding of the discipline of geography.

Laura went on to say,

> *one of the best features of the mapping is that it shows really explicitly the stages of the learning, linking it to the concepts, and linking the concepts to each other, and then*

if there is something missing that has been far more explicit... it has rendered my planning much more efficient and I feel far more successful as a teacher.

Laura

Laura also explained the way she used inferential mapping in her planning, and in doing so, highlighted the significance of the interdependence of concepts, and its importance for teaching.

The way I concept map is in terms of my key enquiry question for the lesson, as my aim is for my learners to be able to answer this question at the end. I work backwards from the question. So, what do my learners need to understand to be able to answer that key question. For example, when considering water scarcity students need to know what the impact of a drought is, they need to know how a drought happens and to be able to link location with physical process, then they need to be able to identify where locations are vulnerable to drought. So, in that respect you can't teach about the impact of drought without knowing what a drought is and why some areas are prone to drought in the first instance.

Laura

Charlotte drew attention to the fact that the mapping out process was something she had already used.

I have used concept mapping before to map out the key things that need to be covered in the lesson, but I wasn't doing it with the inferentialism idea behind it. It's made the planning process better; it's made me aware of more things to consider. It is definitely a much better framework for me in terms of planning than what I did before.

Charlotte

She also emphasised the way it impacted on her lesson planning.

The intervention has given me more confidence in a specific structure to use in a situation where I'm starting to plan the lesson from scratch or where it's a topic which is quite complex... And also for planning a series of lessons.

Charlotte

Like Laura, in recognition of the significance of the intervention Charlotte described the specific ways it was actualised in her planning.

I'm thinking more about the idea of inferential relations and the importance of reasoning, and what they [the students] know already about that. So, it's unpicking that more and then looking at links and building up reasoning. Taking into account prior knowledge maybe wasn't something I thought about so much before this either.

Charlotte

She went on to say:

> *Actually, that's a key point. Before, I was sort of mapping out lessons more academically from my perspective, and now I am bringing in what the students know as well. So, the focus on inferential relations probably has additional things in there – the need to be concerned with what students already know. It's enriched the whole planning process basically.*
>
> Charlotte

Here, Charlotte is acknowledging not only the importance of inferential relations to the development of students' reasoning and conceptual understanding, but in addition an omission in her previous planning. Charlotte is indirectly giving emphasis to a specific category of conceptual change, the transformation of existing knowledge structures from everyday experience due to the acquisition of disciplinary ideas through the development of subject-based reasoning. Charlotte's comments would suggest she has not elevated the students' existing knowledge above the subject knowledge, a concern Mitchell and Lambert (2015) have in relation to the established practices of teaching geography in schools (p. 370).

Having begun to trial the intervention Charlotte not only acknowledges her increased confidence in planning lessons, she drew attention to the fact that she has begun to question her thinking that has supported the planning process and her teaching.

> *What we have to take into account when we are planning lessons is that we are not delivering required content or helping students to construct knowledge but building up their understanding of and reasoning behind concepts.*
>
> Charlotte

There is a well-defined set of arguments behind Charlotte's statement and she seems to have a grasp of the 'backstory'. In effect, she is drawing attention to recent curriculum change, which in itself was a response to what Mitchell and Lambert describe as 'the emptying-out of school subject knowledge' (p. 374), that is to say how teachers have turned away from considerations of knowledge in recent times (p. 371). For Charlotte, both the curriculum revisions and the stronger policy emphasis on essential knowledge and the development of content delivery models of teaching in many schools (*'delivering required content'*), and the previous heavy emphasis on the learning process and the overwhelming concern for engaging young people through connection to their own experiences (p. 367) (*'helping students to construct knowledge'*) appear to be less helpful for identifying what is important in her own subject teaching. We are mindful, however, that in future it may be more difficult for Charlotte (and new teachers in general) to be able to step back from the bureaucratic and performative concerns of schools and what is regarded as 'effective teaching' in the way she has in the intervention study.

Nicole confirmed that the intervention had been helpful *'to some extent'*, that she had *'enjoyed using the concept mapping idea'*, except *'I still think I need to refine it myself, stripping it even further back and saying, ok what are the links the students need to make and be able to reason with'*. Nicole remained most circumspect about the significance of the intervention. She produced several concept maps for the first two lessons in the sequence but afterwards did not use concept mapping. Nicole explained why she did not make consistent use of concept mapping in her planning, *'I don't necessarily work well by drawing a concept map. For me it's the thinking space — the time — that I have for myself that's important.'* Clearly, the potential of concept maps as an educational tool to enable the visual display of information, concepts and relations had to repay the effort of its construction in terms of *'thinking through the geography of each lesson'* and the achievement and expansion of her students' learning. For Nicole, it wasn't the diagrammatic representation of her thinking that was important so much as the thinking time itself.

> So that thinking space is not actually just about the students, it's for me as well, and I feel like the tool could probably be switched down. I mean the links are the important bits, but physically sitting and writing is not so important — for me it's the thinking time that's important.
>
> *Nicole*

She pointed out, however, that her attempts at mapping out the inferential relations of the conceptual content of the lessons did change her approach to planning her lessons:

> I think it streamlined my lesson planning… it solidified the direction and purpose of the lesson… rather than what I had been doing before, which was: ok, what do I need to cover in this lesson according to the examination specification, or according to the existing scheme of work.
>
> *Nicole*

Nicole's statement may be indicative of her first-hand experience of the nature of subject teaching and its role and contribution to students' education in her secondary school placements; and more broadly her understanding of what she described as *restrictive discourses* around subject teaching.

The pre-service teachers began to teach with a stronger conceptual schema of the geographical knowledge to be learned. However, they talked much less about how the inferential mapping had altered their teaching, other than in very general terms as outlined above. An example from Laura offers more specific comments about how it began to impact on her teaching. The focus is what she described as *teacher talk*, namely her instructions and explanations.

> It streamlined my thinking, rendered the key geography far more explicit and allowed me to bring the underpinning concept(s) of each task to the forefront in lessons… I hope

that as I continue to use it I'll also be able to make the geography I'm talking about far more explicit to the learners as well... To me this is exactly what my train of thought is... In terms of lessons and sequences of lessons, everything follows on far better.

Laura

The comment illustrates how Laura is considering the development of her students' geographical reasoning in terms of the externalisation of her own reasoning, that is to say, through giving explicit reasons, explanations, and justifications for the focus of the lesson (the enquiry question) and in modelling geographical reasoning during the lesson. This is not to suggest she sought to dominate classroom dialogue to the detriment of student participation; rather she had recognised through the intervention how the quality of teacher talk can be a powerful resource for learning through a cycle of teaching and learning. The reference to learning tasks suggests she had also begun to consider how the development of reasoning in students is externalised through their discussion and reasoning with others, but there are no further references to task design.

In summary, mapping out the inferential relations of the concepts gave the pre-service teachers a diagrammatic representation of their understanding of the geographical content of the lessons to be taught and were helpful in revealing relationships between concepts that hitherto, as they came to appreciate, had not been acknowledged or if acknowledged, had not been give attention in previous teaching. The mapping out process provided the pre-service teachers with a clearer connective navigation as they sought to establish and represent the functional structure and relationality of the concepts to be taught.

The process encouraged a more specific identification of the geographical knowledge the students were to learn, as well as supporting more thought about students' subject knowledge development within lessons. In this way, the pre-service teachers found mapping out the inferential relations of the conceptual content to be taught helpful in respect to planning both a single lesson and a sequence of lessons in a scheme of work.

In relation to teaching, what is noticeable is that the pre-service teachers efforts were focused on developing the strategies with which they were most practised, and they believed, most competent. Collectively, these were, in relation to whole class teaching and the support of individual students, giving explanations, the emphasis on geographical terminology in teacher–student questioning (by themselves and the students), modelling reasoning and giving a synopsis of the subject knowledge content of the lesson itself.

Students' reasoning and conceptual development

Similarly, what is apparent in these accounts is that the efforts of the pre-service teachers to develop the geographical reasoning of their students was largely confined to their teaching; there was very little emphasis on what the students were to do or on task design itself. Two examples are used as illustration. Laura emphasised that because '*concept mapping links the lesson so closely to the concepts the geographical themes and ideas are explicit in what I'm teaching*'. In consequence, '*I am far more confident in what I'm teaching*'. Going on, she stated

> And because I'm more confident... I feel I encourage my students to also make those more explicit links, to challenge themselves, and to use more academic geographical language.
>
> Laura

In this respect Laura thought that '*the quality of what the students are learning improved because it's generally more geographical*'. But what is not articulated is how she encourages the students to make these more explicit links and to challenge themselves – what the students were doing to develop their reasoning and the reasoning that took place.

Nicole remarked that what her planning did '*was to slow down lessons, in a way, in that I was giving the students time to consider things, to talk about things, far more than I had done before*'. This meant that the students '*were actually able to make the links in class, rather than me expecting somehow for them to make the necessary conceptual jumps*'. She went on to say:

> essentially the things that are inferred by me throughout the lessons need to be made more explicit, in order for students to be able to reason and really get to the depth of the concepts themselves, and how they link together.
>
> Nicole

Nicole's reference to the students' making the necessary conceptual jumps themselves highlights an assumption that has informed her planning and teaching (this may also have been the case for Laura and Charlotte), namely that students can 'draw out' the intended geographical learning for themselves. There is an acknowledgement that she is saying to herself 'students can do these things [this thinking] with this content so that's what I want them to be doing. They will be seeing the complex explanatory scenario I can see' (McCrory, 2017: 38; emphasis added). The emphasis on making her own inferential thinking more explicit is recognition that Nicole knows what geographical reasoning needs to take place but her instructional design lacks a path to ways of working with students to support their reasoning and conceptual development (she recognises the conceptual judgements she has made in coming to know). As yet she seems to have a limited sense of how to induct students into realising these geographical ways of thinking other than the reference to slowing down lessons and the emphasis on student discussion, but without any explanation.

The intervention research challenged the pre-service teachers' existing understanding of their nascent pedagogic practice but they experienced difficulty in reframing how they would work with students. Inferentialism suggests that making claims and asking for reasons enables students to access the meaning making that is valued in the disciplinary discourse in which they are they participating. While the pre-service teachers appreciated the argument of learning as a growing understanding of the inferences that comprise currently accepted meaning, they lacked understanding of *how* this might be done. The pre-service teachers were versed in the workings of the tenets of inferentialism but not in being able to put the tenets to work.

The difficulties arose due to the intervention rather than the pre-service teachers. In introducing inferentialism more attention should have been given to, first, the importance of knowing the students' starting points – their prior knowledge; Charlotte's disclosure is evidence for this; and second, how conceptual movement 'from' and 'to' different meanings occurs (McCrory, 2017: 38). These were given attention in the workshop session, but more emphasis should have been given to the actual conceptual movement that would be required by the students. This conceptual movement, however, can only take place if pre-service teachers formulate the specific detail of the required subject content and its structure in relation to the learning tasks, beyond the use of labels to specify it in a lesson plan. This is what McCrory describes as teachers' 'content-activity pairings'. This has particular significance, as the pre-service teachers seemed to lack appreciation of the significance of the relationship between prior and required subject knowledge for students' learning and instructional design – the starting points and the thinking steps appropriate. It is here, we argue, that the discourses of constructivism and performativity, perhaps, are at their most powerful, whereby pre-service teachers circumvent the necessary thinking about the conceptual movement of their students from 'where they are at' to 'where they would like them to be'. The task of working through inferentialism's implications is recent in geography education and there is much work to be done.

The accounts of the pre-service teachers were similar in many respects and indicate aspects of a changed understanding of their practice; in particular the need to intensify discipline specific insights into their planning and teaching and a stronger subject specific structure and coherence to the geography lessons taught, as well as some appreciation of how students may be supported to grasp difficult and complex concepts. The progress that the pre-service teachers made was catalysed by their participation in a University-led course. While the standardisation of teaching and teacher education is paramount in government policy terms, such courses do offer a potential distancing from the reductive discourses troubling teaching and subject knowledge.

Concluding thoughts: instructional design, teacher education and professional knowledge

The importance of knowledge in education is, of course, not only a matter of its purpose and access within the school curriculum, but also in the curriculum of universities and programmes for the education of future and existing members of the teaching profession.

Inferentialism gives us a new language with which to scrutinise instructional design. It has much to offer pre-service teachers and their university tutors. 'Drawing on Brandom, Derry suggests that making claims and asking for reasons enables students to access the meaning making that is valued in the discourse in which they are participating... the concern with learning as a growing understanding of the inferences that comprise currently accepted meaning, not only has strong implications for how students are engaged as learners' (Childs et al., 2014: 36); it also connects with the future and development of teacher education and its engagement in the practices of schooling (ibid.).

'It raises questions about what university Departments of Education should be about, what they should be researching, what they should be teaching, and how this is to be stipulated' (Young and Muller, 2016: 177), together with their relationship with knowledge stakeholders. Methods of knowledge production and dissemination have been the subject of heated debate for some time. 'The global pressures currently being exerted on higher education are well documented... [though] it is risky to generalise the effects of these pressures on curriculum reform given the complex interplay between global, national and institutional imperatives' (Shay, 2014: 142). In responding to the centrality of knowledge in schools, colleges and universities there is now a need, as Young and Muller (2016) argue, for the development of 'an approach to "knowledge about knowledge" in education, and in particular the differentiated and specialised forms it takes' (p. 3; original emphasis).

What is palpable is that 'policy-makers internationally who are preoccupied with finding ways of strengthening the relationship between education systems and the economy are increasingly focusing on workplace learning as a way of improving organisational performance and, at an aggregate level, national economic success' (McNamara et al., 2014a: 2). In this respect, teacher professional learning has become an area of strategic importance in the debate. In England, 'recent governments of all political persuasions have, with increasingly radical ideological fervour,... pursued a more extensively work-place model of teacher pre-service and continuing professional learning' (ibid.: 1). There is a complex context here that cannot be discussed within the confines of this chapter, other than to say that conceptually, pedagogically, intellectually and even architecturally' (ibid.: 2) teacher professional learning is 'in an evolutionary state' (ibid.) with continued intermittent 'skirmishes between teacher-educators and policy-makers' (Childs et al., 2014: 29).

There are two points that follow from these brief comments about teacher professional learning. First, the recent acceleration in the rate of change in teacher pre-service courses is perhaps rendered more perplexing given that postgraduate pre-service teachers already spend two-thirds of their training in the workplace on professional placement. The logic is also baffling given the confidence reported at the time, by the government's own inspectorate of pre-service teacher education, in the quality of university-based training routes compared to school-based routes' (McNamara et al., 2014b: 184). Second, the ideological position framing the government's recent reforms of pre-service teacher education is that 'teaching and learning to teach is essentially a "craft" rather than an "intellectual" activity' (McNamara et al., 2014: 191). As McNamara et al. emphasise, 'this is an "adaptive" model of learning' (p. 191) focused on mastering or replicating behaviours in particular practice schools as pre-service teachers 'work with' the school-based mentor and other teachers. As previously stated, it is a model that privileges performativity, practical and experiential knowledge.

Childs et al. suggest that it is time to take up the challenge of teacher professional learning and examine how we might build learning environments that draw on the expertise to be found in both schools and universities to create thinking, decision-making professionals (p. 30). In this regard, as Burn and Mutton (2015) emphasise, one of the prominent challenges in teacher preparation programmes is the need 'to facilitate and deepen the interplay between the different kinds of knowledge that are generated and validated within the different contexts of school and university' (p. 217). In their concern with the professional learning of pre-service teachers and the achievement of this kind of knowledge integration Burn and Mutton discuss a range of approaches in and beyond the UK. Attention is given to those programmes where integration has been developed most systematically, what Burn and Mutton describe as 'research-based clinical practice' initiatives. Such initiatives aim to provide the scope for pre-service teachers to focus on the processes by which professional knowledge of all types is created, to interrogate such knowledge, to bring it to bear on interpreting and responding to their classroom experiences and in adopting a problem-oriented approach to professional practice (adapted from Burn and Mutton, 2015). The context of school practice and the aim to provide an opportunity for beginning teachers to engage in 'research-informed clinical practice' (Burn and Mutton, 2015) are two essential elements of the research intervention presented here.

Recently, work has taken place to reconceptualise the Oxford Internship Scheme and Childs et al. (2014) have called attention to this development, stimulated by ongoing research by university tutors and school-based teacher educators. The suggestion here is that pre-service teachers can be part of this ongoing research, which could make the entire professional learning process more secure and sustainable. The intention to work even more closely with schools is dependent on what Childs et al. describe as a 'strong theory of learning' (p. 30),

> the theory is the configuration of approaches that gather under the label of 'cultural historical' understandings of learning and practice, which draw their inspiration from Vygotsky's research... At the core is the recognition of a dialectic between learner and learning environment: we are shaped by the practices we inhabit, but also shape them. But this is no simple notion of person-context interaction. These dialectical relationships stretch, as Lave puts it, among semiotic systems, social structure and political economy. The rethinking is therefore radical, and we hope far more productive than the skirmishes that have shaped teacher education of late.
>
> *Ibid.*

What is of importance for this chapter, beyond the context of the developmental work taking place and 'how university-school relationships may be reconfigured within a more systemic notion of teachers' professional learning' (p. 33), is the emphasis on Vygotskian thought and its significance for education. It is here through the work of Derry (2008, 2013) that we can draw strong connections to recent developments in philosophy and specifically with Brandom's theory of inferentialism. Her reassessment of the significance of Vygotsky's philosophical background show us how we can link ideas about learning to epistemology and at the same time take issue with a range of widely held beliefs about representationalism and the social construction of knowledge. Vygotsky had a far more sophisticated appreciation of reason and its remit than critical characterisations of his work imply. This opens up new frontiers in educational theory and practice.

The professional learning of pre-service teachers would benefit from discussion about alternative conceptions of learning, knowledge and reason. We are particularly interested in the idea that 'the distinctive character of human psychological and intellectual powers resides in our responsiveness to reasons, a capacity that develops in children as they are initiated into traditions of thinking and reasoning' (Bakhurst, 2011; backcover) and to explore its potential in respect to teaching and learning to teach.

Notes

1 The term subject knowledge is used variously in teacher education. Here, 'subject knowledge' is used to refer to disciplinary knowledge and its recontextualised forms that commonly constitute the school subject. We recognise that the relationship between the two is not always direct (Stengel 1997). Equally, how such subject knowledge is held in an intellectual way by prospective and practising teachers will vary, at least in part, due to their experience of the discipline/subject in university and school classrooms.

2 We would emphasise both prospective and practising teachers.

3 With a change of government in 2010 and the publication of a Schools White Paper, *The Importance of Teaching*, which outlined the policy for education in England, this signalled a renewed emphasis on 'traditional' subjects and the acquisition of 'the essential knowledge and understanding that pupils should be expected to have to enable them to take their place as educated members of society' (DfE 2010: 42). Along with changes in the policy setting of pre-service teacher education it has been seen as indicating that it may be possible to anticipate a 'knowledge turn'.

4 Huckle (2017) is critical of geography educators who have given attention to social realism and 'powerful knowledge' as a means to address the neglect of subject knowledge. He argues that they have drawn on the sociological strand of the socially realist argument but not the philosophical strand, whereby the concept of powerful geographical knowledge remains ambiguous. His specific concern relates to a 'capability' perspective on school geography introduced by Lambert and Morgan (2010) and developed in the GeoCapabilities Project (GCP, 2017; Lambert, Solem, & Tani, 2015). It is apparent; however, the argument is targeted more widely. Huckle uses Leesa Wheelahan's (2010) advocacy of critical realism as the philosophical strand of her social realist thesis to contend that 'it is the philosophy of critical realism that should shape a critical and powerful school geography' (p. 9). There is not the space to consider the arguments here, though they do need to be addressed.

5 This intervention research was carried out with support from the University of Oxford Department of Education Small Grant Research Fund.

6 Laura taught a scheme of work on Wild Weather, Charlotte on Glacial landforms and processes and Nicole on Tourism in Antarctica.
7 Constructivism is being used as an umbrella term but we recognise the range of constructivist and socioconstructivist positions on offer.
8 The key concepts are: place, space, scale, interdependence, physical and human processes, environmental interaction and sustainable development, cultural understanding and diversity. This Key Stage 3 curriculum for 11–14-year-olds was taught between 2008 and 2014. It removed large areas of prescribed subject content, which was replaced with a framework of more general principles, based on seven 'key concepts'.

References

Amos, S. J. (2014) *Teacher educators in higher education: a study of their practice and contribution during school placement visits.* Unpublished Doctorate in Education, The Open University. Available online: http://oro.open.ac.uk/42769/1/S_Amos_EdD%20Thesis.pdf

Bakhurst, D. (2011) *The Formation of Reason*, Chichester: Wiley Blackwell.

Bakker, A. and Hußmann, S. (2017) Inferentialism in mathematics education: introduction to a special issue, *Mathematics Education Research Journal,* 29(4): 395–401.

Beauchamp, G., Clarke, L., Hulme, M. and Murray, J. (2013) Policy and practice within the United Kingdom. *Research and Teacher Education: The BERA-RSA inquiry.* Project Report. London: British Educational Research Association.

Beck, J. (2009) Appropriating professionalism: restructuring the official knowledge base of England's 'modernised' teaching profession, *British Journal of Sociology of Education,* 30(1): 3–14.

Brandom, R. (1994) *Making It Explicit: Reasoning, representing, and discursive commitment,* London: Harvard University Press.

Brandom, R. (2000) *Articulating Reasons: An introduction to inferentialism,* London: Harvard University Press.

Bransen, J. (2002) Normativity as the key to objectivity: an exploration of Robert Brandom's articulating reasons, *Inquiry,* 45(3): 373–392.

Brown, T., Rowley, H. and Smith, K. (2016) Sliding subject positions: knowledge and teacher educators, *British Educational Research Journal,* 42(3): 492–507.

Burn, K. and Mutton, T. (2015) A review of 'research-informed clinical practice' in Initial Teacher Education, *Oxford Review of Education,* 41(2): 217–233.

Childs, A., Edwards, A. and McNicholl, J. (2014) Developing a multi-layered system of distributed expertise: what does cultural historical theory bring to understandings of workplace learning in school-university partnerships? in O. McNamara, J. Murray and M. Jones (eds) *Workplace Learning in Teacher Education: international Practice and Policy,* London: Springer.

Connell, R. (2009) Good teachers on dangerous ground: towards a new view of teacher quality and professionalism, *Critical Studies in Education,* 50(3): 213–229.

Department for Education (DfE) (2012) *Teachers' Standards.* Available online: www.gov.uk/government/publications/teachers-standards [Accessed 2 July 2017].

Department for Education (DfE) (2011) *The National Strategies 1997–2011 Final Report,* London: Department for Education.

Department for Education (DfE) (2010) *The importance of teaching. The Schools White Paper* 2010 (Cmnd 7960), London: DfE.

Derry, J. (2017) An introduction to inferentialism in mathematics education, *Mathematics Education Research Journal,* 29(4): 403–418.

Derry, J. (2013) *Vygotsky: Philosophy and education*, Chichester: Wiley-Blackwell.

Derry, J. (2008) Abstract rationality in education: from Vygotsky to Brandom, *Studies in Philosophy and Education*, 27(1): 49–62.

Fernandez, C., Cannon, J., & Chokshi, S. (2003) A US-Japan lesson study collaboration reveals critical lenses for examining practice, *Teaching and Teacher Education*, 19(2): 171–185.

Firth, R. (2015) Constructing geographical knowledge, in G. Butt (ed.) *MasterClass in Geography Education Transforming Teaching and Learning*, London: Bloomsbury Publishing.

Firth, R. (2014) Disciplinary knowledge and task design in geography, in I Thompson (ed.) *Designing Tasks in Secondary Education Enhancing Subject Understanding and Student Engagement*, London: Routledge.

Firth, R. (2011) Making geography visible as an object of study in the secondary school curriculum, *The Curriculum Journal*, 22(3): 289–316.

Hardy, I. (2018) Governing teacher learning: understanding teachers' compliance with and critique of standardisation, *Journal of Education Policy*, 33(1): 1–22.

Huckle, J. (2017) Powerful geographical knowledge is critical knowledge underpinned by critical realism, International Research in Geographical and Environmental Education, DOI: 10.1080/10382046.2017.1366203

Lambert, D. (2011) Reviewing the case for geography, and the 'knowledge turn' in the English National Curriculum, *The Curriculum Journal*, 22(2): 243–264.

Lambert, D. and Morgan, J. (2010) *Teaching Geography 11-18: a conceptual approach*. Maidenhead: Open University Press.

Lambert, D. and Solem, M. (2017) Rediscovering the teaching of geography with the focus on quality, *Geographical Education*, 30: 8–15.

Lambert, D., Solem, M. and Tani, S. (2015) Achieving human potential through geography education: a capabilities approach to curriculum making in schools, *Annals of the Association of American Geographers*, 105, 723–735.

Lewis, C. (2009) What is the nature of knowledge development in lesson study? *Educational Action Research*, 17(1): 95–110.

Lewis, C., Perry, R. and Murata, A. (2006) How should research contribute to instructional improvement? The case of lesson study, *Educational Researcher*, 35(3): 3–14.

Luckett, K. (2016) Making the implicit explicit: the grammar of inferential reasoning in the humanities and social sciences, *Universal Journal of Educational Research*, 4(5): 1003–1015.

Lyle, J. (2010) Stimulated recall: a report on its use in naturalistic research, *British Educational Research Journal*, 29(6): 861–878.

Maton, K. (2014) *Knowledge and Knowers: Towards a realist sociology of education*, Abingdon: Routledge.

Maton, K. (2010) Analysing knowledge claims and practices: Languages of legitimation, in K. Mato and R. Moore (2010) *Social Realism, Knowledge and the Sociology of Education: Coalitions of the Mind*, London: Continuum, pp. 35–59.

Maude, A. (2018) Geography and powerful knowledge: a contribution to the debate, *International Research in Geographical and Environmental Education*, 27(2): 179–190.

Maude, A. (2016) What might powerful geographical knowledge look like? *Geography*, 101(2): 70–76.

McCrory, C. (2015) The knowledge illusion: who is doing what thinking? *Teaching History*, December 2015: 37–47.

McCrory, C. (2017) Using a beginning history teacher's consideration of students' prior knowledge in a single lesson Case study to reframe discussion of historical knowledge, *Revista Electrónica Interuniversitaria De Formación del Profesorado*, 20(2): 29–44.

McNamara, O. and Murray, J. (2013) The School Direct programme and its implications for research informed teacher education and teacher educators, in Florian, L. and Pantić, N. (eds) (2013) *Learning to Teach Part 1: Exploring the history and role of higher education in teacher education*. The Higher Education Academy.

McNamara, O., Murray, J. and Jones, M. (2014a) Framing Workplace Learning, in O. McNamara, M. Murray and M. Jones (eds) *Workplace Learning in Teacher Education: International Practice and Policy*, London: Springer, pp. 1–28.

McNamara, O., Murray, J. and Jones, M. (2014b) Workplace Learning in Pre-service Teacher Education: An English Case Study, in O. McNamara, M. Murray and M. Jones (eds) *Workplace Learning in Teacher Education: International Practice and Policy*, London: Springer, pp. 183–206.

McPhail, P. (2016) The fault lines of recontextualisation: the limits of constructivism in education, *British Educational Research Journal*, 42(2): 294–313.

Meyer, E. and Land, R. (2003) *Threshold concepts and troublesome knowledge: linkages to ways of thinking and practising*. Enhancing Teaching-Learning Environments in Undergraduate Courses, ETL Project, Occasional Report 4, May 2003. Last accessed March 2018.

Menter, I. (2017) *The Role and Contribution of Higher Education In Contemporary Teacher Education*. For the Scottish Council of Deans of Education. Available online: www.scde.ac.uk/wp-content/uploads/2017/05/Report-Ian-Menter-2017-05-25.pdf

Mitchell, D. and Lambert, D. (2015) Subject knowledge and teacher preparation in English secondary schools: the case of geography, *Teacher Development*, 19(3): 365–380.

Moore, R. (2009) Towards the Sociology of Truth, London: Continuum.

Moore, R. (2013) Social Realism and the problem of the problem of knowledge in the sociology of education, *British Journal of Sociology of Education*, 34(3): 333–353.

Morgan, J. (2017) Preserving with Geography, *Documents d'Anàlisi Geogràfica*, 63(3): 529–544.

Muller, J. (2000) *Reclaiming Knowledge. Social theory, curriculum and education policy*, London: RoutledgeFalmer.

Noorloos, R., Taylor, S., Bakker, A. and Derry, J. (2014) An inferentialist alternative to constructivism in mathematics education, in P. Liljedahl, C. Nicol, S. Oesterle, S., & D. Allan (Eds.). *Proceedings of the 38th Conference of the International Group for the Psychology of Mathematics Education and the 36th Conference of the North American Chapter of the Psychology of Mathematics Education (Vol. 4)* (pp. 321–328). Vancouver, Canada: PME. Available online: www.pmena.org/pmenaproceedings/PMENA%2036%20PME%2038%202014%20Proceedings%20Vol%204.pdf.

Oancea, A. (2014) Teachers' professional knowledge and state-funded teacher education: a (hi)story of critiques and silences, *Oxford Review of Education*, 40(4): 497–519.

Peregrin, J. (2012) What is Inferentialism? Available online: jarda.peregrin.cz/mybibl/PDFTxt/580.pdf

Puttick, S. (2018) Student teachers' positionalities as knowers in school subject departments, *British Educational Research Journal*, 44(1): 25–42.

Qualifications and Curriculum Authority (QCA) (2007) Geography Programme of study for key stage 3 and attainment target.

Rata, E. (2017) Knowledge and Teaching, *British Educational Research Journal*, 43(5): 1003–1017.

Shay, S. (2014) Curriculum in Higher Education: Beyond false choices, in P. Gibbs and R. Barnett (eds) *Thinking About Higher Education*, Chapter 10, pp. 141–157, London: Springer.

Sellars, W. (1956/1963) Empiricism and the Philosophy of Mind, in W. Sellars *Science, Perception and Reality*, London: Routledge and Kegan Paul, 1963, pp. 127–196.

Stemhagen, K., Gabriel, Reich, A. and Muth, W. (2013) Disciplined judgment: Toward a reasonably constrained constructivism, *Journal of Curriculum and Pedagogy*, 10(1): 55–72.

Stengel, B. (1997) 'Academic discipline' and 'school subject': Contestable curricular concepts, *Journal of Curriculum Studies*, 29(5): 585–602.

Taylor, S. D., Noorloos, R. and Bakker, A. (2017) Mastering as an inferentialist alternative to the acquisition and participation metaphors for learning, *Journal of Philosophy of Education*, 51(4): 769–784.

Wheelahan, L. (2010) *Why Knowledge Matters in Curriculum. A social realist argument*, London: Routledge.

Young, M. (2008) *Bringing Knowledge Back In: From social constructivism to social realism in the sociology of education*, London: RoutledgeFalmer.

Young, M. and Muller, J. (2016) *Curriculum and the specialisation of knowledge: Studies in the sociology of education*, Abingdon: Routledge.

9

THE PROBLEMS AND POSSIBILITIES OF CONDUCTING SMALL-SCALE CLASSROOM-BASED RANDOMISED CONTROL TRIALS IN CONTRIBUTING TO EVIDENCE-BASED PRACTICE

One school's experience

Elizabeth Samuel, Christina Watson and Ann Childs

1. Introduction

Often, when describing how an innovation is implemented, the analogy of a journey is used and the metaphor, although perhaps clichéd, is apt as we[1] describe two examples of action research contextualised in our attempt to build a community of research practice at a Cumbrian, co-educational school for 11 to 18-year-olds, which had around 1,420 students at the time of the research reported in this chapter.

The chapter begins by describing the school's involvement and commitment to evidence-informed practice through the formation, and ongoing evaluation, of Teaching and Learning Communities (TLCs) at whole school and department level. We argue that this commitment contributed to the decision to be involved in a nationwide initiative, Closing the Gap: Test and Learn. Closing the Gap: Test and Learn was the first programme in the UK to work collaboratively with schools to conduct randomised controlled trials (RCTs) and evaluated the effectiveness of seven interventions designed to close the gap in attainment of disadvantaged pupils. Alongside the school's involvement in the national project we also joined what was termed the 'early adopter' group of schools, 50 in all, which conducted small-scale RCTs in their own schools. The Early Adopter programme was funded by the National College for Teaching and Leadership (NCTL). We reflect on how our involvement in conducting our own small-scale RCTs has opened up other avenues for our professional learning and the chapter concludes by looking at how, post Closing the Gap: Test and Learn, the TLCs have moved on in our school. We also reflect on the value and the challenges in being able to continue to conduct small-scale RCTs in the school as part of a portfolio of methods which contribute to evidence-informed practice.

2. Background – the history of the development of the TLCs

In this section we outline the history of the development of TLCs and show how the ongoing commitment to research informed practice, both at whole school level and in departments, seemed to provide fertile ground for the work we undertook for the Closing the Gap: Test and Learn project.

When reflecting on why the journey started we are agreed that a variety of factors created two research believers before 'the polite revolution' of ResearchEd[2] made more teachers consider the benefits of engaging with research critically. One of us was the product of a PGCE course at the University of Bath which promoted the keeping of a reflective diary, followed by a masters degree which promoted Action Research and the other came from a background of a lifetime of teaching social science enquiry after a degree in 'Education Alone' at Lancaster. Both of us wanted to take a breather in the post National Strategy[3] days when educational initiatives came too thick and too fast, without proper explanation, with insufficient time to embed and with no time to evaluate.

Both of us believed that becoming an effective teacher was an ongoing process and that life in general is a self-improvement journey. This is more articulately expressed by Fullan (1993), who wrote:

> Lifelong learning is essential because in complex, ever-changing societies mental maps 'cease to fit the territory' (Pascale 1990, p. 13). Teachers as change agents are career-long learners, without which they would not be able to stimulate students to be continuous learners.
>
> *Fullan, 1993, p. 4*

At first our ambitions were no more than to offer teachers 'better' learning experiences than we thought one-off twilight professional developments sessions were providing. Ironically, our initial thoughts were based on no more than a gut feeling that the ideas teachers were exposed to did not have much impact.

When we started the journey in 2010 there was no obvious road map: this was in the days before the Teacher Development Trust had commissioned and published its report 'Developing Great Teaching: Lessons from the international reviews into effective professional development', which identifies the:

> several design features in the delivery of a professional development programme (appropriate duration; rhythm; designing for participants' needs; creating a shared sense of purpose; and alignment across various activities) that make it more likely it will have a lasting impact on teacher practice and student outcomes.
>
> *Teacher Development Trust, 2014, p. 11*

However, an Osirus[4] conference on assessment in 2010 led by Dylan Wiliam provided the kernel for a possible plan: the Teaching and Learning Community (TLC). This was presented as part of a ready to use School, Students and Teachers' Network pack which was to be used to embed formative assessment. It stressed the need for the iterative professional development sessions and it was suggested that a series of sessions on the same topic over an academic year would allow time for teachers to reflect and improve their practice. Each session was to have a predictable format where new learning/research would be included. Teachers were to be given time to plan how they could apply what they had learned to their day-to-day teaching and then commit to try out what they had planned with the expectation they would report back on what they had done at the next session.

The TLC meeting agenda is outlined below:

- *Introduction (5 minutes):* Agendas for the meeting are circulated and the learning intentions for the meeting are presented.
- *Starter activity (5 minutes):* Participants engage in a warm-up activity to help them focus on their own learning.
- *Feedback (25 minutes):* Each teacher gives a brief report on what he or she committed to try out during the 'personal action planning' section at the previous meeting, while other participants listen appreciatively and then offer support to the individual in taking the plan forward.
- *New learning about formative assessment (25 minutes):* To provide an element of novelty into each TLC meeting and to provide a steady stream of new ideas, each meeting includes an activity that introduces new ideas about formative assessment.
- *Personal action planning (15 minutes):* The penultimate activity of each session involves each participant planning in detail what he or she hopes to accomplish before the next meeting.
- *Summary of learning (5 minutes):* In the last five minutes of the meeting, the group discusses whether participants have achieved the learning intentions they set for themselves at the beginning of the meeting. The model chimed with us as the work of Black and Wiliam (1998) stressed the need for teachers to take their work on assessment and to adapt it to their context; it included a research element and harnessed reflection and peer pressure. After recruiting leaders who were interested in either research or improving teaching and learning we made two key refinements to the model presented above. The time we had for TLCs sessions, at the end of the school day, was limited and we had to shorten the sessions but we still included the key elements from the agenda outlined above. All sessions had some time built in for feedback, there was always some time built in to bring in new material from research to inform the group's thinking and the group always had to develop some kind of action which they were going to put in place for the next session. Experienced leaders were left to incorporate these key elements and structure the sessions for themselves. We worked more closely with the less experienced TLC leaders ensuring the key

elements were in place. Secondly, we wanted to move away from the focus on assessment and, after a coincidental conversation with an Inspector from the Office for Standards in Education (OfSTED), who signposted the work of John Hattie via the work of Petty (2009), we investigated Petty's work. Petty's work provided us with accessible research evidence o n a wide number of areas.

Whilst we were perhaps unsure of the destination, we were clear that we needed to evaluate the impact of anything we did, and to encourage others working with us to do the same, not least so we could change direction if needed. Our success criteria will seem simplistic in the current climate: we decided that if the sessions had impact on the teachers then there would be impact on the children in the classroom. Now having been exposed to the ideas of Guskey (2000) via the blogesphere[5] we recognise how modest were our initial aims.

2.1 TLCs at whole school level

The first round of TLCs saw all staff opt in to work in interdepartmental groups of various sizes, ranging from 6–20, looking at differentiation, KS5 teaching (teaching with students aged 16–18 years old), independent learning, student discussions, evidence-based practice and behaviour management. The groups presented their finding in short presentations to other staff on June 2012. From a research and development perspective, the presentations were analysed for what they showed in terms of the extent to which:

- the group seemed to be working from existing research or thinking;
- staff appeared to have developed ideas and applied them in the classroom; and
- the presence of evidence of impact on practice (essentially rudimentary action research).

In the first round of evaluations there was much evidence of the use of research to structure the sessions in the groups working on differentiation, KS5 teaching, evidenced based teaching and discussion work. It was also clear that the structure allowed teachers to take away ideas from the group and apply them. Several staff had been surprised by the way the ideas had impacted on students with anecdotal evidence of students taking more responsibility and developing creative ways to present work. In terms of impact, most groups noted little more than teaching methods 'suited some students and not others'. The group looking at behaviour management perhaps had the most well-evidenced impact on practice as the group used a survey to analyse areas of personal strength and weakness in teachers' approaches to behaviour management as a basis for development. Two members of staff in particular talked about how this had changed practice and recognised the impact in improving behaviour in the class. The behaviour group had found through their analysis that, within their lessons, incidents logged on discipline forms and withdrawals had fallen at a time when there was a small rise for the rest of the school.

2.2 TLCs at department level

By 2013 we moved some TLC time to departments, while retaining some at whole school level, as we felt that Heads of Department (HoDs) were sufficiently familiar with the structure to run sessions which could focus on what was needed within a subject and departmental context. The evaluation focused on the extent to which staff had been involved, the application of an evidence base, the impact on classroom practice and lessons for development next year. The evaluation was completed in two stages. A sample of HoDs were asked to complete a brief evaluation sheet and then to discuss their responses in a meeting of HoD and leaders of the professional development programme. Individual informal interviews, of 40 minutes, were then completed with a different sample of HoDs who were selected to represent a cross-section of departments in the school. HoDs were initially invited to talk about what they had done and how their TLC had worked.

The initial study and the interviews both suggested that all staff engaged in the department TLC sessions, although the level of involvement varied by individual and by department. Similarly the use of an evidence base was variable. Some departments built on the whole school TLC and used that evidence base in a departmental context. TLC leaders often used an external course or input to provide an evidence base. The initial study showed that teachers had come back to the TLC and discussed changes they have made in the light of TLC input. HoDs had observed changes in classroom practice but some had doubts about whether this was becoming fully embedded. Reflecting on the TLC, HoDs often identified aspects that they hoped to develop next year. Issues of planning time and difficulties in monitoring impact were identified as was the challenge of summarising research in a useable form. The burden of 'homework' between sessions was also identified. Taken overall, this evaluation covered all but two departments in the school. It identified a wide range of innovation and experimentation which had taken place in the spring and summer terms directly resulting from department TLCs. As one HoD summed it up, 'it was a really valuable opportunity to develop departmental work'.

2.3 The continuing whole school TLCs

In 2014 we undertook some qualitative research with TLC leaders. This focused on their perceptions of how leading a TLC impacted on their practice. As leaders they were not a homogeneous group: four were members of Senior Leadership Team, four were middle leaders (one with an Advanced Skills Teacher designation), two were teachers without formal leadership roles and one was a member of the support staff. The structured interviews, based on the work of Wenger et al. (2011), looked at issues associated with leadership and the impact on the leaders' pedagogic knowledge and classroom practice. Analysis of the findings showed that there were a number of issues associated with the leadership of the TLCs. Firstly, members of the Senior Leadership Team felt that being a TLC leader was a part of their leadership role and so reflected their responsibilities in the school. In terms of impact on leaders' practice, a typical comment was: 'leading makes you reflect on self and stand in front of others and say I haven't got it right yet.' In terms of what they could offer as a leader of a TLC one leader identified that they had brought 'no experience or knowledge' of the issue – what they perceived they had brought was an interest in methodology and action research.

All leaders interviewed identified an impact on their own classroom practice because, for example, membership of the TLC involves 'challenging yourself and getting out of your comfort zone' and partly because running a TLC 'reinforces reflective practice'. All leaders could list changes they had made in their own classrooms as a direct result of running a TLC – and one respondent suggested 'What you get out of running a TLC is far beyond what you get from being a member'.

However, gauging wider impact beyond these perceptions remained problematic. A number of leaders identified that working with the TLC had offered a level of realism about impact as they discovered some staff had a low level of skills, a very different perception of their role, or a resistance to particular approaches. However, these same respondents also identified how enjoyable it was to see people take an interest, use equipment much more or gain confidence in techniques. One leader identified the TLC as a 'testing ground for something that might move onto a wider stage'.

The accounts above of the work of the TLCs give the background of the school's commitment at whole school, department and leadership level to research informed practice. In the next section we argue that this seems to have provided fertile ground for us to become involved initially in the nationwide Closing the Gap: Test and Learn project, and then to move on to designing and conducting our own small-scale RCTs as part of the Early Adopter Programme.

3. Closing the Gap: Test and Learn

In setting the scene for our own involvement in conducting our own small-scale RCTs this section begins by looking briefly at the origins of the nationwide pro-ject Closing the Gap: Test and Learn. This project employed RCTs to measure the impacts of various interventions which had shown promise in closing the gap in attainment for disadvantaged learners. It then goes on to look at some of the arguments for and against the use of RCTs in education and then specifically looks at the emergence within the Closing the Gap: Test and Learn project of what became called 'the Early Adopter programme'. We joined this programme and, as a result, designed and conducted two small-scale RCTs within our own school, which we describe in the final part of this section.

3.1 RCTs in education and the Closing the Gap: Test and Learn project

In 2013 the then Education Secretary Michael Gove commissioned a paper by Dr Ben Goldacre on the use of RCTs as a key methodology in educational research (Goldacre 2013). Goldacre, medical physician, academic and journalist, had contributed already to a published paper 'Test, Learn, Adapt', which set out an argument for the use of RCTs as a basis for social policy across the public service (Haynes et al., 2012).

In *Building Evidence into Education* Goldacre outlined key arguments for teachers being engaged themselves in RCTs when he said:

> I think there is a huge prize waiting to be claimed by teachers. By collecting better evidence of what works best, and establishing a culture where this evidence is used as a matter of routine, we can improve outcomes for children, and increase professional independence.
>
> *Goldacre, 2013, p. 7*

This argument particularly attracted us in that it seemed to be a possible way forward for providing additional evidence for the impact of the work being done in the TLCs. In addition, Goldacre clearly saw RCTs as a tool to empower teachers:

> Firstly, evidence based practice isn't about telling teachers what to do: in fact, quite the opposite. This is about empowering teachers, and setting a profession free from governments, ministers and civil servants who are often overly keen on sending out edicts, insisting that their new idea is the best in town. Nobody in government would tell a doctor what to prescribe, but we all expect doctors to be able to make informed decisions about which treatment is best, using the best currently available evidence. I think teachers could one day be in the same position.
>
> *Goldacre, 2013, p. 7*

More recently the rationale for using RCTs have continued, specifically in relation to the Closing the Gap project in a book on the programme, *Mobilising Teacher Researchers* (Childs and Menter, 2018). Higgins (2018) and Connelly (2018) both recognise that, RCTs have a particular place in educational research and they certainly do not dismiss more qualitative approaches. Higgins (2018), for example, sees them 'as a necessary but not sufficient research design for drawing conclusions about effective educational practice' (p. 97). He goes on to use a toolbox metaphor for their use:

> I see the different types of educational research methods as a toolbox which needs to be matched to a particular educational inquiry question. Randomised experimental trials have a particular function and are best suited to questions of causal impact – was approach X responsible for effect Y?
>
> *Higgins, 2018, p. 97*

Connelly (2018) agrees and then nicely distils out the contribution RCT methodology can make which complements more qualitative methods:

In this sense, if RCTs are the 'gold standard' for determining whether an intervention has had an effect, then qualitative methods – and particularly in-depth ethnographic case studies – are the 'gold standard' for helping us understand causal mechanisms and processes and thus for understanding why

Connelly, 2018, p. 199

We saw too that RCTs offered us another tool for enriching the research in the TLCs in addition to the qualitative approaches we have previously used.

At the time we became part of the Closing the Gap:Test and Learn national trial RCTs were already a part of the educational research landscape. For example, The Education Endowment Fund (EEF) and the National College for Teaching and Leadership (NCTL) had both run large-scale trials where RCTs were managed by academic researchers. The EEF was established in 2011 using funds provided by the Department for Education (DfE), directed through the Sutton Trust, and had a focus on:

supporting projects that show promising evidence of having a measurable impact on attainment or a directly related outcome. We are interested in testing projects' effectiveness through robust independent evaluations, where appropriate as randomised controlled trials. If they are shown to have an impact, they should be able to be replicated and scaled up to improve outcomes for other disadvantaged pupils.

23.06.15: https://educationendowmentfoundation.org.uk/apply-for-funding/

However, Closing the Gap: Test and Learn went one step further than the EEF and built in collaborative work on RCTs with schools and school teachers 'to trial multiple interventions simultaneously using a wholly collaborative approach across a large number of schools'(Churches, 2016, p. 10).

The seven interventions chosen for the national trial were:

- 1stClass@Number (1stClass)
- Achievement for All (AfA)
- Growth Mindsets
- Inference training
- Numicon intervention programme (NIP)
- Research lesson study (RLS)
- Response to intervention (breakthroughs in literacy) (RTI).

Collaborative RCTs were then conducted to evaluate these interventions and we took part initially in the national RCT trial for the intervention, Growth Mindsets, which we briefly describe below.

However, we were also aware that the use of RCTs in education was not uncontroversial and there are a number of key dissenting voices who question the use of RCTs in educational research. For example, Pring (2000) and Biesta (2010) question whether the use of RCTs in medicine can have similar parallels in educational research. Biesta (2010) in particular argues that education is a very different human process from medicine and that any analogy with education may be a very misleading one. Lingard and Gale (2010) and Gale (2018) worry that RCTs will become the gold standard for educational research and push other forms of interpretation and inquiry to one side despite the views offered by Higgins (2018) and Connelly (2018) above. Indeed the concerns of Lingard and Gale (2010) are grounded in the way RCTs have been adopted in the USA:

> For example, as Jean Anyon (2009) has recently pointed out, the Bush government in the USA attempted to construct 'empirically randomised control trials' as the 'gold standard' for assessing educational research and for evaluating all research applications and failed to recognise the significance of theory to social explanation in educational research.
>
> *p. 33*

Gale (2018) also has many other concerns which resonate with those of Pring and Biesta. In particular he questions again whether RCTs, used in the physical world of medicine, really can be used in the social world of education:

> RCTs do not regard the physical and the social as different worlds … and favour a particular view of reality – which is 'out there' to be discovered (by particular methods of discovery) – of what things are and how they are related (e.g. Hammersley, 2013).
>
> *p. 211*

In this the social world Gale argues that RCTs assume that, like the physical world, students do not have a mind of their own and 'when they are exposed to the same circumstances they are presumed to respond in the same ways' (p. 212). However, Gale argues that, unlike the physical world, 'people have a mind of their own (see Taylor 2002 on predictability, changing self-understandings, etc.), which means they can and do act in ways that are unexpected, although not always' (p. 212). Finally, Gale is also concerned that there are simply too many contextual factors to take account of in schools. As a result he argues that any significant change in achievement ascribed to an intervention is 'a leap of faith of elephant proportions' given the numerous contextual factors which could also account for these changes (p. 230).

Whilst we are aware of these debates our main motive for being involved in the Closing the Gap: Test and Learn project was to extend and enrich our experience of research methodologies, akin to Higgins' (2018) toolbox analogy. However, in response to Gale's concerns we perceived that, as teachers on the ground, we knew our students very well as individuals. As a result we are very well attuned to the contextual factors in our schools and classrooms and could, as a result, mitigate some of Gale's concerns. We will come back and reflect later in the chapter on these issues.

3.2 Growth Mindsets – the national trial

As said, it was perhaps the commitment to research-informed practice fostered and sustained in the TLCs and, in addition, our concerns about how to measure the impact of educational interventions effectively that led to our initial involvement in the nationwide Closing the Gap: Test and Learn project. Growth Mindsets is a programme developed from the work of Carol Dweck based around the following ideas outlined by Dweck (2015) herself:

> We found that students' mindsets—how they perceive their abilities—played a key role in their motivation and achievement, and we found that if we changed students' mindsets, we could boost their achievement. More precisely, students who believed their intelligence could be developed (a growth mindset) outperformed those who believed their intelligence was fixed (a fixed mindset). And when students learned through a structured program that they could 'grow their brains' and increase their intellectual abilities, they did better. Finally, we found that having children focus on the process that leads to learning (like hard work or trying new strategies) could foster a growth mindset and its benefits.
>
> *p. 24*

The large nationwide trial that was part of the Closing the Gap: Test and Learn project was designed to assess the impact of a school wide 'mindsets project' on students. It compared the impact of mindsets training on students formally identified as disadvantaged (pupil premium students[6]) with the impact on students not identified as meeting the criteria for pupil premium.

3.2 Growth Mindsets – our own small-scale RCT

As well as being involved in the nationwide trial of Growth Mindsets we also conducted our own small-scale RCT on Growth Mindsets as a result of our involvement in the Early Adopter programme which grew out of the Closing the Gap: Test and Learn project. Churches, Hall and Higgins (2018) describe how the Early Adopter programme emerged from the main project:

> The Early Adopter programme developed from four half-day training modules delivered at Research Development Networking Events over the course of the programme. Although these sessions were initially only intended as a means of developing teacher's understanding of experimental research (including RCTs), the significance of the events rapidly became clear. Almost immediately after the first few events, Teaching School began to

use the materials and try out experimental forms of design research. In turn, interest in the practical use of the materials increased considerably during the first year of the programme resulting in requests for funding from some schools.

p. 114

We were one of these schools and the National College for Teaching and Leadership (NCTL) allocated £2,000 grants for us to complete a study that looked at the impact of mindset training in the context of our school. At the time we conducted our small-scale RCT the results from the national trial had not yet been published so we were unaware that these would show that, at a nationwide level, current school practice (the control condition) was better than the intervention. In fact, when we began our small-scale RCT on Growth Mindsets before the national results were published there were early indications that mindset training was beneficial for disadvantaged students. Indeed, to support this, Dweck's (2016) own work could be interpreted as suggesting that some students of high attainment are unwilling to challenge themselves because they do not wish to fail and thus they are resistant to developing a growth mindset and so mindset training may indeed be more beneficial for lower attainers. These arguments, coupled with the fact that in our school context most disadvantaged children on free school meals are of lower prior attainment, led to the decision to investigate whether children of lower prior attainment were more likely to move towards a growth mindset after mindset training than higher attaining students. Therefore, the small-scale RCT, which we designed, assessed the impact of mindsets training on Year 7 (aged 11–12) students drawn from different attainment bands according to prior attainment. Using a quasi-experimental design and existing pre and post test data, this study investigated whether children of lower prior attainment gained more benefit from experience designed to foster a 'growth' mindset than higher attaining students. The dependent variable of prior attainment was operationalised as the Key Stage 2 (8–11-year-olds) English National Curriculum Levels of Attainment. Table 9.1 below summarises these levels expected for Key Stages 1, 2 and 3.

TABLE 9.1 Key stages and levels of attainment for the English National Curriculum

Key stage	Age range	Range of levels	Expected attainment at the end of the key stage
1	5–7 (Year groups 1–2)	1–3	2
2	2–5 (Y groups 3–6)	2–5	4
3	3–7 (Year groups 7–9)	3–7	5/6

To achieve further differentiation levels were further subdivided into a, b and c. So, for example within level 4 there are sublevels 4a, 4b and 4c, with level 4a being the highest sublevel. Students in Year 6, in primary schools, sit national Standard Assessment Tasks (SATs) which assign levels at the end of Year 6. We used the results of these tests as the prior attainment levels of the Year 7 students involved in the RCT and designated levels 5a and 5b as high prior attainment and 4a, 4b and 4c as low prior attainment. Students with a prior attainment of 5c were excluded to create a clear difference between the groups.

All students had been tested on their first day in school using the test designed by Portsmouth University as part of the CTG project which was a 15 item test (with a Likert scale) which assessed the extent to which each student had a growth mindset. The school then ran six sessions of mindset training in humanities lessons for the Year 7 students and, after a break of a further six weeks, the test was run again. The high prior attainment group included all 33 students for whom we had complete sets of data. For each of these students a matched student of lower prior attainment was selected from the lower prior attainment cohort. Matching used the criteria of gender and primary school attended. A paired student was then chosen at random to create the sample for the lower prior attainment group.

A Wilcoxon signed-rank test (one tailed) indicated no significant difference ($p=0.441$) in the impact of mindsets training on students of lower prior attainment when compared with students of higher prior attainment. The effect size indicates ($r=-0.009$) that the impact of mindsets training was similar for both groups. As there was no significant difference between the growth in mindsets between high and lower attaining students, though we had expected a difference, the research described above made a considerable contribution to a decision to continue with this intervention for all students as they went forward into Year 8, as well as to repeat the intervention with Year 7 in the following year.

Running the intervention with this new Year 7, we became aware of how much work had been done on mindsets with this cohort in their primary schools. One of the advantages of school-based research is sensitivity to a changing context and a questioning of whether existing research conclusions still hold true. Didau (2015) perhaps would argue that professional judgement should suffice, if we suspect that it is no longer working then we should abandon the project. We would argue that one of the benefits of small-scale research is that skim of objectivity which it brings to professional judgement. Following from reading Jones' (2015) blog on 'humble inquiry', Christina coined the term 'humble research' in our use of RCTs – teachers trying to minimise bias and preconception and genuinely (though perhaps not expertly) discover what is going on in classrooms and schools. As Jones suggests, we need to look at a range of evidence to inform improving learning in our classrooms and for us 'humble research' continues to be part of the mix. So despite the criticisms outlined above of RCTs we see these as part of a range of evidence on which we can draw as professionals to make judgements about practice as both Connelly (2018) and Higgins (2018) would agree.

3.3 Dedicated Improvement and Reflection Time (DIRT) – a small-scale school-based RCT

As a result of our involvement in the Early Adopter programme we were also able to conduct a very small-scale RCT that looked at the impact of giving Dedicated Improvement and Reflection Time (DIRT) when KS5 students (16–18 years old) had written feedback that they could apply to develop their work further. A within-subjects design with post-test only was used, the independent variable (DIRT) being operationalised by creating two conditions:

> IV level 1 – when work was returned students were encouraged to work out the meanings of the marking codes (control condition)
> IV level 2 – when work was returned students had to work out the meaning of the marking codes on their work and then re-write a paragraph so that it demonstrated a higher level of skill (experimental condition)

Undoubtedly, one of the advantages of completing a RCT in a classroom con-text is the level of reflection and planning for learning that it encourages. The DIRT research involved designing a comparable and reasonably objective method to provide feedback on Advanced Level[7] written work. With 30 years' experience of Advanced Level sociology, the second author learned a lot from analysing 90 pieces of written work to a standard format, not least that many answers looked superficially good but lacked thorough explanation. Two groups studying Advance Subsidiary Level sociology took part in the study. The groups contained a similar balance of predominately female students and were of similar prior attainment, as measured by General Certificate in Secondary Education (GCSE) scores. In total, 24 students completed all of the tasks in the study and therefore had results that could be included.

Five lessons were planned for the study and delivered to both groups in the same way by the same teacher, as shown in Table 9.2 below.

Two scores were produced for each student using exam board criteria and these were ranked to create post-test ordinal data with 1 as the best piece of work. The first score was for a piece of work completed when they had received only written feedback on the previous work (task 3 for teaching group 1 and task 2 for teaching group 2). The second score was for a piece of work completed when they had received written feedback and DIRT after their previous piece of work (task three for teaching group 1 and task two for teaching group 2).

As long as teachers apply the concept of 'fair test' and constantly evaluate their work, studies like this are often relatively straightforward to design. However, there are some issues and challenges. Firstly, there are compromises to be made frequently in the sample size against a totally matched experience for the control and experi-mental group. Specifically in this case the need to use a within subject design here for sample size, did lead to compromise and acceptance of the fact that the group that experienced DIRT after the first task may have been advantaged with both

TABLE 9.2 Organisation of lessons and provision of DIRT for each teaching group

Teaching Group 1	Teaching group 2
Lesson 1 – Students were given guidance on completing a 'methods in context' (mic) question and then set task one (completing a mic question)	Lesson 1 – Students were given guidance on completing a 'methods in context' (mic) question and then set task one (completing a mic question)
Lesson 2 – This answer was returned during the following lesson with each paragraph coded so students could identify the quality of the content and the range and sophistication of the skills demonstrated. Group 1 was given DIRT time to follow up by writing an improved version of one of their paragraphs.	Lesson 2 – This answer was returned during the following lesson with each paragraph coded so students could identify the quality of the content and the range and sophistication of the skills demonstrated. Group 2 was not given DIRT time but asked to work out how the codes applied to their paragraphs.
Lesson 3 – set task two (another mic question)	Lesson 3 – set task two (another mic question)
Lesson 4 – feedback no dirt	Lesson 4 – feedback with dirt
Lesson 5 – set task three (another mic question)	Lesson 5 – set task three (another mic question)

tasks 2 and 3. Secondly, the study also had to fit within the normal teaching scheme of work and could not involve more than five hours of teaching time so options for design were limited. Thirdly, while it is relatively easy to understand how to design a study, the statistical analysis of the results is a more technical proposition and it was here, for us, that the expertise of a colleague from EDT (who ran the training events for the early adopters part of the Closing the Gap project) and the macro[8] that was produced to complete the statistical analysis were invaluable.

However, the learning from this study was much greater than the statistical outcomes might suggest. For 10 hours, the first author taught classes knowing that she was formally measuring the impact of her work. She was sure the heightened awareness led to her noticing more and reflecting more on the impact she was having on individuals. The students for whom DIRT was not working seemed suddenly more noticeable. After this study, the second author came to watch a lesson where DIRT time was again being used to see if she could observe the impact on individuals. As is frequently the case, it proved very difficult to identify learning happening by watching students at work. Indeed one of the key pieces of professional learning that occurred as part of this project was more focused and effective observation as it raised the issue of whether learning within the lesson can ever be truly visible. One result of this is that teachers were offered the opportunity to bring post lesson observation student work to the lesson observation discussion. It has also opened up a discussion in school with those who observe lessons to consider whether they are predisposed to decide learning has happened when the observed teacher delivers a lesson in a way the observer prefers.

However, as mentioned above we were aware of some potential ethical issues in this study. Fancourt (2018) reflects on the ethical issues raised with the use of control group in the Closing the Gap: Test and Learn project and how this was resolved in that study:

> This was addressed in the early training rounds by drawing on a medical analogy, and particularly highlighting that the control group schools were not conceived to be 'doing nothing', instead they were entitled and indeed encouraged to do as much as they could for their pupils, acting on their own professional judgement: the interventions needed to be better than the schools could provide themselves.
>
> *p. 163*

In addition, because we were uncomfortable with the potential ethics of doing RCTs in school, we decided to fully debrief the students. They were fascinated by the process that we had gone through and keen to offer their view of DIRT and its impact. Their feedback was far more incisive and relevant than the response normally gained from a student survey. They raised issues such as individual differences in reactions to be asked to redraft work during DIRT time. It was clear that some students, though keen to take on board feedback on how to improve their work, would be much more willing to work on a new task than go back to improve a task already completed. The RCT attempts to control variables and look at the impact of one input and discussion with students raised the issue of the multitude of confounding variables affecting any learning situation, and is a key issue identified earlier by Gale (2018).

Having listened to the students, reflected on observations and applied an objective measure very carefully, the feeling was that the impact of DIRT was quite variable. Some students made considerable progress after having the opportunity to apply feedback but for others the gains were less obvious. This does support Gale's (2018) comments that RCTs make the assumptions that students, 'when they are exposed to the same circumstances they are presumed to respond in the same ways' (p. 212). The issue here for us is that, because we are conducting RCTs in our own context, we can also draw on more qualitative and contextual evidence on which to make judgements about practice. It is also important, however, to acknowledge that, without the RCT, professional judgement would have been considerably less informed and probably wrong because, like many teachers innovating in the classroom, we might tend to think new things are working. The RCT helped us understand something of the complexity of the learning process and, hopefully, added sophistication to the way we think about work with students.

While, initially at least, the DIRT study was one teacher using research as a tool to reflect on her own teaching, the mindsets RCT was designed to assess whether an intervention being used for all Year 7 students should instead focus on a particular cohort. It was interesting to reflect on the way in which these studies had an initial impact – one focusing down and looking at classroom practice in minute detail, the other at more general patterns across a year group. However, both studies, in different ways, impacted on the systems and policies of the school. We would certainly agree with Childs and Menter (2018) when they say that teachers' collaborative involvement in RCTs has had the following benefits for the school:

> Furthermore, if teachers are involved in the collaborative way Connelly advocates above, or indeed go further to design and carry out RCTs themselves, then there is opportunity for them to see, at first hand, the methodological and ethical challenges RCTs present. RCTs are now a part of the research landscape and it could be argued that teachers can only be critical and aware of their strengths and limitations if they are involved in their design and implementation.
>
> *p. 231*

4. TLCs and RCTs into the future

The DIRT research was built back into the TLC structure with a research and development group designing similar classroom-based projects. By this stage we were deliberately introducing less experienced staff to running TLCs to try to broaden both the skills of our less experienced leaders and broaden the range of staff experiencing the deeper levels of commitment and learning that we knew leading a TLC offered. In 2015 we returned to look at the impact of interdepartmental TLCs which were looking at 'Life Beyond Levels'[9], Citizenship, Outdoor Learning, 'Sticky Learning' (developing students' long-term memory), Flipped Learning, Coaching, and Research Using IRIS.[10] The evaluation was done at the beginning of a staff meeting when those present were asked to provide information about what they had done or learned as a direct result of being a member of a TLC this year. They were also asked to describe anything they had planned for the future that built on the work of the TLC. Those who had led the TLC groups were asked not to complete a return as we knew from previous research that those who run TLCs learn a great deal from the process and apply this learning in their own teaching and leadership roles.

There were 51 returns, meaning that feedback from about 70 per cent of the membership of TLC groups was analysed. A representative sample of the staff who attended TLC groups attended the staff meeting. Analysis of the responses showed that more than half of the respondents identified an impact that might be judged as significant as teachers felt that had moved beyond experimenting with new ideas and made structural change in the organisation of learning. Those working on 'Life Beyond Levels' identified changes to their practice including:

- re-designing feedback to students about progress/levels;

- using SOLO (Structured of Observed Learning Outcomes) to plan KS3/KS5 Scheme Of Work; and
- developing resources for Year 8 and Year 10 which focus on SOLO in preparation for assessment.

Staff working on 'Sticky Learning' identified they had changed the way they revise with students; the way they set homework and the way in which they were assessing work. At the time we believed these examples showed an impact on the organisation of learning. The TLCs that worked on coaching, research and using IRIS were perceived not to have the potential to have this sort of significant impact on the organisation of learning. However, staff identified impacts such as growing in confidence, working more efficiently and already coaching two individuals. All those involved with IRIS suggested they would continue to use a system like this to analyse their teaching and members of the research group identified impact on work for next year and planned to undertake further research.

It was interesting to compare data from this survey with our previous work in TLCs as, for the first time, this survey suggests that most TLCs were having a significant impact on the way colleagues reflected on learning and the way they planned and organised programmes. The evidence base that the TLCs attempt to develop was supporting substantial actions that should improve progress.

Our conclusions at this point were that:

- the data suggested that a comparatively small commitment of time (five x 50 minute sessions) was having a real impact on working practice for most staff;
- staff were learning about the evidence base or developing their skills in ways that they saw as improving learning; and
- there may be a small group of staff who need a more directed approach to encourage them to apply their learning, but for most staff, there was evidence to justify continuing to build on the TLC approach.

2015 also saw us share the work of the TLCs and other research more widely via the QKSLearning blog which had a regular readership of at least 60 staff. By the summer of 2015 our thinking had got to the place where we saw the value of research but recognised that it needed to be used with school data and with institutional knowledge. Listening to Stephen Tierney at ResearchEd Scotland and reading his subsequent blog[11] struck a chord with us when he concluded:

> improving teaching is a complex process in which research, data, feedback and experience all have a part to play. It is the integration of these four aces that leads to a research, data, feedback and experience deeper wisdom at the root of an enriching school culture that leaders must take responsibility for building.

However, 2015 also saw the beginning of a period of massive change for the school and our own roles within it. This forced us to reflect on what had been achieved, to select elements for focus as we moved forward and fight for the aspects of an evidence base that we believed to be essential in a school facing difficult times. For much of 2015–16, we found ourselves challenged by change and fire-fighting organisational demands, clinging to our core values which included commitment to an evidence base, but unable to move forward in any meaningful way.

5. Concluding remarks

This chapter discussed two different types of interventions and two different approaches to evaluative research. The TLC programme, an intervention designed to improve student learning through more reflective teaching, was evaluated through a variety of research strategies: many of them qualitative.

The two classroom interventions (MINDSET and DIRT) used the RCT as the lead research approach. Our conclusions are about the value of the research approaches and the impact of the interventions.

Unfortunately we have not found the formula which has allowed research to become embedded and research informed practitioners to flourish. It took almost five years to embed and develop the TLC format to the extent where we could see it having an impact in most teachers' classrooms. It is a model which encourages committed staff to take responsibility for their own professional learning but it proved a difficult model to sustain with those less willing or able to commit to the ethos. We remain committed to a belief that a strong evidence base is essential, of which RCTs should form a part, as we moved to a more directive style of delivery for a short period in order to ensure a consistent message across the school in the short term. However, as we reflected on what we had achieved as we wrote this chapter we were reminded of the value of the TLC and that, teachers leading and committing to following up through changes in classroom practice, has a key impact in classrooms and on teachers' professional development. Therefore, we returned to a TLC based model in September 2017 and whilst an evidence base remains a given for all innovations, the new TLCs will have much clearer focus on improving areas of weakness within our organisation. A new group of leaders has been thinking about the issues surrounding adult learning and are keen to lead staff to consider the practical and theoretical issues around 'Closing the Gap: Test and Learn'; 'Stretch and Challenge'; 'Meaningful assessment' and 'Creating a Learning Culture'. The work we have done has informed a new approach to whole school planning. Our School Development Plan now identifies areas of focus; the evidence base to be used to evaluate impact and the timeframe in which impact will be measured. Whilst this approach is embryonic, we are hopeful that it will provide a blueprint that will help leaders reflect on the impact their actions have on the organisation. We know that we cannot assume that this will happen and will continue to evaluate its impact every step of the way. The work on mindsets is embedded and is part of the ethos of the school. Feedback and DIRT is an area of continued focus.

Sadly, we have done no further work with RCTs. This partly reflects our changing roles in our organisation but also, on reflection, flaws in the way that we tried to develop the research agenda in school. The statistics and scientific design of RCTs are not immediately accessible to many teachers and the expert support we had through Closing the Gap: Test and Learn is difficult to replicate in a busy school environment. It worked while we championed and organised the projects but the steps to getting others to follow our path were too steep. Our experience is mirrored in the national frame. Without a Ministry of Education to champion and fund expertise, RCTs for education seems to be quietly disappearing from our agenda at least. Goldacre (2013), Higgins (2018) and Connelly (2018) have made clear that RCTs are not the only way to research but are an approach with potential to trigger real progress in education and our experience supports his view. The RCT is perhaps one way as close as we can get to objective evidence in education and, used in association with subjective insight from all participants, and alongside informed professional judgement, our own contextual knowledge and school data, has the potential to offer a base where decision making in school can be appropriately justified. The work that we did stimulated much thought and has been a continuing influence on our practice.

Notes

1 The use of 'we' in this paper this refers to the first two authors. The role of the third author was in helping with the reflective process and putting the research in a wider research context.

2 ResearchEd is an organisation in the UK whose goal 'is to bridge the gap between research and practice in education. Researchers, teachers, and policy makers come together for a day of information-sharing and myth-busting' (https://researched.org.uk/about/how-it-works/).

3 The national strategies was a change management programme in education from 1997–2011. The programme was run by a national team of experts and a regional expert who worked with local authorities in providing training, support and professional development to schools and settings.

4 Osirus educational is an independent training provider for teachers in the UK.

5 Joeybagstock.wordpress.com/2016/04/09/evaluating-cpd-hard-but-not-impossible/, accessed 31 January 2017.

6 The pupil premium scheme began in 2011 by the then UK government. The pupil premium is a sum of money given to schools each year by the government to improve the attainment of disadvantaged children from low income families where research has shown that these students perform less well at school than their peers. Schools are given a pupil premium for children who have qualified for free school meals at any point in the previous six years and children who are 'looked after' and under local authority care for more than one day.

7 Advanced subsidiary and Advanced levels are qualifications taken by students in England at age 17 and 18 respectively. General Certificate in Secondary Education (GCSE) examinations are normally taken by students at age 16.

8 The macro was designed by the Closing the Gap: Test and Learn team for the school in the Early Adopter programme and consisted of an excel spreadsheet where the teachers had to answer a series of questions about the data they had collected. The macro then directed the teachers to an appropriate statistical test to perform on this data.

9 'Life Beyond Levels' refers to the removal of attainment levels in the English National Curriculum and the need for teachers to think about new ways to assess pupils without levels.

10 IRIS Connect is a system designed to facilitate the professional development of teachers using video and audio recordings to enable teacher reflection and collaboration.

11 Leadinglearner.me/2015/08/29/four-aces-for-improving-the-quality-of-teaching-redscot/, accessed 23 April 2017.

References

Biesta, G. (2010) *Good Education in an Age of Measurement*. Colorado: Paradigm.

Black, P. & Wiliam, D. (1998) Inside the BlackBox: Raising Standards Through Classroom Assessment. *Phi Delta Kappan*, 80(2), 139–144.

Childs, A. & Menter I. (2018) *Mobilising Teacher Researchers: Challenging Educational Inequality*. Abingdon, Oxon: Routledge.

Churches, R. (2016) *Closing the Gap: Test and Learn: Research Report*. London: Department for Education/National College for Teaching and Leadership. Available online: www.gov.uk/government/publications/closing-the-gap-test-and-learn (accessed 24 July 2017).

Churches, R., Hall, R. & Higgins, S. (2018) The potential of teacher randomised control trials in education research. In A. Childs & I. Menter (Eds.), *Mobilising Teacher Researchers: Challenging Educational Inequality* (pp. 113–140). Abingdon, Oxon: Routledge.

Connelly, P. (2018) The future promise of RCTs in education: some reflections on the Closing the Gap project. In A. Childs & I. Menter (Eds.), *Mobilising Teacher Researchers: Challenging Educational Inequality* (pp. 197–206). Abingdon, Oxon: Routledge.

Didau, D. (2015) Do all good ideas need to be researched? (blog) www.learningspy.co.uk/research/should-good-ideas-be-researched/ (accessed 14 May 2015).

Dweck, C.S. (2015) Carol Dweck Revisits the 'Growth Mindset'. *Education Week*, 35(5), 24.

Dweck, C.S. (2016) *Self-Theories: Their Role in Motivation, Personality, and Development*. Abingdon, Oxon: Routledge.

Fancourt, N. (2018) Research ethics in Closing the Gap: equipoise in randomised control trials in education. In A. Childs & I. Menter (Eds.), *Mobilising Teacher Researchers: Challenging Educational Inequality* (pp. 159–174). Abingdon, Oxon: Routledge.

Fullan, M.G. (1993) Why teachers must become change agents. *Educational Leadership*, 50(6), 1–13.

Gale, T. (2018) What's not to like about RCTs in education. In A. Childs & I. Menter (Eds.), *Mobilising Teacher Researchers: Challenging Educational Inequality* (pp. 207–223). Abingdon, Oxon: Routledge.

Goldacre, B. (2013) *Building Evidence into Education*. Available online: http://aka.education.gov.uk/inthenews/a00222740/building-evidence-into-education

Guskey, T. R. (2000) *Evaluating Professional Development*. Thousand Oaks, CA: Corwin.

Higgins, S. (2018) Room in the toolbox? The place of randomised control trials in educational research. In A. Childs & I. Menter (Eds.), *Mobilising Teacher Researchers: Challenging Educational Inequality* (pp. 113–140). Abingdon, Oxon: Routledge.

Jones, G. (2015) The School Research Lead – Evidence Informed Practice and Humble Inquiry (blog) http://evidencebasededucationalleadership.blogspot.co.uk/ (accessed 17 May 2015).

Lingard, B. & Gale, T. (2010) Defining Educational Research: A Perspective of/on Presidential Addresses and the Australian Association for Research in Education. *The Australian Educational Researcher*, 37(1), 21–49.

Petty, G. (2009) *Evidence-based teaching: A Practical Approach*. Oxford: Oxford University Press.

Pring, R. (2000) *Philosophy of Educational Research*. London: Continuum.

Taylor, C. (2012) Understanding the other: a Gadamerian view on conceptual schemes. In J. Malpas, U. Arnswald & J. Kertscher (Eds.), *Gadamer's Century: Essays in Honor of Hans-Georg Gadamer* (pp. 279–297). Cambridge, MA: MIT Press.

Teacher Development Trust (2014) *Developing Great Teachers*. Available online: http://tdtrust. org/wp-content/uploads/2015/10/DGT-Summary.pdf (accessed 24 July 2017).

Wenger, E. Traynor, B. & Laat, M.De (2011) *Promoting and Assessing Value Creation in Communities and Networks: A Conceptual Framework*. The Netherlands: Ruud der Moor.

10

COMMENTARY

Classroom-based interventions in different subject areas: Sharing meaning across researchers and practitioners

Merrilyn Goos

This book offers a rich collection of accounts of classroom-based interventions in different subjects taught in UK secondary schools. In more traditional research, interventions are often defined as occurring outside the normal teaching context and therefore requiring an outside expert for their design and evaluation, typically using experimental or quasi-experimental approaches (e.g., Hattie, Biggs, & Purdie, 1996). In contrast, the classroom-based interventions described in this book were created and implemented by teachers in collaboration with academic researchers or teacher educators, and the term 'intervention' was interpreted simply to mean an action taken to improve a situation. This commentary chapter situates the intervention studies within wider debates about relationships between research and teaching, and uses the following questions as a framework for examining the studies' contribution to these debates:

(1) What is the nature of collaboration between academic researchers and teachers on classroom-based interventions?
(2) What kinds of knowledge are produced by such collaborations, and how is this knowledge shared and used?

Framing the debate: The (ir)relevance of educational research to classroom practice

Education research is frequently criticised for its lack of impact on classroom practice. Explanations for the apparent research–practice gap sometimes highlight the different processes used by researchers and teachers to improve educational practice. For example, Richardson (1994) suggested that, whereas formal research aims to contribute to an established and general knowledge base, the practical inquiry of teachers is focused on solving immediate day-to-day problems. The object of research, unlike in teaching, is not to solve problems but to create knowledge that helps us understand a problem (Labaree, 2003).

Referring to mathematics education, Wiliam and Lester (2008) take a more critical stance in arguing that educational research has failed to influence practice and policy because it has been more concerned with the pursuit of theoretical knowledge than 'moving people – teachers, teacher educators, school administrators, policy makers, etc. – to action' (p. 32). There are tensions here in what counts as knowledge: on the one hand, research promotes a view of knowledge as universal truth validated by appeal to scientific rationalism; on the other hand, teachers know that context matters and they justify knowledge claims by reference to personal experience in specific situations. Acknowledging the complexity and contextual contingencies of educational phenomena can help researchers understand why findings obtained in one situation don't always transfer to another. But it is not surprising that many teachers instead prefer to seek knowledge sources that offer immediate practical insights into what might work with their own students in their own contexts.

If educational research is perceived to have little relevance to classroom practice, then questions can also be raised about the place of research in teacher education and development. In the UK, the inquiry into the role of research in teacher education conducted by the British Educational Research Association (BERA) and the Royal Society for the Encouragement of the Arts, Manufacturing and Commerce (RSA) argued that self-improving education systems need teachers who are research literate and schools that are research-rich environments in which to work (BERA, 2014). The inquiry identified four main ways in which research could make a contribution to initial and continuing teacher education:

- First, the content of teacher education programmes may be informed by research-based knowledge and scholarship, emanating from a range of academic disciplines and epistemological traditions.
- Second, research can be used to inform the design and structure of teacher education programs.
- Third, teachers and teacher educators can be equipped to engage *with* and be discerning consumers *of* research.
- Fourth, teachers and teacher educators may be equipped to conduct their own research, individually and collectively, to investigate the impact of particular interventions or to explore the positive and negative effects of educational practice. (p. 11)

The third and fourth approaches are exemplified in the classroom interventions reported in this book: they imply that teachers and teacher educators need to be both research literate and research engaged. Developing a research-rich culture in schools and education systems is critical at the present time when the emergence of narrow, data-driven approaches to accountability could divert teachers' and school leaders' attention away from the deeper disciplinary affordances of educational research. These concerns are not unique to the UK; for example, Mills and Goos (2016) critiqued the assumed role of research in initial teacher education in Australia as being confined to informing the content and structure of programmes, with little evidence that teachers or teacher educators should be expected to engage with or be discerning consumers of research beyond analysing student achievement data in order to modify teaching strategies.

What is the nature of collaboration between academic researchers and teachers on classroom-based interventions?

The BERA/RSA report provides a powerful endorsement for teachers and teacher educators to engage in inquiry-oriented practice. But it is probably not feasible to expect that all teachers, throughout an entire education system, should develop research skills and conduct classroom-based inquiries on their own without the support of academic specialists. Research-rich school environments might be more likely fostered through collaborative partnerships between teachers and teacher educator-researchers, aimed at improving classroom practice – as argued by Molway, Mutton, Woore, and Porter in Chapter 3 of this volume. Yet one should not overlook the challenges of coordinating the different purposes, perspectives, and practices of these two communities in order to move 'towards synergy of scholarly and craft knowledge' (Ruthven & Goodchild, 2008, p. 561).

Collaborative activity with the aim of improving classroom practice and involving teachers and university researchers has been the focus of a number of initiatives internationally. A recent example from mathematics education is the survey on the topic of *teachers working and learning through collaboration* that was commissioned for the 13th International Congress on Mathematical Education (ICME-13). The Survey Team, comprising academic researchers from the UK, Italy, Canada, Argentina, Australia, Japan, and South Africa, identified 316 sources published from 2005–2015 in journals, conference proceedings, books, and handbooks. Sources were selected only if they reported on research in which collaboration was 'an *explicit and deliberate* part of the research design, and which explores, and explicitly reports on, the influence of the collaboration with respect to the teachers' learning and/or working practices' (Robutti et al., 2016, original emphasis). Despite efforts by the ICME-13 Survey Team to locate and include non-academic sources, the materials discovered were overwhelmingly research reports in which the collaborations were initiated and/or led by academic researchers rather than teachers. As a result, teachers' voices were largely missing (Jaworski et al., 2017). In contrast, the chapters in this volume largely give priority to teachers' own accounts as practitioner researchers conducting interventions in their own classrooms, albeit in collaboration with an academic colleague.

The ICME-13 survey generated a rich and diverse picture of collaborative classroom-based research, not only in terms of the theories and methodologies informing the studies and the impact on teachers' knowledge, thinking, and practices, but also of collaborative ways of working and how these were created.

Fundamental characteristics of these collaborations included cycles of activity and the activation of reflection by colleagues working with teachers – such as teacher educators, mentors, supervisors, or critical friends. Expert figures were found to serve as reference models for teachers, for example, by introducing theoretical lenses, observing the teachers' practices, and sharing their interpretations of these practices to stimulate reflection and subsequent planning of tasks and lessons. The first of these characteristics – cycles of activity – was evident in many of the studies reported in this volume that adopted an action research methodology (e.g., Burn, Carrier, and Fielding in Chapter 7; Haydon and Childs in Chapter 4; Molway et al. in Chapter 3). The second characteristic, which relates to the role of the 'other', more expert figure, was less often addressed by the authors of these chapters. An example can be seen in the chapter by Haydon and Childs (Chapter 4), who explicitly reflected on their own learning as teacher-researcher and university academic during their collaborative study. These authors identified the complementary expertise they initially brought to the research enterprise – the teacher's deep contextual knowledge of the students and school and the academic's knowledge of research literature and methods. They also noted that their research goals, initially focused on developing the teacher's practice, evolved over time towards mutual growth of their understanding and expertise. A different approach is illustrated in the chapter by Samuel, Watson, and Childs (Chapter 9). Here, the first two authors were teacher-researchers participating in a nationwide project while the third author, a university-based education researcher, joined the writing team later to support the teachers in reflecting on the broader implications of their work. These two examples provide tantalising glimpses of the nature of research collaborations between teachers and university academics, and yet in most of the studies in this book the roles of these participants remains largely unexamined. This would be a fruitful area for further inquiry, as an understanding of the rationales, goals, and roles for collaborative work appears to be crucial to the success of projects in which academic researchers and teachers work together (Robutti et al., 2016; see also Goos & Geiger, 2006; Geiger & Goos, 2006, for examples of such inquiry).

To explore the collaboration between academic researchers and teachers who conducted the classroom-based interventions documented in this volume, I will refer to the analytical framework I previously developed for this purpose (Goos, 2013). The framework is a synthesis of the questions and issues that were identified by participants of various working groups on the topic of *Teachers researching with university academics* that met during conferences of the International Group for the Psychology of Mathematics Education from 2005–2009. The dimensions of the framework are summarised in Table 10.1.

The first dimension, *beginning the partnership*, asks how and why each participant enters into the relationship and who initiates the research. The most traditional form of educational research involves university-based researchers recruiting teachers into projects that have already been planned. Less commonly, a teacher might seek out a university-based researcher to support a classroom-based intervention. The third category refers to a situation where teachers are encouraged or

TABLE 10.1 Framework for analysing researcher–teacher relationships

Beginning the partnership	Participants	Purposes of the research
Why? • Researcher motivation • Teacher motivation How? • Researcher seeks teacher • Teacher seeks researcher • Education system selects participants	Roles & expectations Language and communication of findings Trust/relationships Communities and asymmetric needs	Topic (who chooses?) Research questions (whose?) Benefits (for whom?)

required to participate in a research project by some part of an education system (at the level of school, district, or state).

The second and third dimensions are intended to capture how the *participants* will interact and the *purposes* of the research. These characteristics are consistent with Wenger's (1998) ideas about communities of practice, and acknowledge that teachers and academic researchers are members of separate communities with intersecting interests but asymmetric needs (Malone, 2000). Participant roles may be separate (teacher or researcher) or shared (teacher–researcher), but there is value in negotiating role expectations at the start in order to build trust and mutual respect. Because the two communities create and validate knowledge in different ways, attention needs to be given to how, and to whom, the research findings will be communicated. The purposes of the research may differ according to who initiated the partnership, and this often influences who chooses the topic and research questions.

The studies reported in this volume are distinctive in that many were initiated by teachers working on problems of practice in their own classroom contexts, most often as part of a supervised Masters project (*teacher seeks researcher*). In these cases it was the teacher who influenced the purpose of the research by choosing the topic and contributing to the formulation of research questions. Sometimes the research was conducted in highly challenging situations, such as in the Brocklehust and Thompson chapter (Chapter 2) that reports on a study aiming to stimulate reluctant readers in English classes in a school that had received a negative government inspection report. Teacher-initiated inquiry may be more likely to be acceptable to a school in such difficult circumstances than research instigated by an outside 'expert'. Other instances of teacher-initiated research were motivated by a desire to experiment with professional learning communities across a school (e.g., Samuel, Watson, and Childs, Chapter 9), leading eventually to participation in a nationally funded scheme to undertake small-scale randomised control trials (a variant of *education system selects participants*).

The roles of teacher and researcher intersect in interesting ways in these chapters. While the academic supervisor of a Masters project has a proxy researcher role, providing guidance on literature, theory, and methodology, it is usually the teacher who collects and analyses the data from the classroom intervention. Thus the academic researcher maintains role separation and remains in the world of research, while the teacher-researcher crosses the boundary and merges these roles.

A particularly symmetrical form of role coordination appears in the chapter by Ingram, Andrews, Rudd, and Pitt (Chapter 6). In this study, although the participants were currently either school-based teachers or university-based teacher educator-researchers, all were experienced teachers with multiple previous roles in teaching, research, and teacher education. Members of this group shared a common interest in supporting students to develop mathematical talk. In order to maintain the equal status of partnerships between participants and to honour the different kinds of expertise that each person brought to the project, the academic researchers avoided telling the teachers about previous research findings and instead focused on building awareness of choice in teacher actions. Thus the teachers, with sensitive support from the academic researchers, found their own pathway towards new practices that were already well documented in research. This approach places a premium on relationships and trust (see the *Participants* dimension in Table 10.1), perhaps at the expense of explicitly fostering synergy between the distinctive practices and forms of knowledge of researchers and teachers.

The role of practitioner researcher is not specific to teachers, as teacher educators also combine research with practice when they undertake classroom interventions with their students. In the chapters that featured academic researchers in this dual role (Molway et al. Chapter 3; Taylor & Hillier Chapter 5; Firth & Strutt Chapter 8) the research was often multi-layered in that the primary intervention was conducted by the teacher educator in a university classroom, with a secondary intervention occurring (whether formally or informally) when pre-service teachers tried a similar approach with the students they were teaching at school. Questions about how and why this research partnership begins, and who benefits, have ethical implications for the power relationships between teacher educator and pre-service teachers. Adler et al. (2005) have suggested that in order to fulfill these dual roles teacher educators need to develop strategies for distancing themselves from what they are looking at, for example, by developing effective theoretical languages or subjecting their own practice to the scrutiny of colleagues in other institutions. By publishing their studies in this volume, the teacher educator authors are going some way towards developing a critical stance towards the research they conduct with their students.

What kinds of knowledge are produced by such collaborations, and how is this knowledge shared and used?

Ruthven and Goodchild (2008) have expressed concerns about practitioner research as lacking in rigour and contribution to what they describe as 'trustworthy public knowledge' (p. 580). They go on to claim that 'in a climate of externally-driven reform and public accountability, teacher research has tended to become uncritical, focused on effecting immediate classroom changes rather than considering fundamental educational rationales' (p. 580). There is little evidence of such an uncritical orientation in the studies reported in this volume, perhaps because it documents collaborative research conducted jointly by teachers and academics that interprets and addresses classroom problems through the lens of theory. Nevertheless, three issues seem pertinent to the question that frames this section: context, scale, and transferability.

Context

To close the gap between research and practice, Burkhardt and Schoenfeld (2003) argued for greater emphasis on classroom-based research in the development of research programs that seek to understand the role of contextual factors in teaching and learning. The interventions described in this volume are at the same time firmly grounded in local classroom contexts while addressing national problems related to curriculum or educational policy changes, or broader educational concerns that transcend the local or national context. In many studies a careful analysis of the context was crucial to understanding the problem, designing the intervention, and communicating the findings to an audience beyond the local environment. For example, Molway et al. (Chapter 3) provide extensive background on changes to assessment in the UK National Curriculum that left teachers with the responsibility for designing assessment frameworks when these had previously been prescribed. Less detailed, but still significant, was Taylor and Hillier's (Chapter 5) reference to the assessment context in GCSE examinations, where multiple choice questions do not require students to construct the kind of scientific explanations that have value within the discipline and that were the focus of their intervention. For Firth and Strutt in Chapter 8, the use of Teachers' Standards to accredit and regulate initial teacher education in the UK established the policy context for their intervention, which addressed the development of subject knowledge by pre-service geography teachers.

In many chapters there are also analyses of actual or potential connections between the context-embedded, discipline-specific intervention and educational issues of broader theoretical or disciplinary interest. For example, Molway et al. (Chapter 3) situate their study of formative assessment in modern foreign languages in the literature on assessment for learning, while Haydon and Childs (Chapter 4) draw on literature on student questions to design their intervention in a science classroom (which in turn resonates with studies of students' problem-posing in mathematics education; e.g., see Weber & Leikin, 2016). Similarly, the interventions reported by Taylor and Hillier (science), Ingram et al. (mathematics), and Burn et al. (history) sought to improve students' written or oral explanations and reasoning within their disciplinary contexts. While contextual factors mattered in each of these interventions, it should also be possible for readers to recognise the 'fundamental educational rationales' (Ruthven & Goodchild, 2008, p. 580) that underpin them.

Scale

The classroom interventions undertaken by authors in this volume were mostly small scale, sometimes involving only one class of students taught by a teacher-researcher. Timeframes for interventions were also frequently very short – sometimes lasting for only a few lessons – due to institutional or examination constraints that limited the time available. If classroom-based interventions are always restricted to these micro-inquiries it is difficult to see how they could enrich the stock of trustworthy public knowledge that moves people to action. But there are three ways in which this situation could be viewed differently.

First, the kind of knowledge generated by small-scale interventions is not only about 'what works' (or not), but also what can be learned from the research process. A striking example comes from the account of Samuel et al. of their school's experience of participating in a national scheme to undertake small-scale randomised control trials of classroom interventions (see Churches, 2016, for the full report of this initiative; and NCTL, 2016, for brief reports of some of the teacher-led micro-interventions aimed at improving feedback to students). Although their feedback intervention did not produce a statistically significant improvement in student attainment, the teachers involved in the study experienced substantial professional growth as a result of their sustained reflection and planning for the intervention. The teachers who led the research were later able to reflect on the flaws in the approach they used to develop their school-based research agenda, and achieved a new understanding of the place of RCT research in education. Authors of other chapters who experienced mixed results or practical constraints in their interventions reported a similar experience, resulting in improved understanding of the problem under investigation (e.g., Brocklehurst & Thompson in Chapter 2; Burn, Carrier and Fielding in Chapter 7).

Second, small-scale interventions focusing on just one group of students can incorporate elements of a larger investigation, as in the study reported by Haydon and Childs in Chapter 4. The intervention itself, focusing on development of students' questioning in one Year 9 science classroom, was informed by a survey targeting all 270 Year 9 students in the school to elicit their perceptions of the importance of questioning in science, the questioning environment in their science classrooms, and barriers to students asking questions. This is an example of movement along the micro-to-macro scale of research engagement proposed by the BERA/RSA report on *Research and the teaching profession* (BERA, 2014), that is, from 'informal small-scale class or group specific enquiries' to 'school or college-wide investigations' (p. 20). Within this framework, the small-scale RCT studies undertaken by Samuel et al. contribute to the kind of macro-research engagement described in the BERA/RSA report as 'participation in large-scale national studies'.

Third, teacher education interventions can grow in scale when they are replicated longitudinally over time with different cohorts, as in the university-based intervention reported by Taylor and Hillier in Chapter 5. Although the chapter reports only on data from the current cohort of pre-service teachers, the intervention is now in its sixth year and well embedded in the course. Thus there are opportunities here for more systematic research into the evolution and impact of the intervention with larger numbers of pre-service teachers.

Transferability

The research studies on classroom-based interventions presented in this volume offer theoretically informed solutions to problems of practice identified and experienced by the authors who are teachers and teacher educators. Do they then succeed in achieving synergy between scholarly knowledge and craft knowledge, as advocated by Ruthven and Goodchild (2008)? At one level, we might say the answer is *yes* because each intervention was grounded in educational theory and also empirically tested. But another way to frame this question is to ask how the resultant knowledge was, or could be, disseminated and with what intent and effect. Are the findings transferable to different contexts? Or are the particularities of the original research setting so unique that the interventions will only 'work' in the context for which they were designed? These are questions that were explicitly considered by the majority of chapter authors.

Many of the studies in this volume demonstrated that the knowledge generated by highly contextualised classroom-based interventions can be shared with others and adapted to different settings. For example, the chapters by Molway et al. and Haydon and Childs both referred to the teacher-researcher sharing their findings with colleagues in their school and also since moving to new schools, which led to the intervention strategies being taken up by other teachers – sometimes across a whole year level. While this is a very direct and personalised dissemination approach that is unlikely to achieve widespread impact on practice, Molway et al. (Chapter 3) argued that impact should not be judged only in terms of the number of people affected. Instead they contend that their intervention achieved real depth of impact, with profound and long-lasting changes in the knowledge, beliefs, and classroom practices of the participants. Teacher education provides another context for translation of practitioner research findings with potential for both breadth and depth of impact, as Haydon and Childs noted in Chapter 4. University-based teacher educators are therefore in a pivotal position, not only in supporting teachers' classroom-based intervention research, but also in bringing the findings of this research into their work with prospective teachers.

Another way to promote transfer of research findings is through journal publications and conference presentations – the staple dissemination strategy of academic researchers. Yet these are rarely accessed by teachers. However, an intriguing possibility is suggested by comparing the dissemination opportunities within different disciplines. Molway et al. (Chapter 3), writing about modern foreign languages education, note that many large- and small-scale intervention studies are conducted in the UK with most of the latter being undertaken by teachers in either initial teacher education or Masters projects. However, the discipline lacks a professional journal as an outlet for practitioner research. This contrasts with the situation in history education in the UK, as explained in the chapter by Burn, Carrier, and Fielding

(Chapter 7), where there are very few large-scale studies conducted by academic researchers but a long tradition of small-scale practitioner research disseminated through the professional journal, *Teaching History*. In the relative absence of funded academic research in history education, this journal has assumed a critical role in making practitioner research accessible and promoting rich and interconnected professional discourse in which teacher-researchers build on each other's work and test small-scale interventions across different contexts. Such an approach seems to offer a powerful means of contributing to both scholarly and craft knowledge, and opens up greater opportunities for the dissemination of practitioner research.

Revisiting the debate

The challenges of linking teaching and research to produce usable knowledge are well documented. While some would argue that the context-bound character of small-scale intervention studies renders them less likely to contribute to scholarly knowledge, others warn that research focusing too much on the pursuit of theoretical knowledge has no influence on educational practice and policy. This commentary chapter has attempted to navigate some pathways through the debates about relationships between research and teaching, drawing on the preceding chapters for examples and discussion points. The aim has been neither to make judgments about the value of scholarly knowledge versus craft knowledge, nor to arrive at prescriptive conclusions about how classroom-based interventions should be conducted, but instead to expose some of the issues faced by researchers and practitioners in sharing meaning across their respective worlds.

It is appropriate now to return to the debate on the apparent irrelevance of educational research to classroom practice with which I opened my commentary. The vivid, reflexive accounts within this book show how research studies mediated by practical and theoretical concerns can have impact as well as rigour. Thus it is clear that classroom-based interventions conducted by teachers, in collaboration with university academics, can indeed be successful in both 'moving people … to action' (Wiliam & Lester, 2008, p. 32) and contributing to 'trustworthy public knowledge' (Ruthven & Goodchild, 2008, p. 580).

References

Adler, J., Ball, D., Krainer, K., Lin, F-L., & Novotna, J. (2005). Reflections on an emerging field: Researching mathematics teacher education. *Educational Studies in Mathematics*, 60, 359–381.

British Educational Research Association (2014). *Research and the teaching profession: Building the capacity for a self-improving education system. Final report of the BERA-RSA Inquiry into the role of research in teacher education.* Retrieved 6 August 2017 from: www.bera.ac.uk/wp-content/uploads/2013/12/BERA-RSA-Research-Teaching-Profession-FULL-REPORT-for-web.pdf

Burkhardt, H., & Schoenfeld, A. (2003). Improving educational research: Toward a more useful, more influential, and better funded enterprise. *Educational Researcher*, 32(9), 3–14.

Churches, R. (2016). *Closing the gap: Test and learn. Research report winter 2016.* National College for Teaching and Leadership. Retrieved 8 August 2017 from http://wednesburyt eachingschoolalliance.co.uk/pdf/closing_the_gap_test_and_learn_full_report.pdf

Geiger, V., & Goos, M. (2006). Living in the gap: A tale of two different types of researchers. In P. Grootenboer, R. Zevenbergen, & M. Chinappan (Eds.), *Identities, Cultures and Learning Spaces* (Proceedings of the 29th annual conference of the Mathematics Education Research Group of Australasia, pp. 254–261). Adelaide: MERGA. Retrieved 8 August 2017 from www.merga.net.au/documents/RP272006.pdf

Goos, M. (2013). Researcher-teacher relationships and models for teaching development in mathematics education. *ZDM Mathematics Education,* 46(2), 189–200.

Goos, M., & Geiger, V. (2006). In search of practical wisdom: A conversation between researcher and teacher. *For the Learning of Mathematics,* 26(2), 37–39.

Hattie, J., Biggs, J., & Purdie, N. (1996). Effects of learning skills interventions on student learning: A meta-analysis. *Review of Educational Research,* 66, 99–136.

Jaworski, B., Chapman, O., Clark-Wilson, A., Cusi, A., Esteley, C., Goos, M., ... Robutti, O. (2017). Mathematics teachers working and learning through collaboration. In G. Kaiser (Ed.), *Proceedings of the 13th International Congress on Mathematical Education* (pp. 261–276). Springer Open. DOI 10.1007/978-3-319-62597-3_17

Labaree, D. (2003). The peculiar problems of preparing educational researchers. *Educational Researcher,* 32(4), 13–22.

Malone, J. (2000). Bridging the gap: A challenge for the dual community. In J. Bana & A. Chapman (Eds.), *Mathematics education beyond 2000* (Proceedings of the 23rd annual conference of the Mathematics Education Research Group of Australasia, pp. 27–36). Sydney: MERGA. Retrieved 7 August 2017 from www.merga.net.au/documents/Keynote_Malone_2000.pdf

Mills, M., & Goos, M. (2016). The place of research in teacher education? An analysis of the Australian Teacher Education Ministerial Advisory Group report 'Action now: Classroom ready teachers'. In M. Peters, B. Cowie, & I. Menter (Eds.), *A companion to research in teacher education* (pp. 637–650). Singapore: Springer Nature.

National College for Teaching and Leadership (2016). *Closing the gap: Test and learn. Teacher led randomized control trials – Feedback.* Retrieved 8 August 2017 from www.gov.uk/government/uploads/system/uploads/attachment_data/file/495902/Feedback_posters_FINAL.pdf

Richardson, V. (1994). Conducting research on practice. *Educational Researcher,* 23(5), 5–10.

Robutti, O., Cusi, A., Clark-Wilson, A., Jaworksi, B., Chapman, O., Esteley, C., ... Joubert, M. (2016). ICME international survey on teachers working and learning through collaboration. *ZDM Mathematics Education,* 48, 651–690.

Ruthven, K., & Goodchild, S. (2008). Linking research with teaching: Towards synergy of scholarly and craft knowledge. In L. D. English (Ed.), *Handbook of International Research in Mathematics Education* (2nd edn) (pp. 561–588), New York: Routledge.

Weber, K., & Leikin, R. (2016). Recent advances in research on problem solving and problem posing. In A. Gutierrez, G. Leder, & P. Boero (Eds.), *The Second Handbook of Research on the Psychology of Mathematics Education* (pp. 353–382). Rotterdam, The Netherlands: Sense Publishers.

Wenger, E. (1998). *Communities of Practice: Learning, meaning, and identity.* New York: Cambridge University Press.

Wiliam, D., & Lester, F. K., Jr. (2008). On the purpose of mathematics education research: Making productive contributions to policy and practice. In L. D. English (Ed.), *Handbook of International Research in Mathematics Education* (2nd edn) (pp. 32–48). New York: Routledge.

11

COMMENTARY

Interventions in education: origins, theoretical perspectives and challenges

Shirley Simon

Introduction

I have welcomed the opportunity to read and provide my own commentary on the chapters in this book. Having undertaken many research projects that involve some aspect of classroom intervention, I have been interested to note the participant researcher roles prominent in many chapters, and the value to professional learning that being involved in research affords. In particular, I have noted that where there is collaboration between colleagues, the impact of interventions and the professional learning gains are more marked. I begin this commentary with a review of how 'intervention' has been interpreted in this book, as the chapters serve to enlarge our ideas of what intervention might mean. I also look at how interventions arose – from contexts, issues and the motivation of participants to design and engage in some kind of enquiry, action research or experimental design. Of particular interest is the way in which interventions are informed by previous research and theory, insights gained from the different reports add weight to the value of research informed practice, however complex and multivariate the process of learning from an intervention might be. I also identify the kinds of challenges and barriers that have been experienced by those undertaking interventions, as there are some school-wide solutions that can help to overcome these challenges. Finally, I wish to highlight the importance of Masters level study, which brings together educational theory, previous research and personal motivation to bring about some desired change in teaching and learning.

What is an intervention?

As acknowledged in the introduction, the term 'intervention' has been used in different ways in research, mostly in the context of studies that involve some kind of pre and post testing. In this book, the guiding notion of intervention is taken from its use in medicine, where an intervention denotes 'action taken to improve a situation' (Stevenson and Lindberg, 2012), here the situation being classroom practice. Thus authors have interpreted 'action' and 'improve' in different ways according to theoretical perspectives that make meaning of the 'situation'. Some authors, for example, Molway et al. (Chapter 3) define their use of the term intervention, 'a conscious change in classroom practice aimed at improving learning and teaching', indicating that the term involves an assessment of outcomes to see whether the intervention has made a difference. I believe that small-scale studies which produce rich findings are valuable – in a volume such as this there is an opportunity to extend our understanding of classroom intervention and the definition of what it means.

In Chapter 4 a more conventional interpretation of intervention underpins the design of action research on student questioning undertaken by Haydon and Childs – as baseline data were sought regarding student questions, and follow-up investigation to see if gains were made post intervention. In Chapters 5 and 6 the intervention is more exploratory where new strategies are tried out, and the perceived impact of those strategies examined, though the approach taken was different in kind in each of these studies. The intervention undertaken by Taylor and Hillier (Chapter 5) focuses on a micro analysis of written and oral explanation in science, with feedback and discussion central to the intervention with both school science students and pre-service teachers. Ingram et al. (Chapter 6) expand the notion of intervention as a process of change through collaboration: 'our approach to intervention was not to offer specific approaches for teachers to enact, but rather to seek to expand the range of choices that were available to them through raising awareness of research findings'.

In Chapter 7, the teacher researcher intervention that is cited by Burn et al. takes the form of action research by a teacher studying for Masters level (M-level), the intervention changing as the impact of strategies was evaluated. A more conventional idea of 'intervention' is adopted in Chapter 9 by Samuel, Watson and Childs, who report on the use of Random Controlled Trials (RCTs) to measure impact of specific interventions adopted within Teacher Learning Communities as part of the Closing the Gap initiative.

The varied approaches to classroom intervention portrayed in the book serve to expand the established understanding of 'intervention'.

Different kinds of intervention: where do they come from?

Interventions are undertaken when there is an issue of concern and where some improvement is perceived to be needed. In the context of classroom teaching and learning, and also teachers' professional learning, how these issues are identified and lead to interventions of different kinds is of interest. In the book we see different examples of how interventions have come about and thus approached in different ways.

In several chapters there are accounts of practitioner intervention, where the author-researcher has problematised an aspect of practice. In Chapter 2, informed by engagement with M-level study, one of the authors undertook an intervention in his own classroom. Molway et al. in Chapter 3 likewise report on practitioner research, but in a context of changing assessment policy. In this chapter Katherine, an M-level student, was concerned that existing assessment practices in Modern Foreign Languages (MFL) might not accurately reflect students' actual skill-related performance. Her concerns regarding these practices were related to the removal of statutory assessment levels and the onus on schools to devise their own assessment frameworks. Her starting point was also the perceptions of lack of motivation. She therefore engaged in action research that focused on students' self-assessment. Action research was also conducted by Haydon and reported in Chapter 4 by Haydon and Childs, where the study arose from an observation of children and students that led to problematising an aspect of school science – students' questions.

The interventions reported in Chapters 5 and 6 both arose from specific aspects of science and mathematics learning. Taylor and Hillier are concerned with developing more scientific explanations with school students and also pre-service teachers. The approach is to understand through discourse analysis how the explanations for specific science phenomena might shift from everyday or partial understandings towards more scientific explanations. This intervention is therefore small scale and very context specific. In Chapter 6 Ingram et al. are concerned with talk in mathematics, prompted by a desire to support students to develop their mathematical talk in lessons, through focusing on the nature of teacher talk. The collaborative approach taken by these researchers is central to this chapter; the theme of collaboration within interventions is strong in many projects and clearly an important feature of the kinds of interventions involving groups of participants undertaking innovative practice.

In Chapter 7 the dearth of research in history education leads Burn et al. to focus on teacher research that has contributed to the professional discourse of history teachers, the examples of classroom interventions (as part of M-level study) being designed to 'tackle specific weaknesses in their students' approach to particular kinds of historical question'. The first example centres on the framing of meaningful history questions by students aged 17–18 years to carry out investigations, the second on the ability to analyse patterns of change and continuity across a period of history. Like the earlier chapters this account serves to highlight how small-scale studies can be revealing in ways that inform future practice.

Chapter 8 represents a departure from classroom issues observed by teachers as a basis for intervention to focus on the ways in which knowledge is understood in geography education, and how pre-service teachers can be better prepared to navigate between the knowledge and discourse of the discipline and of student learning. The concern was to help pre-service teachers to balance the need to motivate students while taking into account learning processes as well as the discipline.

The interventions reported in Chapter 9 took place within a whole school initiative to develop Teacher Learning Communities (TLCs) that would develop and share practice across a range of teaching and learning issues. The specific interventions developed and tested through Random Control Trials (RCTs) in this context were part of the Closing the Gap initiative. These interventions were designed to close the attainment gap for students with low achievement in literacy and numeracy. The work reported here focused on two interventions chosen to address specific areas of learning: Growth Mindsets and Dedicated Improvement and Reflection Time (DIRT). The approach taken in the Growth Mindsets intervention was to implement and assess the impact of mindset training with different groups of students. The DIRT intervention was also implemented over a series of lessons that involved students in coding their work, reflect and make improvements. In each case RCTs were used to assess impact.

Theoretical basis of interventions: how important is this?

In this book there is a clear thread of linking research to practice in all the interventions undertaken, be they in different disciplines and utilising different approaches. In this section I aim to pull out some of the ways in which previous studies have informed both the interventions themselves and the analytical processes that are used to evaluate their impact.

In Chapter 2 Brocklehurst and Thompson focus on how to stimulate reluctant readers in Year 7 (11 to 12 years). This is built on strong theoretical foundations derived from Vygotsky, and conceptions of learning as being individual and situated. These authors synthesise a conceptual framework from Vygotsky's *principle of double stimulation* – being set a problem or dilemma, and being provided with mediational tools or artefacts to solve it, and also Engestrom's *theory of expansive learning* – to take account of the social context of the system in which the intervention takes place. The notion of 'transforming the activity' is applied to the study of classroom reading, in which the use of literature circles is seen to develop skills that help individuals to engage in reading through collaborative activity. The theory is put into practice in this study by having older students involved in the literature circles, the theoretical perspective being put in practice is nicely captured by the authors in the following excerpt:

> The intention was for the older students to act as a secondary stimulus within the activity system of a collaborative reading group to support processes such as inference and criticality employed by successful readers.

In Chapter 3 Molway et al. point out the importance of mediated classroom interventions being both research-informed and practitioner-informed, where practical concerns are mediated by research understandings, and vice versa. The background they draw on relating to assessment research informed the strategies developed in the intervention. Likewise in Chapter 4, the background research on student questioning provides a basis on which the action research intervention is approached. In this study, where data pre and post the intervention are collected to investigate the impact, the instruments used are clearly informed by the research literature – the instruments needed to be theoretically aligned with the intervention strategy to provide validity. In this case, the intervention builds on a 'training model' for students to develop their questioning, which was obtained from previous research. In Chapter 5 Taylor and Hillier use systemic functional linguistics to analyse discourse within students' science explanations – this might be too fine-grained and time consuming to be widely applicable, but reveals the possibilities of understanding in more detail how explanations flow and change as a deeper scientific understanding emerges.

The intervention process reported in Chapter 6 uses video analysis which builds on Mason's (2002) discipline of noticing, and other research on teachers' professional learning. In addition, Ingram et al. draw on interaction studies to identify specific strategies that would be developed within the intervention, such as the silences between turns. The connection between research and practice is made explicit in this intervention through sharing of literature between researchers and teacher participants. Ingram et al. also refer to personal and collaborative theorising by participants as they analysed practice using the videos and engaged in coding transcripts of interactional episodes of teaching. The researchers also draw on Clarke & Hollingsworth's (2002) model of professional growth to focus on changes in how teachers valued outcomes, a model that has been used worldwide to understand the connections between changes in beliefs, practices and valued outcomes in professional learning.

In Chapter 7 on history education, Burn et al. draw attention to the limited research reported in this discipline which can be translated into small-scale classroom intervention studies. This is clearly unlike the situation regarding mathematics and science education, as we have seen in terms of background research in earlier chapters (Haydon and Childs, Ingram et al.). The research they do cite was important in the 1990s as part of a multi-discipline ESRC initiative to examine progression in different subjects, including science and mathematics (Simon et al., 1996). This work is clearly still influential across disciplines and studies of conceptual understanding. The authors do acknowledge recent successful research into Holocaust Education, and smaller scale studies of classroom interventions but their focus in the chapter highlights the importance of the journal *Teaching History* in publishing teacher research, with examples that contribute to the professional discourse of history teachers. These studies were clearly influential to the participating teachers developing their own classroom interventions.

In Chapter 8 the authors set out to use inferentialism as a theoretical resource in an intervention study based within a teacher preparation programme, so that participants would focus on geographical reasoning in their planning and teaching. Firth & Strutt focus on the interaction between disciplinary and pedagogical knowledge in relation to teaching geography as a basis for this intervention. The Growth Mindsets intervention reported in Chapter 9 by Samuel, Watson and Childs is based on previous research by Dweck using mindset training.

The wealth of theoretical perspectives that have informed the intervention studies across different disciplines can provide a basis for further research in classrooms, and also other learning environments including initial teacher education.

Interventions: what roles do teachers take?

The interventions that are classroom based in this book involve teachers taking on different roles as they focus on the intervention. It is worth drawing attention to these as there are ways in which teachers undertaking classroom interventions can gain insights regarding focus, collaboration and cycles of action research when planning future interventions.

In Chapter 2 Brocklehurst and Thompson point out the different roles that teachers can take whilst developing critical reading in the literature circle. The presence of the teacher can inhibit or change student talk, but it can also be beneficial if the 'role of a fellow reader' is taken, and the teacher listens and takes on mediational guidance. The study also explored how an older student could replace the teacher in the literature circle, taking on the role of a more capable peer (Vygotsky). In one circle the older student was limited in this role (Jack); this contrasted greatly with the older student in the other circle (Emily), whose approach was to gain trust and create an atmosphere of trust between members of the circle. This approach was transformational for some students (Chris). The study shows the complexity of approach that is required to engage reluctant students into a learning scenario where they lack knowledge, skills and confidence. There is much to be learnt with regard to teaching approach in this study. Brocklehurst and Thompson point to the need for 'conceptual clarity' in the role of the mediator in the learning process and point to features that characterise a 'capable peer'. Advancing the role of the student in leading the discussion and questioning is part of the teacher role in Chapter 4. The excerpts show how the teacher engages in a number of processes – modelling asking questions, using reflective statements to transfer answering responsibility to the students. This strategy appears effective in providing a learning environment in which students do then ask questions to problem solve. This environment also allows the teacher to take on the role of questioner, an important role as once encouraged, students do ask questions that might be beyond the knowledge of the teacher, but her role can be that of co-investigator once a questioning stance is legitimated and encouraged as part of classroom discourse.

In Chapter 3, Molway et al. show how in both their cases, participants were able to take some degree of ownership of how the intervention (assessment framework) was implemented. The role of both the masters and student teachers was outside of the mainstream teaching and learning in their schools, but they were supported by their engagement in the university programme to which they were linked. In Chapter 5, Taylor and Hillier also identify different roles on the part of the teacher. The classroom study involved collaboration between two experienced physics teachers, who began by constructing their own explanation of the phenomenon under study, in order to provide a benchmark for comparing students' explanations. The style of tracking the students' emergent explanations overtime clearly expands their role in the intervention to research analysis. The collaborative nature of Ingram et al.'s work, where teachers shared in the literature background, analysis of video and coding of their own lesson transcription, portrays a different kind of role that teachers can take in an intervention but that also involves them in the research process. The examples cited in Chapter 7 also show the kind of role practitioner researchers can take in an intervention that involves action research.

Clearly the research process involved in classroom interventions as described in this book must be valued such that teachers become engaged in the process and are willing to devote time needed for intervention. Collaborative roles seem to be key in bringing about this engagement.

Interventions: how are outcomes judged?

Whatever way any intervention is conceptualised and approached, there is a need to identify the impact of the intervention. The chapters in this book show many ways in which such an impact can be judged, according to the style and focus of the intervention.

In Chapters 2 and 3 the impact is evaluated by looking at individual students' learning and engagement that the authors can directly attribute to the intervention, and relating these to the intervention practices. For example, in Chapter 2 these are features that enabled poor readers to engage and become more critical and practiced, whereas in Chapter 3 these are the confident responses of students who had been guided through new self-assessment strategies. The main outcome of the two cases in this study is in terms of the participants' professional learning, rather than student outcomes, respondents reported positive impacts on their teaching. Intervention studies of practice do often come down to how teachers perceived their value, changes in their own beliefs and practices, rather than direct evidence of impact on students. Specific examples of teacher learning are found in this chapter.

In Chapter 4, the outcomes of the intervention are judged using a number of data sources, observations and classroom dialogue, focus groups and post-test. The strategies building on previous research, the training model, were shown to be effective in developing students' thinking and range of scientific questions. Other positive student outcomes were evidenced by observation of behaviours during practice. Moreover there was evidence of professional learning. The specific outcomes of the intervention reported by Ingram et al. in Chapter 6 are directed more towards research, though there is also a professional development implication. The authors' discussion of how students are introduced to and use mathematical vocabulary and on different types of pauses within classroom interactions, highlight the 'complexities of connections between classroom practice and research'.

The outcomes identified by teacher practitioners in Chapter 7, where they undertook action research in history as part of M-level study, though specific to the study, are clearly applicable to other teaching and learning history contexts as well as across disciplines where students need to develop independent learning and the use of metaphors and analogies to characterise change. In their discussion of the two practitioner interventions Burn et al. highlight the limitations regarding the testing that accompanies interventions, but that the qualitative approaches necessitated by individual small-scale studies can provide insights on the impact of interventions.

The assessment of the impact of the two interventions using RCTs reported by Samuel and Watson in Chapter 9 used statistical methods to compare control and experimental groups. Though the statistical analysis showed no significant differences, the authors highlight the benefits of being involved in the intervention using RCTs. The teacher involved in the DIRT intervention, Liz, became more aware of the impact she was having on her students, and was able to identify students who were not responsive to more reflection time. Moreover, as the researchers interviewed students about the intervention, they were able to appreciate how the 'multitude of confounding variables' were affecting learning situations, thus the RCT 'helped us understand something of the complexity of the learning process'.

Intervention challenges: what are the barriers?

Most authors in the book acknowledge that interventions meet certain challenges, and this will always be the case. However when interventions can be aligned with school policy, shared with colleagues by working collaboratively, and motivated by external support, the challenges that are presented can be more easily addressed. In this section I have pulled out some examples of the key challenges that might create barriers to successful classroom intervention.

In Chapter 2 Brocklehurst and Thompson point out the problems of carrying out an intervention whilst a school or department is under inspection scrutiny. In these cases, the intervention has to be recognised as having value and being commensurate with school policy. Thus Brocklehurst and Thompson developed an intervention that was 'aimed at an identified issue of whole school improvement'.

Barriers can also be in the form of how an intervention is perceived, for example in Chapter 2, literature circles might focus on roles, which can dominate the work – and require teachers to understand the value of direct mediation with students as they talk (as opposed to teachers asking questions about the text). In Chapter 3 the complexity arising from the power relations between student teachers, university tutors and school mentors, led to ethical issues and also the problem of 'control' that many teachers are unwilling to relinquish – either themselves or on the part of others, such as student teachers. This need to retain control can be a real barrier to innovative practices that are part of interventions. Teachers need to be convinced of their value in order to devote time and energy to participating in and supporting interventions, as highlighted in the case of Katherine's colleagues, who had insufficient interest in engaging in her intervention.

Challenges presented to Ingram et al. in their study of talk in mathematics were in terms of the ways in which students used mathematical words, so participants addressed this issue through strategies focusing on mathematical language. This issue is also common to science, the authors draw on Lemke's (1990) work on talking science to draw out meaning from observations regarding conceptual networks and relationships between ideas. Challenges identified by the examples in Chapter 7 make reference to the newness of the school and lack of established approaches, and also existing positions of colleagues about student limitations regarding independent approaches to history inquiry.

Many of the challenges identified by those undertaking small-scale action research projects as interventions lie in the systems within which they are carrying out their research. If they experience limited value, support and interest by colleagues this can mean carrying out an intervention is a lonely process. Moreover, sharing the process and outcomes of an intervention by working collaboratively is likely to lead to more sustained impact. The work of TLCs reported in Chapter 9 by Samuel, Watson and Childs suggests that many teaching and learning issues can be addressed if there is the will to be collaborative and reflective on a school-wide and or department basis. The value of such initiatives to professional learning, a reported outcome of many interventions in this book, must be a priority of senior leaders in schools.

The power of Masters level (M-level) study

In this section I want to highlight the value of postgraduate study in education, in particular for M-level qualifications that underpin many of the accounts in this book. The value of M-level work on critical reflection and enhancement of practice (Turner and Simon, 2013) has been shown to help teachers focus on issues of practice and ways of designing inquiry or interventionist studies that can really change practice and enhance student experience.

In Chapter 2 Brocklehurst had learned about a collaborative reading activity that he had been made aware of during his teacher education programme and took on the role of practitioner researcher, as did authors in Chapter 3 (Molway et al.), who highlight the role of practitioner research guided by M-level study for professional learning. The M-level student, Katherine, though working on her own with little professional discussion, experienced effective professional learning.

The importance of M-level study can go beyond participant teachers' professional learning, when it makes a wider contribution to professional discourses within subjects, as exemplified in Chapter 7 by Burn et al. In this chapter the authors highlight the dearth of research into history education that the publication of teacher research (often from m-level study) in the journal *Teaching History* seeks to address.

Conclusion

This set of chapters demonstrates what is possible regarding classroom research and what indicators exist to promote the importance of this work. Together they show how valuable interventions can be facilitated by promoting the culture of research informed practice, and participant engagement with wider theory and research to enhance teaching and learning.

I began this commentary with a review of how 'intervention' has been interpreted in this book, and I believe the chapters serve to enlarge our ideas of what intervention might mean. I also looked at how interventions arise – from an individual's observation and reflection of practice, or as part of a school-wide initiative such as a TLC. I have highlighted some examples of how interventions are informed by previous research and theory, some analytical frameworks and procedures in different studies illustrate the variety of ways in which the outcomes of participant research can be harnessed and interpreted. I also identified the kinds of challenges and barriers that have been experienced by those undertaking interventions, and I believe there is an agenda here for those involved in enhancing learning to address at many levels. In particular, I think we should value the motivational and theoretical richness of interventions that are undertaken in the wealth of small-scale studies that abound as part of M-level work. Indeed they form a substantial part of the *Teaching History* publications, as cited by history educators in Chapter 7.

In summary, the book offers a wealth of ideas for classroom intervention across different disciplines using a variety of approaches and theoretical perspectives.

References

Clarke, D. & Hollingsworth, H. (2002). Elaborating a model of teacher professional growth. Teacher and Teaching Education. *Teaching and Teacher Education*, 18, 947–967. https://doi.org/10.1016/S0742-051X(02)00053-7

Lemke, J. L. (1990). *Talking Science: Language, learning, and values*. Norwood, NJ: Ablex.

Mason, J. (2002). *Researching Your Own Practice: The discipline of noticing*. Abingdon: Routledge.

Simon, S.A., Brown, M.L., Black, P.J. & Blondel, E. (1996). Progression in learning mathematics and science. In M. Hughes (Ed.) *Progression in Learning*. Clevedon: Multilingual Matters, 24–49.

Stevenson, A. & Lindberg, C. A. (Eds.). (2012). *New Oxford American Dictionary* (3rd ed.). Oxford University Press. Retrieved 12 February 2013, from www.oxfordreference.com/view/10.1093/acref/9780195392883.001.0001/acref-9780195392883.

Turner, K. & Simon, S. (2013). In what ways does studying at M level contribute to teachers' professional learning? Research set in an English University. *Professional Development in Education*, 39(1), 6–22.

INDEX

Printed in Great Britain
by Amazon